JAMES A. REILLY is Professor of History at the University of Toronto and specialises in the social history of Syrian cities. He travelled widely in Syria between 1974 and 2010, living there on two separate occasions, and is the author of *A Small Town in Syria* (2002) and *The Ottoman Cities of Lebanon* (I.B.Tauris, 2016).

'James A. Reilly's *Fragile Nation, Shattered Land* is a gem. Reilly does what only a master historian who has studied Syria for a lifetime could do: he condenses 500 years of history into 200 pages, and almost every page delivers a sparkling insight set off by a simple and elegant style. This book should be read by anyone wishing to understand the deeper social and cultural dimensions of Syria's modern crisis. I will be assigning it in my Modern Middle East class.'

Joshua Landis, Director of the Center for Middle East Studies,
University of Oklahoma and author of *Syria Comment*

'James A. Reilly is a leading historian of modern Syria, and this book will be a certain, and immediate, classic. It is likely to be the best book published on Syria for a long time, and it is obvious the author has been an acute and wise firsthand observer of Syrian politics and society over the past several decades. The scope and breadth is outstanding and it makes an enjoyable and fluid read, giving the reader plenty to think about.'

Michael Provence, Professor of History,
University of California, San Diego

'An epic history of modern Syria, this book is vital to understanding the roots of what has become the most devastating conflict of the twenty-first century. From Syria's history under Ottoman Turkish and European rule up until its experience of military dictatorship, Reilly helps explain the roots of Syria's tragedy and the possible futures that may await it.'

Murtaza Hussain, *The Intercept*

'None of Syria's current problems were born yesterday. Almost everything that the people of Syria are fighting about today is deeply rooted in history – a history that needs to be constantly revisited, re-taught and deeply comprehended to understand why and how Syria collapsed in 2011. That's what makes this book particularly important, because it reaches back to the sixteenth century, giving a comprehensive academic background to readers, penned by none other than James A. Reilly, a veteran Syriologist with seminal works on nineteenth-century Damascus. Generations have grown up hearing his lectures in Toronto and reading his scholarly articles, which have become overnight classics and must-reads for historians of Damascus.'

Sami Moubayed, author of *Under the Black Flag* (I.B.Tauris, 2015)
and founder of The Damascus History Foundation

'With his deep understanding of Syria, James A. Reilly has produced a masterpiece that illuminates the country's convoluted past and tragic present. It would be hard to find a more lucid and gripping guide to the roots of the Syrian predicament. If there is one book you have to read about Syria to better understand the reasons behind its fragility, this is it.'

Omer Taspinar, Professor of Security Studies, US National War College;
non-resident Senior Fellow, The Brookings Institution and author of
***The Mirage: Misunderstanding the Middle East* (I.B.Tauris, forthcoming)**

FRAGILE NATION, SHATTERED LAND

THE MODERN HISTORY OF SYRIA

JAMES A. REILLY

I.B. TAURIS
LONDON · NEW YORK

Published in 2019 by
I.B.Tauris & Co. Ltd
London • New York
www.ibtauris.com

ISBN: 978 1 78453 961 0
eISBN: 978 1 78672 450 2
ePDF: 978 1 78673 450 1

A full CIP record for this book is available from the British Library
A full CIP record is available from the Library of Congress

Library of Congress Catalog Card Number: available

Typeset by Riverside Publishing Solutions, Salisbury, Wiltshire
Printed and bound by by CPI Group (UK) Ltd, Croydon, CR0 4YY

To Noah Ahmed Reilly

CONTENTS

LIST OF MAPS

LIST OF PLATES

1 View of Aleppo from the south-west (photographed pre-1914). The medieval citadel looms in background and two sixteenth-century Ottoman mosques are identifiable by their pencil-shaped minarets. On left: the Adiliyya. On right: the Khusrowiyya. (Library of Congress)

2 Nawfara coffee house in Damascus (1938 photo). This café, in the shadow of the Umayyad Mosque, is still in business in the same location today. (Library of Congress)

3 Rural life: threshing wheat in a northern Syrian village (1930s photo). (Library of Congress)

4 General view of Damascus from above Salihiyya, nineteenth century. (Library of Congress)

5 Damascus courtyard house, late nineteenth–early twentieth century. (Library of Congress)

6 Pilgrims in Damascus on their return from Mecca. In the background is the Mahmal, symbol of the sultan's patronage and protection of the Mecca pilgrimage. Photograph from 1903. (Library of Congress)

7 French authorities publicly display corpses of slain rebels, Damascus 1925 (© Bettmann / Getty)
is 515982298

8 Ruined Damascus neighborhood after the French bombardment of October 1925. Courtesy of the Otrakji family collection.

9 Husni Zaim, author of the first military coup. (© Stringer/ Getty)
#: 51398288

10 Nasser receiving a hero's welcome in Damascus, 1958, with Quwatli at his side. (© Bettmann / Getty)
#: 515303010

11 Cult of personality: Hafez al-Assad's image looms over Damascus in 1999.
(© RAMZI HAIDAR / Staff)
#: 51398513

12 Bashar billboard, Damascus, 2006. (© Anthony Asael/Art in All of Us / Getty)
#: 534929022

13 Government soldiers in rubble of the eighth-century Umayyad (Great)
Mosque in Aleppo, after capturing it from rebels in 2017. (© Youssef
Karwashan / Stringer)
#: 629499134

ACKNOWLEDGEMENTS

A wide-ranging account like this one cannot come from one author's head alone. I am indebted to the dozens of scholars whose work I have mined and synthesized to build arguments and reach conclusions. Because this is a book meant for a general readership, not a specialist academic audience, I have minimized the use of endnotes and references. References to other works are found only when the text is quoting someone, usually a historical actor. Scholars of Syria will see their fingerprints on a number of unreferenced passages. The bibliography offers readers the names of authors and titles that have been essential for putting this book together. I hope that readers will be tempted to look more deeply into topics that interest them, and the bibliography will be a place to start.

Over the course of my career I have accumulated many debts, more than I can recount here. In the specific process of writing this book, I wish to thank for their input or suggestions Joshua Landis, Jeannie Miller, Dana Sajdi, Steve Tamari and Nina Youkhanna. Camille Otrakji made available a historical photograph from his family's collection. My students at the University of Toronto have been patient sounding-boards for this material, and their questions and comments have sharpened my thinking.

At I.B.Tauris Tom Stottor has been a keen-eyed editor, and as a result of his efforts this book is pithier and more focused than it otherwise would have been. He also has pushed production along at a rapid clip, which I appreciate. Cartographer David Cox produced the fine maps, and Arub Ahmed lent a sharp editorial eye to the manuscript as it moved toward publication.

Three referees contracted by I.B.Tauris have improved the work and saved me from error. To all of them I am grateful, including one (fellow historian Michael Provence) who revealed his identity.

None of those named or thanked is responsible for the book's remaining shortcomings, errors, or omissions, or for my judgments and conclusions.

Finally, thanks are due to my wife Sabah, who supported me in the completion of this work that claimed a big chunk of time and energy over many months.

A visitor to Syria since her childhood, she has been my companion in our decades-long experience and exploration of the country. Thanks also to our son Kamal, who spent a happy year in Damascus in the second grade during the 1990s. He came away with fond memories of Syria. I hope that one day he might be able to visit there again, this time with his own little boy, in conditions of peace, security and recovery.

MAPS

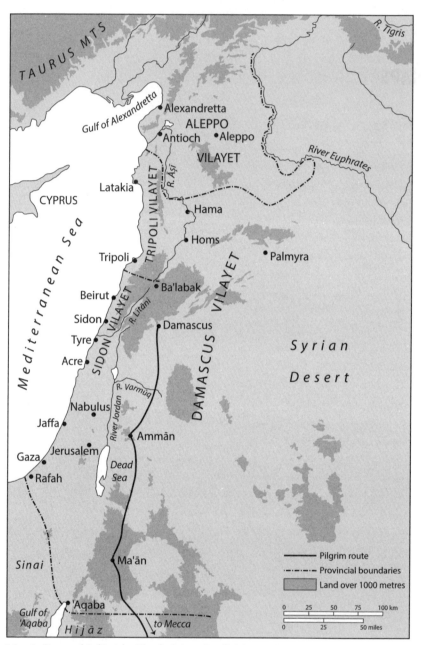

Map 1 Geographic 'Syria' with administrative divisions, 1800

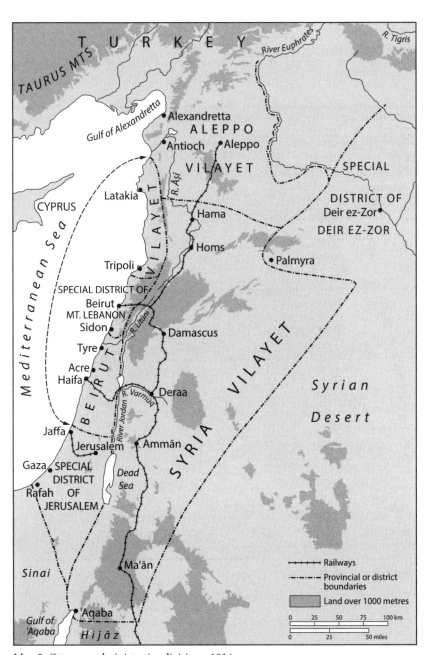

Map 2 Ottoman administrative divisions, 1914

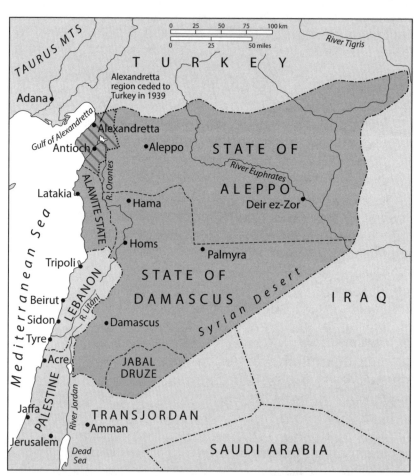

Map 3 French Mandate Syria

Map 4 Syria, 2007

INTRODUCTION

On the night of 23 July 1920, Yusuf al-Azmeh, the Minister of War of the recently proclaimed independent Syrian kingdom, marched westward from Damascus to a mountain pass to confront an advancing French army. As he left his home in the hillside Muhajirin neighborhood of Damascus, al-Azmeh commanded a disparate force of a few thousand men and a small number of women. His forces included elements of an official army that until recently had been supported by Britain, as well as volunteers mobilized by national committees. More than one week before, the French commander had sent an ultimatum to the Arab king of Syria, Faisal, demanding that he disband his army and permit France to march on Damascus, fulfilling the terms of an Anglo–French agreement that awarded Syria to France. Aware of the weakness of his position Faisal agreed, but his capitulation did not dissuade the French, determined as they were to make a show of force. Meanwhile, popular committees mobilized Damascenes, urging them to resist the advancing colonial power and to wage a holy struggle, a jihad, in defense of the city and country.

As al-Azmeh marched out of Damascus at the head of his rag-tag and hastily assembled force, he was rushing to the defense of Syria. But what did the name 'Syria' mean? Nationalists had declared statehood the previous March, but Syrian statehood was unrecognized by the Great Powers who were poised to redraw the Middle Eastern map. Much of what nationalists called 'Syria' was now under French and British military occupation, former Ottoman territories shortly to be designated as Lebanon and Palestine, respectively. For most of the previous 55 years there had been an Ottoman province (vilayet) named Syria, with its capital at Damascus, but this Syria had not included the coast (administered from Beirut) or the north (administered from Aleppo). Northern resistance to the French was being waged in the name of Syria, to be sure, but also in the name of Muslim solidarity under the symbolic leadership of the Ottoman caliphate in Istanbul. The notional Syrian 'state' was at best an afterthought in northern rebels' Ottoman restoration project (a project not shared, it should be said, by the Ottoman sultan himself as he coped with the British occupation of Istanbul). As al-Azmeh and his troops marched out of Damascus, many of the city's traditional powerbrokers – who had been Ottoman loyalists to the very end – hung back. They had viewed with alarm the arrival of Faisal in the baggage, as it were, of the British army. They mistrusted the political operators around Faisal who hailed from distant regions of the Hejaz and closer regions like Palestine, regarding them as opportunists and outsiders who threatened to displace the city's old notable grandees.

Al-Azmeh and his ill-prepared forces were defeated in a mountain pass west of Damascus known as Maysaloun. The French troops, stronger thanks to tanks and artillery, scattered al-Azmeh's forces, killing him in the process, and entered Damascus on 25 July. Faisal and his allies fled and took refuge with their British friends and patrons. A remaining delegation of city notables surrendered Damascus to the French army, formally inaugurating the period of French colonial rule in Syria.

Al-Azmeh died a martyr to the cause of Syrian independence, and years later he would be honored with songs, statues, street names, and a token (but never actually opened) government museum. But the Syria for which he had died was not the Syria that came into being. In 1920 France and Britain determined the boundaries of what was Syria and what was not-Syria. In the years that followed France repeatedly adjusted the new country's political frontiers, sometimes shrinking them and sometimes expanding them according to political and colonial expediency. When French rule finally ended after 1945, France had created a Syrian *state* but French policy had discouraged the formation of a Syrian *nation*. In three short decades Syria had gone from being a narrowly defined Ottoman province, to being a theater for a sudden, brief and tumultuous assertion of Arab national identity (under British auspices), had experienced deliberately divisive French rule, and came out on the other side as a nominally independent state with a contested sense of nationhood.

The roots of political instability in Syria today are undoubtedly located in the modern state's colonial origins and experiences. These left Syria and its political class ill-equipped to navigate the newly formed Middle Eastern state system after independence. Syria's politicians worked in an unforgiving environment that included weak Arab states with contested borders and acute internecine rivalries, Israel's ethnic cleansing of Arabs from neighboring Palestine, and Israel's serial defeats of Arab armies that created and consolidated a Jewish-majority state there. But it is impossible to fully comprehend the present-day civil war and destruction in Syria without knowledge of the country's intricate, longer-term and pre-colonial history. A centuries-long period of Ottoman rule came to an abrupt end in 1918, leaving in its wake a complex social and institutional legacy. These inherited difficulties and divisions were subsequently denied, exacerbated and exploited by various foreign powers and claimants to national authority and legitimacy.

This book's distinctiveness is that it tells the story of Syria's modern history over many centuries, linking Ottoman, colonial and independence eras to explain the present and to trace contours and possibilities for the future. The 500-year history is told here for the first time in all of its color and complexity. Also noteworthy, the social and cultural dimensions of Syrians' experiences, and not just their political and institutional histories, are key parts of this account.

Syria's pre-twentieth-century history is one of relationships: between people and the land, between cities and countryside, and between local inhabitants and their imperial Ottoman rulers. Calling these populations 'Syrians' prior to the nineteenth century is of course a case of backward historical projection since the idea of Syria, as a place and an identity, did not receive full articulation until the mid- to late-1800s. Medieval Arab geographers called this region 'the lands of Sham' (*Bilad al-Sham*), originally a reference to areas 'north' (*shamal*) of the Arabian Peninsula. Later, the word Sham (also spelled Cham) became a synonym for Damascus, acknowledging the historic and geographic centrality of the city. The peoples of Syria/*Bilad al-Sham* thought of themselves in other ways: as inhabitants of a city, or a village or region, as members of clans or tribes, and as members of religious communities. Only in the nineteenth century was the name Syria attached to an administrative unit centered at Damascus, and only then did some avant-garde intellectuals propose 'Syrian' as a civic identity for people of the country. But Syria (or *Bilad al-Sham*) as a geographic space is found in historical sources and in the historical imagination. We can call the people who live there Syrians, without necessarily imposing anachronistic concepts of nationhood and identity on them.

My own usage of the place-name Syria will be more or less elastic, depending on the era. While the focus throughout is on the cities and regions that came to be identified as territorial Syria after 1920, the pre-1920 narrative will draw on examples from a wider canvas including what later were defined as Palestine and Lebanon to illustrate points about the Syrian lands or *Bilad al-Sham* prior to the demarcation of modern frontiers. After 1920, references in this text to Syria refer to the country internationally recognized by that name, corresponding mostly to the borders of present-day Syria.

Starting with the Ottoman conquest of the 'Syrian' lands from the Mamluks, this book will show why the Syrian nation is a fragile one: born recently, defined arbitrarily, contested repeatedly and vulnerable to internal schism and external intervention. At the same time, Syrian society is resilient, with a continuous history that spans the centuries. Readers of this book will gain an appreciation of both sides of the paradox.

1

SYRIA BECOMES OTTOMAN, SIXTEENTH TO SEVENTEENTH CENTURIES

CLASH OF ARMIES ON THE PLAIN OF DABIQ

In August 1516 the Ottoman army, led by Sultan Selim I, marched eastward. Claiming that his army was moving to confront the Persian Safavids, he had deceived the Mamluk sultan of Egypt and Syria. But as he approached the Ottoman–Mamluk frontier, Selim showed his true intentions by mistreating an envoy sent by Mamluk Sultan Qansuh al-Ghawri. Wheeling southward, Selim's army confronted Qansuh's army that had marched north from Aleppo. Unknown to Qansuh, his Aleppo governor Khair Bey was in touch with Selim and preparing to betray the Mamluk sultan. The armies clashed at Marj Dabiq, the 'plain of Dabiq,' on 24 August 1516 and Khair Bey's defection sealed Mamluk Sultan Qansuh's fate. He died in battle and his body was never recovered, though somehow his head was reportedly delivered to Selim. The elaborate mausoleum that Qansuh had built for himself in Cairo never received the Mamluk sultan's remains. Selim's victory opened up 400 years of Ottoman rule in Syria.

By the time it conquered Syria from the Mamluks, the Ottoman Empire had emerged as the heir of the Byzantine Empire, whose capital Constantinople (today's Istanbul) had fallen to the Ottomans in 1453. Ottomans (a name derived from the ruling dynasty's founder) were a ruling stratum of soldiers and administrators of various ethnic backgrounds, whose administrative language was Turkish and whose official religion was Islam. Prior to their conquest of Syria, the Ottomans had already subdued rival principalities in Anatolia (Asia Minor, roughly corresponding to modern Turkey) and in the Balkans or southeastern Europe. Subsequently, Ottoman rule expanded further and turned the Black Sea into an Ottoman lake, captured most of northern Africa from Egypt to the borders of Morocco, and incorporated most of the Red Sea coast on both Arabian and African shores.

Therefore in 1516–17 Syria became part of a far-flung sultanate, whose political, administrative and economic structures would condition Syrians' entry into the modern world. Syria's present borders were drawn in the twentieth century, but Syrians' experiences of modern statehood began before that, here, in the preceding period of Ottoman rule.

The Ottomans' conquest of Syria grew out of various regional and international challenges confronting the sultanate in the early sixteenth century. Established already in Anatolia, the Ottomans led by Sultan Selim I (r. 1512–20) faced a threat in the east from the newly emerging state of Safavid Iran. The Safavids (1501–1722) had developed out of a militant religious movement who regarded their founder (Ismail, d. 1524) as a source of religious authority and esoteric knowledge inherited from his ancestor, the Kurdish Sheikh Safi al-Din (d. 1334). In the Islamic mystical tradition, known as Sufism, saintly charisma was typically ascribed to a founding sheikh's descendants if descendants' lives and deeds proved their worthiness. Under Ismail Safavi, this particular Sufi movement consolidated into a version of Shiism that emphasized ideological loyalty to and obedience of the Safavid dynasty. Turkish-speaking Shiite tribesmen, loyal partisans of Ismail Safavi, threatened Ottoman Sultan Selim's hold on eastern Anatolia.

The Ottomans themselves had also emerged from a Sufi-infused frontier religion (fourteenth century). As they grew into their role as successors of Byzantium, which they had toppled in 1453, Ottoman sultans institutionalized the trappings of state-sponsored Sunni Islam. Sunnis recognized different sources of religious authority than did Shiites,[1] and over time these differences led to variant interpretations of Islamic religious law (the sharia). Ottomans patronized the Hanafi school of Islamic law (the Hanafi 'rite'), and Ottoman imperial schools and religious officials identified with Hanafi Sunnism.

Despite their Sunni–Shiite differences, however, the political quarrel between the Ottomans and the Safavids was not ideological at its root. Their clashes grew out of simple militarized competition for land, population and resources, although the introduction of a Sunni–Shiite ideological dimension into their rivalry allowed both dynasties to identify friends and foes in the borderland regions.

As he prepared to conquer Syria, Sultan Selim correctly suspected the (Sunni) Mamluk Sultan in Cairo of working with the (Shiite) Safavid Shah (king) to hem in and weaken the Ottomans. Selim's victory at Marj Dabiq opened the Ottomans' way to the riches of Egypt, the heart of Mamluk power, and to the Hejaz, home of the Muslim holy cities of Mecca and Medina. Two months after his victory at Marj Dabiq, Selim's armies overwhelmed Damascus. The Mamluks' capital Cairo fell in April 1517 and the Mamluk sultanate came to an end.

The downfall of the Mamluks and the arrival of the Ottomans marked the boundary between Syria's medieval and early modern histories. Now Syria was part of an empire that straddled three continents, whose peoples spoke multiple languages, and whose rulers pursued imperial interests in the Indian Ocean, on continental Europe, around the Black Sea and across the length of North Africa. But Selim's conquest was epochal only in hindsight. A notable Syrian eyewitness to these events, the prominent Damascene scholar and historian Muhammad Ibn Tulun (d. 1546), was unperturbed by Selim's arrival. Ibn Tulun visited the sultan's camp when Selim mustered outside the city walls. His account shows that Damascenes were curious about the new ruler, not fearful or 'defeated' (defeat belonged to the Mamluks). Ibn Tulun referred to Selim as the 'King of Rum'[2] and reserved judgment about the implications of the new kingship, but he felt reassured by Selim's respect for Islamic norms and by the sultan's efforts to present himself as a 'just ruler' in the Muslim tradition. The chronicler dryly reports Selim's arrival, his departure for Cairo (where he decisively defeated the Mamluk sultanate), and then his return for a sojourn in Damascus, during which time Ibn Tulun speaks highly of the sultan's charity and good works. Importantly Ibn Tulun did not see the *Rumis* as alien to the cultural, religious and political traditions that he took to be proper and legitimate. His attitude anticipated an ongoing relationship of close cooperation between Syria's Arabic-speaking urban leaderships and Ottoman authorities within the evolving imperial system.

ENTER THE OTTOMANS

In December 1557, an envoy sent to Istanbul from the sharif of Mecca was following the pilgrimage route from the Hejaz through Syria to Anatolia. As they approached Damascus from the south on their camels, the envoy, Qutb al-Din al-Nahrawali, and his party slogged through cold, mud, darkness and rain. The downpour was so heavy and the night so dark that at one point they were forced to halt in the open for a few hours. Resuming their journey they came to a small fort, a way-station for the annual pilgrimage caravan, and a resident cook there prepared for them a spare meal of beet soup. The weary travelers were eager to reach Damascus, so they consumed the soup without dismounting from their camels, then continued on their way. Finally, al-Nahrawali wrote, 'we entered Damascus the divinely protected following the evening prayer.'[3] As emissaries from the sharif of Mecca, the traveler and his companions were lodged in the Ottoman governor's guest house. The governor plied them with food, provisions and supplies and invited them to winter in the city before resuming their onward journey. For the next few weeks the sharif's envoy made the social rounds in Damascus, met the city's literati and its learned men, and recorded his encounters with them. Typical of learned people of the time, al-Nahrawali and his interlocutors competed with each other to compose poetry, to show their respect for each other and to express their mutual esteem. Addressing the chief judge or *kadi* of the city, al-Nahrawali compared Damascus to the Kaaba of Mecca, as a place of sanctuary. Praising the judge, al-Nahrawali's poem continued:

> In determination and high-mindedness hath he surpassed old men [...].
> With him hath Syria become an object of pilgrimage, both major and lesser.[4]

Clearly Damascus loomed large in al-Nahrawali's imagination, and it represented a stronghold of civility, comfort, learning and administration.

Damascus and Aleppo, Syria's other great inland center, were the thriving hubs of the Syria that the Ottomans conquered, and the Ottomans divided Syria into two provinces, one governed from each. Selim appointed a turncoat Mamluk official, Janbardi al-Ghazali (d. 1521), to govern Damascus. For two years until Selim's death in 1520, Janbardi administered Damascus in the name of the sultan. For him, retaining power was the main thing, not loyalty to a newly arrived dynasty. After Selim's death Janbardi revolted against his successor, Sultan Suleiman 'the Magnificent,' in a doomed attempt to restore the Mamluk sultanate.

Selim's initial appointment of the capable and opportunistic Janbardi illustrates the Ottomans' penchant for adapting many of the existing Mamluk practices, and even using their personnel. Another example of administrative continuity was the Ottomans' recognition of a principal chief of the Mawali Bedouin as the 'emir (commander) of the steppe.' In principle, this honoree was to ensure the safety of trade and communications routes in the Syrian steppe and desert. In this manner the Ottomans (as did the Mamluks before them) symbolically integrated pastoral Bedouins into their ruling hierarchies.

With the suppression of Janbardi's revolt and his execution in 1521, Ottomanization of Syria's administration proceeded apace. In its mature and settled form, which emerged during the long reign of Suleiman, Ottoman rule was characterized by a duumvirate at provincial and district levels: the governor (or district governor) and the chief (or deputy) judge.

The governor was a high-ranking military administrator, usually with the rank and title of pasha, who was responsible for criminal and fiscal matters. He reported to the Grand Vizier in Istanbul, the seat of power often referred to as the Sublime Porte (literally, the 'high gate' of the sultan's palace). Supported by imperial garrisons of elite infantry called Janissaries, by mercenary formations, and – later – by locally recruited troops, the *pasha* was responsible for maintaining order and security and remitting taxes to Istanbul. Alongside the governor, the *agha* (commander) of the Janissaries was usually a powerful military figure in his own right. The Porte rotated governors frequently to discourage them from 'going native' and from forming close ties to local power centers. In Syria's first Ottoman century, governors tended to be drawn from the sultan's household and from graduates of imperial schools in Istanbul. Their experiences in various provinces gave the most ambitious of them opportunities to rise further in Ottoman ranks. Bosnian general La La Mustafa Pasha was governor of Damascus in the 1560s, and later he became Grand Vizier for three months in 1580. Albanian general Sinan Pasha had already been Grand Vizier when he fell from favor and was appointed governor of Damascus from 1589–93. Subsequently his political fortunes turned and he became Grand Vizier again on various occasions in the 1590s. The Bosnian Khusrow Pasha became governor of Aleppo, then of Damascus in the early sixteenth century, and rose to a high rank in Istanbul though he never quite made Grand Vizier. La La Mustafa established an endowment in Damascus that centuries later became a revenue base for one of his descendants (Jamil Mardam Bey) who became a leading political figure in twentieth-century Syria. Sinan built a landmark mosque in Damascus that remains a prominent feature of the old city's skyline. Khusrow Pasha built Aleppo's first Ottoman landmark, a mosque-madrasa that stood prominently at the base of the citadel until destroyed in Syria's civil war after 2012.

Both Damascus and Aleppo were prestigious postings: Aleppo for its size and wealth and Damascus for its historical associations and its status as a gateway for the annual Muslim pilgrimage caravan to Mecca. Notable governors created imperial endowments in both cities, and often when the governors moved on some of their relatives or other household members stayed behind to administer the endowments, establishing a multi-generational presence among local urban elites. A comparable dynamic (though on a smaller scale) was seen in district administration, where lower-ranking soldiers (typically with the rank of *bey* or title of *agha*) took on functions of district governors assisted by detachments of local and imperial military forces.

Alongside the governor, the second pillar of Ottoman provincial administration was the chief judge. Like the governor, the *kadi* was appointed from Istanbul to Damascus, Aleppo and other provincial centers. Typically, chief judges had been trained at the major schools of Istanbul, and they were specialized in Islamic religious law of the official Hanafi rite. Chief judges were part of a hierarchy of learned men or *ulama* that extended from district and provincial centers back to the chief jurisconsult of the empire, the Sheikh al-Islam in Istanbul. The Sheikh al-Islam occupied the apex of the *ulama* hierarchy in much the same way as the Grand Vizier was at the apex of the military/administrative governors' hierarchy. Like provincial governors, chief judges served time-limited terms. They oversaw sharia law courts, which had wide discretion in a range of judicial and civil matters. The judges' courts acted as notary offices, oversaw inheritances, adjudicated property disputes and public morality, monitored endowments and settled (or registered settlements of) civil suits. Judges also were responsible for the officials who inspected markets and buildings in response to complaints or legal queries. On the ideological plane, judges came to be seen as symbols of the 'justice' that rulers invoked to legitimize the rule of the Ottoman sultans and their representatives.

Between them, governors and judges represented the Ottoman dynasty in Damascus, Aleppo and other Ottoman provincial capitals. During the initial Ottoman decades, governors and judges sent to Syria typically were *Rumis*, products of imperial institutions in the capital. With the passage of time, though, distinctions between what was imperial and what was local began to blur.

Cities and Towns, Local and Imperial

The heart of Ottoman administration of Syria lay in the major cities, anchored by Damascus and Aleppo. Both cities laid claim to the distinction of being the 'oldest continuously inhabited city in the world.' Both lay astride major trade and communications routes. The Ottoman-era 'Sultan's Road' (*al-tariq al-sultani*) joined the two cities and linked them to Ottoman Anatolia (and eventually to Istanbul) in the north, and to Palestine and the Muslim holy cities of Mecca and Medina in the south. Prominent in each city were fortified citadels that housed imperial garrisons and served as symbols of military authority.

Information about early Ottoman Syria is most abundant for the provincial centers of Damascus, Aleppo and Tripoli, and for the district centers of Hama and Jerusalem. These centers all displayed common patterns, revealing an Ottoman institutional stamp. Ottoman officials interacted with local society through a network of intermediary collective bodies. Heads of neighborhood quarters, heads of guilds, leaders of recognized descendants of the Prophet (a group known as *ashraf*), heads or elites of non-Muslim religious communities, and military/tribal heads of localized garrisons were the representatives who mediated or occupied the space between imperial demands and local requirements. The importance of these collective bodies produced a lively sense of local group solidarity and membership.

These groups were collectively obliged to discharge their obligations (typically fiscal) to the rulers' treasury. At the same time, they were held accountable for other services and demands. Informal dispute resolution mechanisms settled differences within and among these various groups or communities. Institutional judicial authority would be invoked (leaving archival records) only when other avenues were stymied, or when someone determined that formal documentation of an agreement, contract or decision was needed.

A key institution in the cities of Ottoman Syria was the sharia law court. In the cities of Aleppo and Damascus there were many such courts, while smaller towns like Hama and Jerusalem each had but one. In Aleppo and Damascus the chief *kadi* was assisted by deputies who presided over separate courts in other parts of the city. In Damascus there were as many as seven courts, and in Aleppo five. Although the *kadi* was usually an Istanbul-trained *Rumi* (i.e., a Turkish speaker), deputy judges were invariably drawn from local scholarly families. Generally it was the more recognized *ulama* families with histories of service who would obtain deputy judgeships. The same recognized families would claim precedence in prestigious teaching posts or in the administration of pious endowments. Often they had *ashraf* status, making them part of a 'nobility of blood,' in contrast to local military families who enjoyed hereditary authority as a 'nobility of status.' Prominent *ulama* families were among the more significant Syrian Arab partners in the system of Ottoman rule. Not only did learned members of these families assist in urban administration, they also played key roles in the ideological legitimization of Ottoman rule in predominantly Muslim Syrian cities and towns.

Major endowments (*waqfs*) provided, both to *ulama* and scions of military families, material support to maintain their lineages' prominence, patronage and station. Under the Ottomans, *waqfs* of all kinds became ubiquitous. The largest and most extensive of them were administered by *ulama*, often *ashraf-ulama*, and by descendants of military/administrative figures who had founded the endowments. Because properties could be endowed to support a founder's descendants, with revenues directed to public or charitable purposes only if descendants died out, endowments also were a way to incorporate family holdings and keep them under the supervision of an overseer. (Otherwise, according to the workings of Islamic law, privately owned properties would be divided among heirs.)

Ottoman officials' use of *waqfs* changed Syria's cityscapes. After his conquest of Damascus Sultan Selim, reflecting his dynasty's encouragement of Islamic mysticism, patronized the tomb of the theosophist Ibn Arabi (d. 1240) in the Salihiyya suburb of Damascus. Selim ordered the construction of the city's first Ottoman monument, the still extant tomb-mosque of Ibn Arabi.

Ibn Arabi's tomb and its associated madrasa (the Selimiyya) was a harbinger of physical changes that Ottoman rule would bring to Syria's two major provincial centers. Damascus boasted the patronage of two sultans: Selim and his son and successor Suleiman. The latter constructed a mosque, hospice, *caravanserai* (merchants' emporium) and madrasa on the site of an old Mamluk palace along the banks of the Barada River. This structure provided lodging for pilgrims preparing to depart for Mecca and became known as the Suleimaniyya. In rapid succession, three sixteenth-century governors of Damascus – Murad, Darwish and Sinan Pashas – built mosques that included madrasas and commercial facilities along the Sultan's Road that extended south from Damascus, a jumping-off point for the Mecca pilgrimage. All of these new buildings were outside the city walls, highlighting the extent to which Damascus grew in the Ottoman era, secure now from foreign attack and invasion.

In Aleppo the first major Ottoman structure, completed in 1546, was built at the behest of governor Khusrow Pasha. It was a massive mosque-madrasa-caravanserai complex southwest of the citadel, which added a distinctive Ottoman architectural mark to Aleppo's skyline. Other constructions by later official patrons followed, whose net effect was to shift the principal axis of Aleppo's streetscape. Formerly it had been North–South, but Ottoman-era constructions shifted the axis to East–West, beginning from the citadel to Antioch Gate – *Bab Antakya* – that became the early modern city's major thoroughfare and the heart of the Old City *suq* (market). Aleppo owed its early modern prominence as Syria's major merchant center to its position within a vast Ottoman-facilitated trade network. The officially patronized infrastructure projects (especially caravanserais) came to define Aleppo's old city until its destruction in the recent civil war.

The *waqf* or endowment was the legal institution that allowed for the construction, reconstruction and maintenance of facilities intended for public benefit. A benefactor – in the case of major projects, typically the sultan, a member of his household, or a locally stationed high official – would endow urban and rural revenue-producing properties for the support of mosques, madrasas and other projects like public fountains. Endowments of this kind were huge projects that remade urban space. The great commercial caravanserais of Aleppo and Damascus were built to encourage the commerce that would generate revenues to support endowers' projects. The *kadi* and his court oversaw administration of endowments, with members of the endower's family or household acting as administrators in some instances. The *waqf* institution fused the interests of military elites and ranking local *ulama*. *Waqfs* permeated urban society, and some people endowed mixed family–charitable *waqfs* as a way of embellishing their status as quarter notables.

Almost any public purpose could be supported by the creation of a *waqf* – whether it was for poor relief or the care of stray cats. In Ottoman times, Christian and Jewish *waqfs* supported the needs and institutions of these communities.[5]

Guilds or craft corporations were another quintessentially Ottoman institution that became a key part of urban governance. Nearly all economically productive men were organized into guilds, each with its own leadership and existing in a complicated hierarchical relationship with other guilds. Guilds grouped together the manufacturers, artisans and tradesmen of the city, and were a point of contact between Ottoman authority and local economic activity. Guilds adjudicated internal disputes and represented their members' interests in constant negotiations with the tax collection authorities. As intermediate institutions, guilds appeared to be a mixture of grass-roots self-government and top-down administrative supervision.

Some guilds, such as the bakers' guild and the butchers' guild, were essential for the provisioning of cities and for food security. Ottoman civil and military authorities took a close interest in the workings of these guilds and insisted that they supply certain quotas and uphold basic standards. Other important guilds included those connected to textile weaving, which was the craft that employed the greatest number of workers. Here, supervision of inputs and outputs and regulation of quality and protection of guildsmen's monopolies were uppermost.

Guilds were self-regulating up to a point, though they were not egalitarian. Within each guild was a hierarchy of craft workers plus the recognized head(s) of the guild, and some guilds were subordinate to others. But guilds did form institutionally recognized interest groups, who might (depending on circumstances) push back against certain tax or payment demands, or at least would determine the individual distribution of tax burdens on their members.

Whereas many guilds were uniformly Muslim, and recognized heads of guilds were always Muslims, membership of some guilds included significant numbers of Christians or Jews. Legal distinctions among religious communities did not have a counterpart in strict social segregation, at least not in the market and workplace. Christians were often found in the textile and construction trades. The 'chief builder' of Ottoman Syrian cities was typically a skilled Christian. Judges and deputy judges of the sharia courts relied on testimony of the chief builder when courts heard complaints regarding sites and buildings, or when courts wanted to assess the state of a property for a legal ruling.

Guilds of tradesmen and shopkeepers offered the means to regulate and adjudicate marketplace conditions in the name of an ideology of economic justice. Merchants themselves were not organized into guilds, but the preeminent merchant would be recognized with the title of *shahbandar* and might witness the formalization of contracts. The different *suqs* had designated sheikhs to act as a local reference point, and to serve as intermediaries between representatives of Ottoman authority on the one hand and shopkeepers and merchants in specific *suqs* on the other hand.

No longer expanding, or expanding only slowly, the Ottoman state could not rely on expensive imperial troops alone to meet its military needs. This was particularly true in a place like Syria, far removed as it was from the main battlegrounds of central Europe, the northern Black Sea shore, Transcaucasia and Iran. Locally recruited military forces commanded by locally rooted military leaders became mainstays of Ottoman administration in Syria's towns and countryside.

In the towns, these local forces frequently acquired guild membership, becoming part-time soldiers and part-time craftsmen (or sometimes, nominal soldiers and full-time craftsmen). Armed soldier–craftsmen developed ties to the local productive economy, sometimes engaging in protection rackets. At times these local recruits were ethnically marked, as 'Moroccans' (*Maghariba*) or 'Albanians' (*Arna'ut*), denoting social identities that came from memories of emigration and settlement. At other times they were recruited as clients of locally powerful (and wealthy) military commanders. The point is that local recruits were local men of long-standing or of recent in-migration, who had close ties to commerce and production.

Multiple and sometimes overlapping sets of affiliations therefore expressed social solidarities in towns and cities.

Intellectual Life

The *ulama* of the sixteenth and seventeenth centuries were supported by an array of madrasas, where they cultivated and taught the Islamic sciences (jurisprudence, exegesis, source criticism, Arabic grammar). Damascus and Aleppo each had scores of madrasas, whose exact number fluctuated from one era to the next. New madrasas were established following the Ottoman conquest, as part of the pattern where *ulama*, or wealthy merchants, or prominent military administrators endowed properties to support them.

In addition to madrasas, Syrian cities and towns saw the spread of Sufism and of Sufi meeting places – imperfectly translated as 'lodges' (Ar. *zawiya* or *khanqah* or *takiyya*). Sufism as a mystical tradition complemented the scholasticism of the *ulama* who specialized in jurisprudence. Sufis emphasized the experience of unity with God, or of feeling God's presence, and typically they were organized into 'orders' (Ar. *tariqa*) that practiced the spiritual exercises of their founders, much as medieval Christian orders of monks and nuns looked to the example of their founding patron or saint. Sufis emphasized the personal authority and insight of the Sufi sheikh, who would trace his authority (and sometimes his bloodline) back to the order's founder. Some Sufism shaded off into esoteric or antinomian practices (bizarre or transgressive public behavior), explained by the mystic's having been 'seized' or 'captured' (*majdhub*) by the Divine.

For the most part, though, Sufism in the early Ottoman period was integrated with the more scholastic pursuits of *ulama*, and many *ulama* enhanced their personal prestige by also being leaders (often, hereditary leaders) of Sufi orders. In Aleppo, one celebrated nonconformist Sufi (Sheikh Abu Bakr b. Abi al-Wafa, d. 1583) was memorialized after his death in a tomb complex outside the city walls, which became in time a respectable place of pilgrimage, serving also on occasion as the headquarters of Ottoman governors. Like madrasas, the Sufi lodges were supported by a network of endowments that were administered by and offered institutional support to *ulama*.

Ulama of Damascus predominated in the intellectual life of sixteenth and seventeenth-century Syria. Though Aleppo was a great administrative, commercial and religious center, Damascus was richer in terms of its intellectual output. Perhaps because of its sacredness in Muslims' imagination, Damascus attracted the persons and institutions that supported a vigorous life of letters. In addition to its many madrasas and Sufi lodges, Damascus was favorably referenced in a canonical statement of Prophet Muhammad who compared it to paradise, and Damascus was a staging point for the annual pilgrimage caravan to Mecca.

Damascus had been the capital of the Umayyad caliphs (661–750) who triumphed over their rivals to establish the first 'royal' Islamic dynasty. The city's venerable Umayyad Mosque was the principal physical vestige of this era. During the Crusades, Damascus had been a rallying point for the Muslim defenders who managed to confine the Crusader states to the coast, and who used Damascus as a political and military base for the reconquest of Jerusalem. Muslim refugees from Crusader depredations in Palestine founded a new quarter of Damascus (Salihiyya) on a nearby mountainside, which soon became replete with mosques, madrasas and Sufi lodges.

During the rule of Saladin (d. 1193) and his successors the Ayyubids (r. 1174–1250), the madrasa system was introduced to Damascus and was further built up under the Mamluks (r. 1250–1516). Damascus's Umayyad Mosque incorporated tombs said to contain remains of John the Baptist (the Qur'anic Yahya) and the Prophet's grandson Hussein (martyred at Karbala in Iraq in 680). On a nearby mountainside above Salihiyya was the grotto where Cain is said to have slain Abel. As noted, when the Ottomans entered Damascus in 1516, Sultan Selim made a point of building an imperial mosque over the tomb of the medieval theosophist Ibn Arabi in Salihiyya, a gesture that enhanced the centrality of Damascus for Sufi mystics, and demonstrated the high religious and spiritual regard that the sultan had for the city.

The issues that sixteenth and seventeenth-century writers discussed included a range of subjects and genres, from the traditional sciences of Islamic law and jurisprudence, to mysticism, poetry, history, travel and pilgrimage, and biography. Modern scholars have closely studied only some of these manuscripts, reflecting modern academic priorities and interests (especially studies of history and of Islamic law). The relative neglect of this era's other writings, compared to earlier centuries of Arab scholarship, reflects a bias that modern thinkers – Arab and non-Arab alike – held about Arabic cultural production in the early Ottoman period. It was said to be intellectually uninteresting especially compared to the vibrant and original work produced in Arabic during the preceding medieval period.

It is true that royal or imperial sponsorship of Arabic scholarship after the thirteenth century diminished, as Mamluk and Ottoman rulers did not surround themselves with Arab scholars and poets to the same degree as their predecessors, favoring instead writing in Turkish and Persian. Though Ottoman Damascus remained a major Arabic scholarly center, its scholars' output could seem 'provincial' compared to Arabic scholarly output of earlier centuries. But intellectual life in early Ottoman Syria (sixteenth–seventeenth centuries) was not stagnant or unaffected by wider trends in Muslim scholarship – quite the contrary.

Arabic intellectual life in the early modern period, including work produced in Syria, was organically linked to what came before and is revelatory about the living intellectual practices, traditions and issues of the day. The depth and scope of Syria's intellectual infrastructure (madrasas, Sufi lodges) and the role of Damascus in Arab Muslims' understanding of the world demonstrates that Arabic thought in these years was a living thing, dealing with changing circumstances within paradigms and frameworks that made sense to contemporaries.

Much of scholarship focused on verifying or elaborating on the works of earlier scholars, marking a continuity of cultural and intellectual traditions. Debates and arguments revolved around the interpretations of these works, what scholars at the time called *tahqiq* – 'verification.' In the wake of the Ottoman conquest and the Ottoman–Safavid wars, Sunni scholars entered Ottoman lands from Persianate cultural areas, bringing new books and styles of scholarship with them. Therefore, Damascene scholars engaged with Muslim thought outside of the Arabophone cultural sphere. At the same time, *Rumi* (Turcophone) scholars were eager to engage with their Arabophone counterparts. Damascus saw the development of lively literary salons in the sixteenth and seventeenth centuries, where male scholars of local and *Rumi* origin met and debated questions of law, theology and interpretation of earlier texts. New canons grew out of these encounters, evidenced by the integration of Syrians' scholarship into the curricula of Ottoman imperial madrasas.

The legacies in Damascus of two archetypal late medieval thinkers offered plenty of material for scholars' discussions and debates. The first, the mystic and theosophist Ibn Arabi, has already been invoked. He wrote about the concept of 'unity of being,' in which the material world of the senses is understood to be manifestations of divinity rather than as a 'creation' separate from the Creator. This insight encouraged his disciples to discover the 'inner meanings' of truths, which might be concealed by outer forms such as the literal meanings of words, or the formalistic demands of religious law. The second, the scripturalist and legalist Ibn Taymiyya (d. 1328), represented a contrasting tradition that sought to determine truth through a close and literal reading of canonical texts that abjured the mystics' goal of finding 'higher truths' through direct experience of the divine. Ibn Taymiyya lived and wrote in the aftermath of the Mongol irruption into the heart of the Islamic world, and he feared for the integrity of Arab–Islamic learning. He and those who followed in his footsteps were critical of the theosophists' relativizing (or watering down of) literal and outward forms of scriptural understanding. (In our own day, Ibn Taymiyya's literalism and hostility to Shiites has made him a popular medieval source for Sunni fundamentalists and sectarians.)

The spread of Sufism and of new Sufi orders in Syria generally during the sixteenth and seventeenth centuries demonstrates a kind of spiritual and intellectual unsettledness, or openness to the new. Two of the most significant new Sufi orders were the Mawlawis and the Naqshbandis, both of which originated outside of the Arabophone sphere. The Mawlawis (*Mevlevis* in Turkish) were an Ottoman order founded by devotees of the Konya mystic Jalal al-Din al-Rumi (d. 1273). They were best known for their ceremonies that combined music and rhythmical movement to produce a mystical state that enabled devotees to experience the sensation of union with the infinite. The Mawlawis were popularized among European travelers and residents as the 'whirling dervishes.' Aleppo became a major Mawlawi center, second only to Konya itself.

The Naqshbandi order (spelled Nakshbandi in modern Turkish) had originated in Central Asia, and came to Syria with pilgrims and travelers from Persian and Turkish-speaking lands as well as with pilgrims returning to Syria from Mecca, where pilgrims from India had established the order. The Naqshbandis emphasized both scriptural knowledge and spiritual exercises that forsook the more dramatic or showman-like qualities of some rival Sufi orders – thus one can think of the Naqshbandis as a 'sober' Sufi order. (They continue to have a significant influence in Syria today.)

All forms of Sufism relied on the examples of their founders, passed along by Sufi masters, to guide practitioners on paths to spiritual enlightenment. In Syria's cities Sufi sheikhs were typically *ulama*, often from families who had a hereditary identification with a particular order and with the 'saintly charisma' associated with it. For example, the Kaylanis of Hama and Damascus were identified with their ancestors' Qadiriyya order that had originated in medieval Iraq. In the countryside, where well-trained *ulama* were rare and where institutions of urban Islam were usually absent, itinerant Sufis or local Sufi shrines might be the principal way in which peasants expressed and experienced their spiritual lives.

The dominant figure in the intellectual life of seventeenth-century Syria is the Damascene Abd al-Ghani al-Nabulusi, whose work bridges the seventeenth and eighteenth centuries. Born in the middle of the seventeenth century, his family had been living in Damascus for many generations after fleeing Crusader rule in medieval Palestine. Abd al-Ghani was from a scholarly and wealthy family, and he could afford to devote his life to teaching and writing. He identified with the official Hanafi rite. The subjects that engaged him were wide ranging and they reveal something about the intellectual horizons of the day. He wrote on Sufism (he was a Naqshbandi who defended Ibn Arabi from charges of heresy), he wrote about law and debated adherents of a literalist or fundamentalist movement that was making inroads in Istanbul and Damascus. Against conservative criticisms he upheld the morality of popular practices such as coffee and tobacco consumption, and literary expressions of homoeroticism. Of tobacco's ubiquity he wrote:

> [Tobacco] has now become extremely famous in all the countries of Islam: in the Holy Cities, Damascus, Cairo, Aleppo, Anatolia. Indeed, it was diffused and spread until it reached from North Africa to the Middle East and to India and the Indus Valley. People of all kinds have used it and devoted themselves to it: those who are known for goodness and piety [i.e., the Sufis] those from among the doctors of law, the chief shaykhs of the muftis and teachers, and [students]; those who possess the positions of commanders, judges, prayer leaders, preachers and muezzins; the rulers of the state; and finally the general population in the markets and homes, as well as soldiers and slaves, from among the elderly, adults, youth and children. I have even seen young children of about five years applying themselves to it.[6]

Against conservatives, and consistent with his Sufi outlook, he argued that Jews and Christians had a path to paradise based on their inner faith which only God could know. He wrote poetry and left accounts of his travels: pilgrimages around Syria, Egypt and the Hejaz in which he recorded the prominent sites, scholars and spiritual leaders that he encountered. Abd al-Ghani taught in the Umayyad Mosque of Damascus and in various madrasas, especially the Selimiyya, the madrasa built by Sultan Selim at the tomb of Ibn Arabi. His lessons were major public events, and he appears to have been genuinely popular among Damascenes (but less so among officials). He had many admirers among his peers, and his reputation transcended the confines of Damascus. (When Abd al-Ghani visited Homs in 1693 it was a memorable occasion in the life of the town, still recalled years later.) But judging by his interventions in public debates, Abd al-Ghani also was a polarizing figure who could draw stringent criticism, particularly from *ulama* inspired by the more literalist or fundamentalist tradition of Ibn Taymiyya.

By the standards of his day Abd al-Ghani was a cosmopolitan intellectual. Keen to explore dimensions of Sufism and the relationship between inner belief and external laws, he engaged with thinkers and ideas from throughout the Islamic lands. He wrote:

> I have seen in this time of ours a community from all ethnic groups, the Arabs, the Persians, the Indians, the Turks, and other ethnic groups as well, all of whom reached – by reading the books of truth [i.e., the Sufi texts] – the levels of the masters, and acquired from [the books] the objects of their hopes. If after that, one supports his knowledge with additional practice and devotional struggle one becomes among the perfect men [i.e., those who have obtained mystical enlightenment].[7]

Yet at the same time, alongside his sense of Islamic universalism and cosmopolitanism, Abd al-Ghani had a strong sense of his ethnic and cultural identity as an Arabic speaker. In a polemic that he wrote against a fundamentalist or literalist Turkish adversary who had accused Abd al-Ghani of unbelief, he responded that as an Arabic speaker he had a deeper affiliation with Islam than did his adversary: 'the *ulama* have established that the Arabs are masters of the Turks and Persians in matters of religion and that it was they who brought the Turks into Islam in the first place.'[8]

Intellectual life of early Ottoman Syria was rooted in the cities. Its participants shared a sense of local identity as inhabitants of these cities and as speakers of Arabic. Syrian (especially Damascus-based) *ulama* engaged co-thinkers and adversaries from the wider Ottoman and Islamic intellectual spheres. Their outlook and world-view was far from what would later be called 'national,' though elements of their early modern discourse (a combination of localism and universalism) would later be evoked by advocates of Arab and Syrian nationalism. Early modern intellectual life expressed the world-view and outlooks of a small but culturally influential group of urban men, in a region and at a time when most people lived outside of the cities, outside the circle of literacy, and absorbed by the challenges of sustenance and survival in environments where the formal structures of Ottoman statehood often were absent or tenuous, or experienced mainly as exploitative or oppressive.

The Countryside

Syria's major cities were the heart of Ottoman administrative, military and legal institutions, demonstrating the centrality of urbanism to the definition and understanding of Ottoman rule. Agricultural areas that adjoined cities – typically irrigated market gardens and orchards – were also closely bound up with and integrated into urban-based Ottoman legal and institutional structures. Cultivators and villagers from nearby gardens and orchards were part of the ebb and flow of human and commercial traffic in the markets of cities and towns.

Legal regulations included sultanic law decreed by the rulers, and sharia law derived from Islamic legal sources. Both types of law sought to balance rights of landholders and peasant cultivators, and these laws were meaningful to the degree that people appealed to them or resolved conflicts by using them. But the further out into the hinterlands one went, the more the interests of rural people and of urbanites became antagonistic or oppositional.

The interplay of needs among city dwellers, peasant cultivators and pastoral nomads could create mutually beneficial relationships. For instance, soap merchants and manufacturers in Aleppo depended on peasants to supply olive oil and Bedouins to supply alkali. Peasants needed a market for their olive oil, and both peasants and Bedouins needed the products of the city.

But relations of power made all the difference, and the more powerful party (typically representatives of the city) could extract what they needed from the less powerful (through taxation, forced confiscation, usurious debt, etc.). The exploitative relationship between town and countryside is reflected in a comment from one of the *ulama* of Damascus in the sixteenth century, Zayn al-Din Muflih al-Dimashqi:

> Allah has located knowledge and tyranny mostly in the city, and revenue and ignorance mostly in the villages. Allah gives the revenue of the villages

mostly to the *ulama*, and in exchange, He gives to the ignorance of the villagers the tyranny of the cities. In this way, it is knowledge that brought revenue to the *ulama* and also to the Turkish military and other inhabitants of the cities.[9]

In rural areas the Ottomans adapted to circumstance, in light of the huge range of lands, climates and resources represented by irrigated areas, rain-watered areas, hilly regions and arid pasturelands (steppes). In northern and central Syria (Aleppo, the districts of Homs and Hama) the Ottomans introduced a system that granted revenues for service. Military men called *sipahis* were granted revenues from groups of villages in return for fulfilling military obligations by sending cavalrymen (including the *sipahi* himself) on campaign. Larger revenue-yielding lands were known as *ziamets*, and their holders were called *zaims*. In hilly and mountainous areas the Ottomans usually identified a powerful clan or family who would be responsible for maintaining order, collecting taxes and remitting these to the treasury.

Clan leaders were recognized as tax farmers, that is, as individuals authorized to collect taxes in return for a payment or tribute to the Ottoman treasury, and they might be awarded official ranks to announce their status. These intermediaries were sometimes already established clans, or at other times leaders of tribal communities whom authorities brought to a region. Elsewhere, districts with varieties in types of terrain and water resources were treated as farmsteads leased or owned by power-brokers who collected rents and revenues from cultivators, and who remitted profits to local treasuries.

In more distant or exposed areas, powerbrokers exercising these rights were often leaders of military units (such as *aghas* or *beys*). The true steppes, where year-round settled agriculture was impractical and where animal husbandry dominated, were in the hands of pastoral nomadic chieftains and tribes who were subject at least in principle to a range of taxes including 'wintering fees' for seasonal camps in the vicinity of more densely populated areas. The Ottoman treasury in fact paid the most powerful pastoral nomads to provide security and transport services, whether these be escorting caravans or keeping the peace by checking upstart or obstreperous rivals.

The overall rural picture is one of military officers or militarized elites (including local clans) who exercised authority in their regions under the umbrella of the Ottoman sultan's authority. Rural clans or households would frequently struggle among themselves to extend their writ at rivals' expense. The more remote the region – either because of its ruggedness or distance from an administrative center – the greater was the potential for rivalries to be expressed as raw power struggles.

These arrangements had a strong regionalist character. The Ottomans' pragmatic adaptation to local circumstances trumped any (impractical) effort to impose administrative or fiscal uniformity throughout the disparate domains.

What these diverse rural administrative arrangements had in common was their military character. The *sipahis*, the *zaims*, the holders of farmsteads, the mountain intermediaries, and the tribal peoples all were armed and all were tied to the Ottomans' military administration in one way or another. Militarization of the countryside allowed the Ottomans to extend their writ across Syria's vast landmass. The regularity of commercial and pilgrimage caravans through Syria and across the steppes into Mesopotamia demonstrates the usefulness of these arrangements for protecting vital routes and interests. Unlike modern states with their police forces and extensive bureaucracies, Ottoman rule did not represent a uniform kind of authority. Although well-entrenched institutions and status hierarchies dominated Ottoman cities and towns, the farther away one moved from urban administrative centers, the more tenuous and symbolic Ottoman authority became. Garrisons and fortresses stood astride major trade routes, but Ottoman rulers acknowledged the reality of rural autonomies. This acknowledgement gave Ottomans officials or representatives considerable leeway in how to express or exercise imperial authority, opening the door for constant negotiations and renegotiations based on shifting balances of power. In times of crisis, armed pretenders to authority could and did arise in the countryside when circumstances favored it, or when an Ottoman appointee with strong local connections feared he might lose his position and rebelled for the cause of self-aggrandizement (including aggrandizement of his allies and clients).

Specific rural areas proved especially challenging. The range of coastal mountains that extended from Antioch in the north to the Galilee in the south – which then continued as hill country through Nablus, Jerusalem and Hebron (today's Palestinian West Bank) – was difficult to administer directly. As far as the authorities were concerned, direct administration was usually not worth the effort and expense of constant military expeditions. In these mountain regions the Ottomans identified local families and tribal chieftains who could represent Ottoman authority and pay tribute or taxes to a provincial governor. But otherwise they would enjoy local authority and exercise leeway in administrative arrangements.

A well-documented example of this practice comes from Mount Lebanon. The Ottomans' need to keep a close eye on Lebanon's coastal mountains led to Tripoli in the north and Sidon in the south being designated as Ottoman provincial capitals in 1579 and 1660, respectively. (The other two provincial capitals in Syria were Aleppo and Damascus.) In Tripoli province the Ottomans recognized the Turcoman military family of Sayfa as Istanbul's representatives. (The Sayfas had arrived in the region from Anatolia in the 1520s, and had acted locally on behalf of the new authorities.) The Sayfas subsequently ruled Tripoli, the northern part of Mount Lebanon and parts of the Ansariyeh mountains in Syria's coastal north for many years, from 1579 to 1625. During those decades their fortunes rose and fell vis-à-vis rival aspirants for power in their mountainous region. Such turbulence was typical of Ottoman provincial politics away from the main cities. In the central parts of Mount Lebanon the Ottomans initially worked with the Shiite military clans of Harfushes and Hamadas, and with the Maans. The latter were an influential, locally rooted Druze family whose most celebrated figure was Emir (or Prince) Fakhr al-Din (d. 1635). With rare exceptions, however, Istanbul did not permit the tax farmers of Mount Lebanon to claim the office of governor of Sidon. Direct appointees of the central government filled the Sidon governorship, and part of these governors' job was to monitor the balance of power in the Mountain and to maintain Ottoman suzerainty by exploiting rivalries between the Maans and other aspirants for authority.

At times of stress, countryside regions fell out of government control, often at the hands of insubordinate military elites. The rebellion of Janbulad Ali Pasha in 1605 is illustrative. His rebellion encompassed northern Syria. The Janbulad family was of local Kurdish origin in the region north of Aleppo, and Janbulad's uncle Hussein had been the first non-imperial (i.e., locally rooted) Ottoman governor of Aleppo. But when the Ottomans executed Hussein for alleged dereliction of duty, his nephew Janbulad launched a revolt supported mainly by his fellow Kurds, in which significant stretches of the northern Syrian countryside fell out of the Porte's control. Janbulad boasted to the Venetian consul in Aleppo that he would emerge as the sultan of the Syrian region, and he appealed to Venice for help. During the months of his 1605 rebellion, Janbulad denied the Ottomans valuable revenues, territory and trade routes in the important Aleppo hinterland. Looking to buy time while mustering resources to defeat him, the imperial government bought off Janbulad and recognized him as governor of Aleppo. Ultimately an imperial force defeated him and he was executed in 1610.

A similar fate awaited the Ottomans' Druze feudatory Fakhr al-Din Ibn Maan. In 1625 Fakhr al-Din had ended Sayfa dominance in Tripoli and added these northern regions of Mount Lebanon to his tax farms. Ottoman officialdom feared he was becoming too powerful. Eventually the Porte brought him down at the hands of an imperial army sent from Damascus in 1633, and executed him in 1635.

As the dramatic stories of Junbalad and Fakhr al-Din illustrate, the rural politics of Syria knew periods of turbulence in the first two Ottoman centuries. Most of the time and in most places, the Porte's writ was enforced, whether through its direct garrisons or through allied military intermediaries. The arrangements were not bureaucratic as much as they were family, tribe and household based, subject to ongoing negotiation (and intermittent fighting) as various parties sought to maximize their advantages.

In due course, the Ottomans recruited more and more of their military forces from the populations of Syria, so that the dividing line between who was 'military' and who was 'civilian' became blurred. Rivalries among local urban militias and factions could cause turbulence, but the extension of their presence in society demonstrated that Ottoman authority was becoming localized and had created constituencies for whom 'Ottoman legitimacy' was a claim to status and benefits.

As for cultivators in rural regions, the basic unit of production was the household. People's access to land and resources in their villages was typically determined by their membership in kin- and clan-based solidarities. This kind of land use was communal, as individuals' fortunes were tied to those of their kin or clan affiliations. Cultivators who lived in the vicinity of cities and or urban 'green belts,' and who were integrated into city-based legal and institutional structures, tended (like townspeople themselves) to have individual rights of cultivation, access and ownership, which they might share with partners or with co-owners. These orchard and market-garden cultivators depended less on clan-based systems of common law or customary practice to distribute and redistribute shares, and more on a combination of customary and sharia law that was adjudicated in the urban sharia courts.

The historical importance of these rural patterns is to highlight the diversity of Syria's rural areas, and the various patterns of power and influence that were found there. Urban areas were the centers of Ottoman administration, but rural areas did not passively submit to city-based authority. A range of intermediaries and local forces contested for rural influence and control, and above all for rural resources: crops, taxes and mastery of trade routes. If cities were centers of imperial (and later, national) imaginings, the rural majority jealously guarded their local interests and local particularisms against demands and pressures of the city, typically viewed as rapacious or exploitative. Urban–rural tensions and contestations would prove to be an enduring feature of Syria's modern history.

Senses of identity and of solidarity among country people in early Ottoman Syria formed around various axes. Village and kinship ties predominated, along with factional allegiances that were especially strong in mountain regions. Factional allegiances are best understood as alliances that permitted mountain populations and their leaderships to form political bonds outside of their immediate locales. In the coastal Ansariyeh mountains east of Latakia, tribal affiliations among the predominantly Alawite population were a source both of inter-village solidarities and rivalries in a rugged and remote district. In other villages on the plains and in the river valleys, wider affiliations might be expressed in kinship or tribal idioms. Especially in the areas where Bedouins were seasonally active, myths of common kinship or tribal affiliation were used to express alliances and patron–client relationships. Other rural tribal peoples in addition to the Arabic-speaking Bedouin were Kurds and Turcomans, whose chieftains were courted by the Ottomans as paramilitary allies. In the seventeenth century, the Ottomans settled Turcomans in the hinterland of Hama in order (the imperial authorities hoped) to provide a reliable paramilitary frontier guard in regions that were exposed to Bedouin raiding.

The social solidarities formed in early modern Ottoman Syria – both urban and rural – would endure and be tested in ensuing periods. New relationships of power reconfigured Ottoman rule in Syria during the eighteenth century, and Syrians responded or contributed to these immediate changes from the vantage point of how different groups saw themselves, their interests and their choices. Even later, and into the twentieth century, aspects of these identities, the relationships that they represented and the world-views that they invoked would continue to influence Syrians' sense of themselves, of their past, and of their present and future possibilities.

2

SYRIA'S 'LONG' EIGHTEENTH CENTURY: POLITICAL CRISES AND LOCAL RULERS

One day in 1717, crowds gathered in Homs to greet and to celebrate the city's district governor as he returned from an expedition against nearby Bedouins. A chronicler who was among the crowd later wrote, 'The poor and the unfortunate – men, women and children – opened the gates and went out to meet him. Some cried, and some blessed him, and they honored him with a great procession.'[1] The writer, a sharia court scribe named Muhammad al-Makki, also wrote with glee about a pasha of Damascus who had slaughtered a different set of Bedouins and took survivors as captives for ransom. One of Makki's heroes, a local military strongman named Ibrahim Agha Suwaydan, impaled obstreperous mountain people who in the chronicler's mind deserved no less. A few decades later in Damascus, a barber and chronicler named Ibn Budayr derided loose morals in the city (Prostitutes! Greed!), and bitterly criticized the powerful governor of the day, local man Asaad Pasha al-Azm, for spending extravagantly on his new palace and for failing to protect the weak from arrogant and undisciplined soldiers.

The 'long' eighteenth century – bracketed by the Treaty of Karlowitz (1699) and the Egyptian invasion of Syria (1831) – was not a happy or tranquil time. Urban–rural tensions and the political ambitions of local military families marked the period. Critically for the future, it was also in this era that foundations were laid for enduring local leaderships who persisted in Syria's cities and hinterlands until the mid-twentieth century. These developments strengthened local forces that attached themselves to, or were legitimized by, Ottoman authority, but that were not 'national' in outlook or in scope.

SYRIA'S NEW POWERBROKERS: THE RISE OF THE AZMS

Ottoman global preeminence faded in the eighteenth century. The seafaring states of Europe came to surpass the sprawling but loose-limbed empire in economic, organizational and technical fields, as well as in dominating the Indian Ocean trade. European merchants and governments obtained new riches and new products from the transatlantic economy, including trade in African slaves and colonial exploitation of the Americas.

In an earlier time the Ottoman imperial system had depended on, and reproduced itself by, conquest and territorial expansion to obtain new resources. But this expansionist era also came to a definitive end, both practically and ideologically, when the Ottomans signed the Treaty of Karlowitz with an Austrian-led alliance. In this treaty the Ottomans lost substantial European territories and agreed to establish fixed boundaries with their Christian adversaries. Henceforth the imperial treasury would have to draw more and more on resources internal to the empire, rather than obtain new resources by conquest. Complicating the task was a shift of international long-distance luxury trade away from Ottoman controlled overland routes to European-controlled maritime routes.

For Syria, these developments meant Istanbul's greater willingness (or need) to rely on local intermediaries, and to accede to these intermediaries' acquisition of land, wealth and provincial resources as part of a devolutionary policy. Indeed no less than the Treaty of Karlowitz, the development of lifetime tax farms (called *malikane*, first introduced in 1695) and the power they bestowed on their owners was an important and revealing signifier of the new era. Crucially they provided a formal, institutionalized and legal way for newly ascendant provincial power-brokers to lay claim to taxation income of cities and countryside, subject to their payment of requisite funds to the imperial treasury.

The most visible political impact of these changes was the ascendance in Damascus, and in north-central Syria generally, of a military family called the Azms who proved (in the main) to be able administrators and effective commanders. When they were successful the Azms could marshal rural food resources to provision Damascus, as well as use their military prowess and political contacts to ensure the safe passage of caravans and pilgrims. The Azms' wealth permitted them to play the political game in Istanbul, where family agents cultivated Ottoman patrons with promises of gifts and gold. Azm governors of Damascus left an impressive legacy of stone buildings – palatial, commercial and educational – in the city as well as in the provincial center of Hama, their earlier political base. The Azms' salience in the eighteenth century also underscores a new centrality of Damascus for Syria's commerce, eclipsing Aleppo.

Even so, Istanbul was not willing to give the Azms carte blanche. Officials at the Porte maintained ties with the family's Syrian factional adversaries to impose some checks on their ambitions. As Ibn Budayr the barber's complaints show, the Azms' rise to power and their aggrandizement of wealth produced a local backlash from those who were excluded or disadvantaged. Damascus developed its own pattern of factional politics rooted in family alliances, neighborhood identities and economic interests, and the Azms and their allies did not consistently maintain their governing positions.

Nonetheless, the persistence of the Azms' political presence in Damascus was a qualitatively new phenomenon, one that helps to symbolize some of the changes that Syria experienced in the eighteenth century, as well as their lasting importance. The Azms and many other powerful families that rose to prominence at this time survived the vicissitudes of empire, colonial rule and early independence. Indeed, the last Azm to be politically prominent in Syria did not depart the scene until 1963.

The emergence of the Azms was part of a broader Ottoman and Syrian phenomenon, characterized as the rise of the notables or *a'yan*. These emerging powerbrokers can be put into two categories, corresponding to the different types of Ottoman-linked elites that readers of this history already have met. The first type were families of military origin (such as the Azms or the Suwaydans), whose leading lights often had the title of *agha* or *bey*, denoting a military rank or position that sometimes was quasi-hereditary. The most ambitious of them would aspire to the highest Ottoman rank of pasha. As noted in Chapter 1, Ottomans began to raise local military forces quite early in their rule. By the eighteenth century Istanbul was ready to appoint some of these local soldiers to positions of high political and administrative authority in their home regions.

The Azms, for example, first came to the Porte's attention because the founder of the family's fortunes, a soldier named Ibrahim Bey, was an effective commander in the region of Ma'arrat al-Nu'man, a village and caravan stop on the Sultan's Road between Aleppo and Hama. After serving as district governor of Hama, Homs and Ma'arrat al-Nu'man, Ibrahim's son Ismail was promoted to pasha. The Porte appointed Ismail Pasha first to the secondary governorship of Tripoli, in whose jurisdiction Homs and Hama then lay. Subsequently, in 1725, Ismail Pasha ascended to the governorship of Damascus, inaugurating Azm rule in the city and province. The rise of a locally rooted family to this position of leadership is all the more significant since, a few years prior to 1725, Istanbul had decided that the governor of Damascus should *ex officio* also be the commander of the annual pilgrimage caravan to Mecca. This association with the pilgrimage enhanced the prestige and prerogatives of the Damascus governorship.

The second strand of powerbroker were those who came from prestigious *ulama* families, sometimes associated with leadership of Sufi orders. The *ulama* had of course long been prominent in the lives of the cities, with illustrious lineages becoming a kind of 'nobility of blood' who passed down their families' prestige, learning and legal-administrative-religious positions from one generation to the next. These notables' prominence as administrators of major endowments made them a major part of the consolidating local elite. The *waqf* endowments encompassed significant swathes of productive urban and rural properties, including workshops, commercial warehouses, farms and villages. Typically the *ulama* notables bore the honorific title of *effendi*, and if they were *ashraf* (descended from the Prophet) they also would be addressed as *sayyid* in recognition of this status.

Between them, elites of military origin and notables of *ashraf* lineage and Sufi backgrounds dominated the scene in Syria's cities during the eighteenth century. As the dominant social forces in the country's urban centers, elites and notables formed alliances and rival factions within their ranks. Combinations of these elites and notables held villages in the hinterlands of the towns, whether outright as private property, or (more often) as a combination of lifetime tax farms, endowment tenancies and leases, and private ownership. Individual notable families might rise and fall in importance, but as a group they retained a presence and exercised local influence for the duration of the Ottoman period – and even beyond. While the most important or renowned elites and notables of this kind were Muslims, prominent Christians and (to a lesser extent) Jews also acted as clients or associates of Muslim patrons or benefactors. In the region of Mount Lebanon a handful of Christian and Druze families even acquired feudal-administrative powers that allowed them to emerge as local powerbrokers in their own right, complete with their own internal factional divisions and contestations.

Accounts of selected military and *ulama a'yan* families in the eighteenth century illustrate the dynamics at work at this level of Syrian–Ottoman society. When Ibrahim Bey al-Azm's son Ismail Bey became district governor of Homs, Muhammad al-Makki (the sharia court scribe who delighted in news of slaughtered tribespeople) praised his generosity. 'He performed a great beneficence for the people of Homs, supporting the poor and unfortunate by sending wheat and barley.'[2] Subsequently promoted to pasha, Ismail was appointed governor of Damascus in 1725 and he served until 1730. The second Azm governor of Damascus was Suleiman Pasha, who first held this office in 1734, then was dismissed, and subsequently served again, dying in office in 1743. He was immediately succeeded by his nephew Asaad Pasha, who served for a remarkably long period of 14 years, and episodically drew the ire of Ibn Budayr, the barber-chronicler. Two other Azms, plus on occasion some of their allies, held the Damascus governorship discontinuously until 1807.

Given the nature of factional politics in Ottoman Syria, and Istanbul's interest in maintaining a balance of power, the Azms fell from favor cyclically but they demonstrated remarkable resilience in coming back. At the peak of their power Azm rulers supported the family's political ambitions with income from endowments, tax farms, villages and trade – including under Asaad Pasha especially monopolistic and speculative economic activities (e.g., wheat hoarding) that inflamed local opinion.

Their rule left its mark on the city: Asaad built his palatial residence in the center of Damascus (the Azm Palace), which remained family property until 1920 when descendants sold it to the French colonial government. (Today it is a folklore museum.) He also built near the palace a celebrated caravanserai to support the Baghdad caravan trade. This structure – today a state-owned heritage site, the Khan Asaad Pasha – demonstrates Damascus's rising commercial preeminence (at the expense of Aleppo) by the mid-eighteenth century.

In both Damascus and Hama, Azm men intermarried with Sufi-linked *ashraf* women, particularly from the Kaylani family who led the Qadiriyya Sufi order. Through such marriage ties, the Azms (like other ambitious political households) extended their contacts and their influence in the Syrian region. Interconnected interests bound together elites of military origin, long-distance traders and prominent *ulama*.

The nearest *ulama* counterparts to the Azms in Damascus were the Muradis. Their founder was Muhammad Murad al-Bukhari, a well-traveled scholar from Samarkand who settled in the city in 1670. He was a cosmopolitan scholar of his day, having studied throughout Muslim lands in Central Asia, India and the Ottoman Empire, as well as in Shiite Iran. He worked in three literary languages (Turkish, Persian and Arabic) and was principally responsible for the introduction of the Naqshbandi Sufi order to Syria. The family's material prosperity was rooted in Muhammad Murad's acquisition of villages in the Damascus region as lifetime tax farms – *malikanes*. The family also accumulated significant interest in *waqf* endowments. Murad himself established two madrasas, both called al-Muradiyya (and distinguished from each another by the adjectives 'Inner' and 'Outer,' a reference to the city walls). In this era students came to Damascus from as far away as Yemen to study in the Muradiyya madrasas. Muhammad Murad's descendants (called the Muradis) were politically aligned with the Azms more often than not.

The consolidation of local leaderships was found in smaller Syrian centers, too. For instance, the town of Hama (a home base and preparatory testing ground for the Azms) saw military elites (including the Azms) and *ulama* elites (including the Kaylanis) predominate in Hama's district administration and judicial offices. Between them the Azms, the Kaylanis and other powerful families dominated Hama's countryside through a mixture of tax farms, endowment administration and tenancies, and landholdings. Similarly in Homs, *aghas* from the local military family, named Suwaydan (whose home base was a village south of the town), were recurring candidates for administrative appointments. Meanwhile, Homs *ulama* families like the Sibais and Atassis filled offices of judge, mufti, and head of the *ashraf*. (Later, descendants of the Atassi and Sibai clans would play prominent roles in the twentieth century, including two Syrian presidents and a founder of the Syrian Muslim Brotherhood, respectively.)

A local dynasty comparable to that of the Azms did not emerge in Aleppo. The city was closer to Istanbul than was Damascus and its administrative area included significant swathes of the Empire's Anatolian heartland (territory that is today in Turkey). Nonetheless Aleppo did witness devolution of power to local forces, especially after 1775. By then Istanbul was distracted by recurring wars and threats of wars on its northern frontiers. While the Porte never conceded Aleppo to local forces, the latter were able to impose themselves at moments of imperial weakness. Among local forces both the *ashraf* and the local Janissaries were organized and numerous enough to assert a self-interested presence in the city. Emerging local elites of Aleppo included more merchant families than at Damascus, and Aleppo's *ulama* establishment was not as self-contained (in terms of intermarriages and family alliances) as its counterpart in Damascus. Nonetheless, eighteenth-century Aleppo offers a variation in degree, not in kind, of the *a'yan* phenomenon.

A dominant *ulama* family in Aleppo were the Jabiris, descended from an Ottoman *kadi* after whom they were named. Men of the Jabiri family were principal *ulama* in Aleppo from the second half of the eighteenth century. They had *ashraf* status, and as early as the 'long' eighteenth century, Jabiris owned considerable urban property, created endowments (including a madrasa), and repeatedly won appointments to prestigious and influential posts. As leaders of the *ashraf*, Jabiris played a role in the politics of Aleppo when the *ashraf* became a political faction (1770s–1805). The Jabiris of Aleppo, like many of their counterparts in other towns, endured. (Aleppo's Saadallah al-Jabiri was a prime minister of Syria during World War II.)

The rise of *a'yan* underscores the significance of powerful families and households in the formation of Ottoman-era Syrian urban elites. Many of them – Azms, Jabiris, Kaylanis and others – remained prominent in Syrian politics and society through the remainder of the Ottoman Empire, during French colonial rule and in the early years of Syrian independence. Marriage alliances allowed prominent families to extend their networks (by marrying out), or to consolidate family resources (by marrying in), or to bring in new wealth to support older lineages that had fallen on hard times. If we understand the *a'yan* households to have been not just 'families' (in the everyday modern use of the word) but political and economic interest groups, then the politics of the notables of eighteenth-century Syria can make sense beyond mere references to 'factionalism'. At a time when government and the state were less bureaucratized than they later became, elite households were centers of administration and wealth, and their internecine rivalries were part of the regular political order. In a sense, this arrangement duplicated on a provincial level the patrimonial model of government associated with the Ottoman ruling house in Istanbul. As the capacities of the imperial center became strained in the eighteenth century, the rise of provincial political households and reliance on these family networks were among the outcomes.

Although the symbolism of the sultan's authority remained significant, these families' rise conditioned the way that modern state formation was experienced in Syria in the nineteenth and twentieth centuries. Eventually, in the second half of the twentieth century rural military officers would launch coups and dispense with the older political households, but in time new intermediaries and powerbrokers took their places. The heterogeneity of Syria's population and countryside, and the difficulties encountered by imperial, colonial and national governments in administering differentiated territories and populations, meant the emergence of local power centers has been a recurring feature of modern Syrian history.

INTELLECTUAL LIFE AND LITERACY

Damascus continued to dominate intellectual life in eighteenth-century Syria. Local families (including the Azms and Muradis) built no less than seven new madrasas in Damascus in the eighteenth century. Damascenes' eighteenth-century literary output showed continuity with the past, as well as evidence of new social currents. *Ulama* debated and argued about textual traditions and mystical insights, and wrote poetry, chronicles and biographical dictionaries. Just as in the political realm, where the newly arrived Azms rose to prominence, carved out a space for themselves, and created stone monuments to their new preeminence, so too in the literary field the older cultural producers (elite *ulama*) were joined by upstart new literary voices from other segments of society. This social broadening of literate discourse was a symptom of the social flux and mobility of the period.

The Damascene *ulama's* cultural production rested on their self-confident position as the guardians and guarantors of public Muslim self-consciousness and scholastic knowledge. From his position in the city's most important teaching post, for example, the conservative jurist Ismail al-Ajluni (d. 1749) defended inherited textual traditions against those (such as Abd al-Ghani al-Nabulusi, cited in Chapter 1) who were attracted to experiential learning and mysticism. In defense of textual tradition, Ajluni wrote:

> I know it has been in the tradition of scholars of *hadith* [= canonical accounts of Muhammad's life] in the past and today to mention their [list of author-ities] and their connections to the imams and the shaykhs, because these chains of transmission are the expression of their lineage to the imams and the shaykhs; and from them and the means by which scholars of *hadith* listen to them and are supported by them.[3]

In other words, Ajluni positioned himself as one speaking with the voice of textual authority, as testified by the soundness of his chain of authorities. Nabulusi, whose life bridged the seventeenth and eighteenth centuries, ranged widely over numerous top-ics as we have seen, and he criticized those whom he regarded as overly rigid in their methodologies and conclusions. He defended popular practices and pastimes, and he also criticized careerism and petty one-upmanship that he saw among fellow *ulama*.

Muhammad Ibn Kannan (d. 1740–1) was a Naqshbandi Sufi of the Hanafi rite, a teacher and writer who drew from the diverse range of Damascus's Islamic learning. He was a dedicated teacher who spent his time lecturing, visiting with fellow schol-ars, and reciting and composing verse. Above all, Ibn Kannan is remembered today because he wrote an account of his life and times in Damascus, carrying on a prac-tice of chronicle authorship that had been a forte of *ulama* since medieval times. Ibn Kannan contributed to a well-established tradition of memorialization that bol-stered *ulama* prestige and solidarity via his authorship of biographical sketches. In these he acknowledged the leading *ulama* of the city, and described their academic connections and training, their personal qualities, and their relationships to Sufism.

Elite *ulama* were economically comfortable, and some were even extremely wealthy. The few exceptions (*ulama* who rose from modest backgrounds to the ranks of peer-recognized scholars) prove the rule. From Ibn Kannan's chronicle, readers can piece together a sense of the world as it was seen and experienced by a member of the Damascene *ulama*. He communicates the rhythms of the scholarly year, with the repeating cycle of lectures and lessons including special series that marked the holy month of Ramadan. He enjoyed scholarly exchanges with peers in the city's verdant gardens. 'On a Saturday [in September 1721],' he wrote,

> I was at the garden of Zayn al-Din with a fairly large group. We read from compilations of works by Abd al-Ghani al-Nabul[u]si and others. [The fol-lowing] Monday I was with a group of good friends in al-Rabwa [garden,

overlooking Damascus] [...] and on Wednesday most of our studying focused on 'Ali Halabi's biography of the Prophet. [*Ulama* companions] read aloud while the rest listened. We spent the night in Mazza [a village then outside of Damascus, but today a neighborhood in the city].[4]

The surroundings of well-appointed madrasas were likewise appealing to a man of Ibn Kannan's stature. He called one madrasa, the Ajamiyya,

a beautiful building with a façade embellished with multi-colored tiles and inscriptions. Inside there is a raised water fountain and the floor of the madrasa is decorated with alternating white, multicolored and marble tiles. The windows are [framed with] steel.[5]

As a member of the *ulama* at the top ranks of his profession, Ibn Kannan embraced the life of the mind and the opportunity to work amidst architectural and natural beauty.

Ibn Budayr the barber (d. ca. 1763) came from modest and unpromising circumstances. He was born in the outskirts of Damascus, along the Sultan's Road that went south to Houran and the beyond to the holy cities of Mecca and Medina. Ibn Budayr did not follow his father's trade as a porter for the annual pilgrimage caravan. Instead he moved closer in, to a neighborhood that adjoined the walls of Damascus. He apprenticed with a barber who worked in the heart of the walled city near the Umayyad Mosque. This central area is where the political, economic and intellectual elites lived and worked. In time Ibn Budayr opened his own shop, or perhaps carried on in his patron's workplace after the latter's retirement. He cut the hair of, and got acquainted with, leading lights of the city's *ulama*. His regular contact with this group appears to have imbued him with the self-confidence to try his hand at writing a chronicle, a literary form that until then had been a near-monopoly of the *ulama*. Ibn Budayr's chronicle is notable for the perspectives it offers on life from a common man's standpoint. He is unsparing in his criticism of Asaad Pasha al-Azm, whom he accuses of greed and profiteering at the expense of the general population. Alongside Ibn Budayr's modest class origins, his animosity to Asaad Pasha might have stemmed from the barber's birthplace and later residence in neighborhoods dominated by the Azms' rivals, 'localist' factions who were linked to the Houran grain trade in the city's southern hinterlands.

The Orthodox priest Mikhail Burayk (fl. 1782) was the first Christian in Damascus to write a chronicle. Although it was an account of his own community, Burayk was cognizant of the wider Muslim-dominated society. He sensed and reflected a change in the air that made his project of writing a chronicle timely. On the one hand, Asaad Pasha al-Azm's friendly attitude toward Christians encouraged the priest. Asaad Pasha eased restrictions on Christians' clothing regulations and church construction; restrictions that had marked them as a dependent albeit 'protected' Ottoman community. But Burayk was worried that emboldened Christian *dhimmis* would press their newfound sense of liberty too far and provoke a Muslim backlash. He was particularly exercised about the public behavior of Christian women, and he criticized their colorful public dress and their recreational smoking and drinking in gardens surrounding the city.

The reign of Asaad Pasha al-Azm got contrasting reviews from the barber and the priest. In his chronicle Ibn Budayr condemned Asaad's greed:

> Asaad Pasha, the governor of Damascus, bought many properties: houses, orchards and mills. He raised the price of wheat and barley while people were asking for relief and imploring for protection, but there is no one to help or guide the people.[6]

The barber had a low opinion of the military in general, and Asaad Pasha was part of the problem:

> The unruly soldiers of Damascus have committed excesses, cursing of religion has increased, the commoners have been oppressed, and no one listens to what they say, and the ruler of Damascus, his Excellency Asaad Pasha, has not confronted any of these matters. Public order has dissipated [...]. He does not move a thing, but sleeps with the sleeping.[7]

Contrast this with Burayk's positive view:

> I have read all of the histories of Damascus since its takeover by the Muslims until now, and I have not read one that reported the degree of wealth, strength, repute, power and mention that the Christians have reached in the past ten years under the rule of Asaad Pasha Ibn al-Azm. His name is Asaad [i.e., more felicitous], and good fortune (*al-saad* [a pun]) is in his face.[8]

In addition to being alarmed about the public behavior of Christian women, Burayk was exercised about the defection of Orthodox Christians to Catholicism. This peeling away of (Greek) Orthodox Christians to form the community later recognized as Greek Catholics (or Melkites) was part of the wider transformations affecting

Syria in the eighteenth century, linked to the growing influence of France and the intensification of Syria's coastal trade with Egypt and the Christian Mediterranean. Greek Catholics became key intermediaries in the trade between Syria and Egypt, and selected Catholics enjoyed French 'protection' under the Capitulation Agreements (an understanding between the sultanate and the French government that specified the rights of French nationals in Ottoman territories) through their association with French merchants at Tripoli, Sidon and Acre.

This disruption of the older Ottoman world may have contributed to Burayk's sharpened historical consciousness. Burayk was perhaps the first Syrian Arabic chronicler to express a sense of historical change, as distinct from 'mere' narration of historical events. His chronicle portends the opening of a new era, however inchoate, unformed or uncertain this liminal moment might have appeared to contemporary observers. Burayk conveyed all of this *in media res*, writing without the benefit of hindsight.

What is striking about these writers is their social and intellectual diversity. The Muslim scholar, the barber and the Christian priest hailed from different walks of life, yet something about living in Damascus in the eighteenth century encouraged all of them to record their thoughts on paper. They wrote in a transitional moment, on the eve of a new age that would see *ulama* lose their virtual monopoly on local literary production on account of the imminent arrival of the printing press and of modern newspapers. The older-style *ulama* chronicle was on the verge of extinction. Ibn Kannan's was the last of that breed. Deeply rooted intellectual traditions of Muslim Damascus would fall silent for a time, as the new world of the nineteenth century overtook it and shook inherited assumptions. Eventually, a new type of intellectual (often called modernist or secular) would find tools of expression and would devise novel categories of historical analysis and understanding, giving rise in turn to a self-consciously 'traditionalist' backlash by the early twentieth century.

LEISURE ACTIVITIES AND LIFE'S PLEASURES

The proliferation of writing from eighteenth-century Damascus allows modern readers to glimpse life's daily rhythms. What we see permits us to gain a sense of shared lives and shared humanity with people who otherwise might seem abstract or depersonalized, due to the distance of time and of cultural context (preindustrial versus industrial). Crucially, this book tells the story not only of institutions, leaderships and governments in modern Syria, but also of its population's humanity as expressed through cultural and intellectual pursuits. Histories of institutions and of politics tell us about people's experiences; but accounts of their cultural and intellectual interests offer windows into their consciousness.

For the well-to-do classes of urban Syria, the eighteenth century had much to offer. Among *ulama* such as Ibn Kannan, picnics in the verdure outskirts of Damascus were commonplace, offering opportunities to pursue a learned style of male sociability associated with scholarly debates, poetry recitations and literary discussions. The beauty of Damascus's natural setting literally moved him to poetry:

> On Wednesday [23 July 1727] I was in a garden [...]. Fragrance billowed from the blushing cheeks of the flowers, which were arrayed like a handful of rings. I was moved by my reverie to recite a love poem.[9]

Material comfort made such leisure possible. The accumulation of fortunes in provincial hands is remarkably demonstrated by the appearance of palatial homes in this era. The two Azm Palaces (Damascus, Hama) were the most spectacular of them, but they were not alone. One estimate is that 17 new mansions were built in Damascus's central city in the eighteenth century, a far greater number than had been erected earlier following the Ottoman conquest. Ibn Kannan described a reception room that he added to his house in 1717:

> [T]he construction of the [reception] hall in our house [...] was completed. It came out to be of extraordinary beauty and grace. It was done in the best of brilliant paints, with ornamented bookcases, extensive calligraphy, the most elegant furniture, colored and decorated plaster, with an octagonal pool and a pretty fountain with copious water.[10]

Other strata of society also enjoyed opportunities for public display. Coffeehouses, controversial in the previous century, became ubiquitous. Though spurned by the elite who regarded them as lower-class venues, they became popular places of male recreation where coffee and tobacco were voraciously consumed. Men whiled away the hours playing chess and other board games, gossiping about the news of the day, and listening to public recitations of poetry and epic tales. In Damascus, coffeehouses were found both in the built-up parts of the city and in its extramural open areas along the Barada river. The English traveler Henry Maundrell (end of the seventeenth century) described one of the riverside establishments:

> [It was] a coffee house capable of entertaining four or five hundred people, shaded over head with trees, and with mats when the boughs fail. It had two

quarters for the reception of guests, one proper for the summer, the other for the winter. That designated for the summer was a small island, washed all around with a large, swift stream, and shaded over head with mats and trees. We found here a multitude of Turks [in this context, read 'locals'] upon the divans, regaling themselves in this pleasant place.[11]

Coffee and coffeehouses were associated with tobacco. Smoking was a popular pastime among men and women. In the eighteenth century tobacco was grown in the hinterland of Latakia and also was imported from Iran. Though both smoking and coffee drinking originally had been controversial (witness Abd al-Ghani al-Nabulusi's earlier writings in their defense), these recreational products were part of everyday life by the eighteenth century. As early as the 1670s Aleppo was estimated to have more than 100 coffeehouses, including a massive complex built as part of an endowment established (1654) by the Ottoman official Ipshir Pasha. In both Damascus and Aleppo tobacco was often laced with opium, offering imbibers an even greater chemical lift than that provided by caffeine and nicotine alone.

Though smoking was commonplace, the practice still bothered eighteenth-century moral conservatives like Ibn Budayr the barber and Burayk the priest, especially when women partook. Groused the barber in 1749: 'Smoking has become one of the greatest scourges in Damascus. Men, women and even girls have begun to smoke.' The next year, he gloomily observed a number of women in an outdoor picnic area, 'greater than the men, sitting along the bank of the [Barada]. They were eating and drinking, and drinking coffee and [smoking] tobacco just as the men were doing.'[12] A few years later, Burayk expressed his discomfort with the phenomenon of women 'who smoked tobacco in homes, bathhouses and gardens, even along the river while people were passing by.'[13] But the spread of private and public tobacco and coffee consumption were part of a broader development of public sociability in Ottoman cities, a phenomenon not unique to Syria that was noticeable in Istanbul as well. The integration of these historically new commodities into everyday life and routines was symptomatic of Syria's wider connections with and participation in the early modern world.

URBAN–RURAL TENSIONS

There were also changes afoot in Syrian hinterlands and regions in the eighteenth century which would have far-reaching implications on the dynamics of Syria in this period and beyond. One dimension of this is the firm grip that military elites obtained on land and its resources in the countryside. Military officials had long been prominent in Ottoman land arrangements (via military fiefdoms and tax farms), but studies of landholdings in the hinterlands of Aleppo, Hama and Damascus in the eighteenth century are consistent in their affirmation of the dominant roles played by regionally rooted military men as owners, administrators, creditors and tax farmers. In principle sultanic and sharia law protections for cultivators remained in place, but peasant flight from cultivable land was widely remarked in the latter half of the eighteenth century. Urban landholders and tax farmers had an interest in ensuring peasant production from year to year, and this as well as the aforementioned sultanic and sharia legal protections could mitigate conditions of oppression and exploitation. Cities were major markets for cultivators' produce, especially in the market garden lands closer to the cities and within their respective 'green belts,' as discussed earlier (Chapter 1). Yet urban-based elites' domination of the farther countryside could be harsh. In more distant regions, urban centers of power (and the military men associated with them) might be seen as little better than rapacious and brutal oppressors. Homs scribe Muhammad al-Makki's enthusiasm for rural bloodletting is a stark example of urbanites' disdain for the 'savage' hinterland.

Tripoli was the provincial seat whose domains included the Ansariyeh coastal mountains north of the Homs gap. The gap is a plain that provides relatively easy access between the coast (Tripoli) and the interior (Homs). The predominant populations in the northern coastal mountains were tribally organized Nusayri (called today Alawite) peasants. Other mountaineers in this region included Orthodox Christians and small communities of Ismaili Muslims.[14] Intermittently after 1799, a strongman from the ranks of the local Janissaries named Barbar Agha dominated Tripoli. Barbar usually was allied with the administration based at Acre (coastal Palestine) against the interests of Damascus during recurring episodes of political and military rivalry between Syria's interior (Damascus) and the coast (Acre–Tripoli). During his periods of ascendancy in Tripoli, Barbar was a tax farmer and district governor who regularly led military raids into the mountains. He fought against Nusayri chieftains and seized villagers' crops and goods in the name of taxation. He and his men would return to Tripoli carrying sacks full of heads of alleged rebels and tax evaders. Targeted villagers left no written record of their experiences, but one can imagine that, to them, 'the state' in the form of Barbar and his men was little more than an excuse for brutal military predation.

A remarkable written record from a pair of Shiite farmers offers a rare firsthand glimpse into rural attitudes toward Ottoman governance in this era. The authors

were a father and son from the Jabal Amil region of what is today southern Lebanon. The father, Haydar Rida al-Rukayni (d. 1783) started the chronicle and his
son (whose full name is unknown) finished it. In those days Jabal Amil was subject
to the authority of the province of Sidon (whose actual administration had moved
to Acre). The Rukaynis' chronicle is unusual because simple farmers had not previously left written records of their lives and times. Perhaps the high incidence of
Shiite madrasas in the Jabal Amil region, combined with the new social mobility
that had encouraged Ibn Budayr the barber and Burayk the priest to write their
chronicles in Damascus, also fueled the farmers' literary ambitions. In the elder
Rukayni's lifetime the principal leader of the Jabal Amil Shiites was allied with a
Galilean merchant, warlord and tax farmer named Zahir al-Umar (d. 1775). Zahir
was a local strongman of Arab tribal origin who had turned Acre into his political
and economic base (more on this below). Zahir and his Jabal Amil allies defeated
an Ottoman expedition sent against them in 1771, when Zahir was in revolt against
the Ottomans after they had tried to dismiss him. Recounting the battle, the
Rukaynis write:

> They [Shiites and Zahir] inflicted a great defeat on these Pashas and they
> subjected the *dawla* ['state'] to humiliation and disgrace because they [the
> Ottoman governors of Damascus and two sub-districts] were utterly abased
> in a manner that had not happened in this age. They threw themselves, their
> horses and whatever they had with them into Lake Hula [in present-day
> Israel]. They were like Pharaoh and his armies: 'We drowned them in the
> sea' [...] 'and they were unable to defend themselves.' They were over-
> whelmed by [the Shiite] battle cries and cowered in their places filled with
> despair and overcome by debasement. And [the victors] took from them
> booty of all kinds [...]. They were overcome with suffering and tribulation,
> and the *dawla* was laid low.[15]

In the Rukaynis' chronicle the Ottoman sultanate is simply referred to without affec-
tion and without ceremony as 'the state' (*al-dawla*). The authors exult in its defeat.
They do not in any way identify with it, and they compare the Ottoman pasha to
Pharaoh who in the Qur'an is an evil tyrant. To be sure, this was not only or merely
a 'rural' view of the Ottoman state, but one that was colored as well by sectarian
animosity: 'Revenge will be taken from the Turks for the House of Muhammad [an
allusion to the Shiite imams] and their oppression by their enemies.'[16] But the larger
point stands: most historical records were generated in the towns and cities and
they reflect urban viewpoints. Rural people, especially in the more remote districts,

had no reason in this era to see representatives of urban state authority as anything but avaricious or murderous adversaries.

In the eyes of urban Sunni Muslim authorities and their supportive *ulama*, the Nusayris and Shiites were heterodox communities whose beliefs and practices lay outside the bounds of normative Islam (as defined by the four accepted Sunni rites or schools of law). But these 'ideological' differences between town and country were not a proximate cause of political conflict. On a day-in, day-out administrative basis Ottoman authorities did not make an issue of these rural communities' non-normative beliefs. However, when political tensions led to military campaigns against them, ideological denunciations of 'heresy' were dusted off and invoked to justify recalcitrant populations' punishments. But quotidian relationships between formal Ottoman authority and institutions, on the one hand, and Shiite and Nusayri tax farmers, on the other hand, demonstrate that the Ottoman state did not actually care what people in these communities thought or believed, as long as they did what authority demanded of them (loyalty, compliance, remission of taxes, etc.). Urban–rural tensions were real enough, rooted as they were in contradictory material interests (rural producers versus urban takers). In this context confessional differences offered ready-made fodder for polemics and propaganda.

Shiites and Nusayris were on the margins of contemporaneous Ottoman historical accounts of the eighteenth and nineteenth centuries. But both communities would become central to political developments in independent Lebanon and Syria in the twentieth century. In the Ottoman era the Shiites of Jabal Amil usually were called Mutawila, the local name for followers of their faith. (In the twentieth century Mutawila came to be seen as a pejorative term, and it fell out of polite or courteous usage.) They were a mostly rural, village-based community who had a robust tradition of Shiite religious scholarship. *Ulama* families maintained traditions of scholarship and of nobility (as *sayyids* or descendants of the Prophet). Their political structure was semi-feudal, based on clans and lineages with powerful military leaders who (like others in Syria's hill country) alternately jousted for power in Ottoman factional struggles, and contested to hold remunerative tax farms. Although in an earlier age the Safavid Shahs of Iran had recruited Jabal Amil *ulama* to preach Shiite doctrines in Iran, this Persian connection was of no political significance in the eighteenth century. (The Safavid dynasty had collapsed, and Jabal Amil was far away from Iran.) The scholarly families in Jabal Amil had ongoing relationships with (and family ties to) Ottoman Iraq, owing to the presence there of the Shiite shrine cities of Najaf (the location of the tomb of Ali, the Sunnis' fourth caliph and the Shiites' first divinely inspired imam) and Karbala (site of the martyrdom of Ali's son and the Prophet's grandson Hussein, the Shiites' third imam).

The Nusayris (Alawites) in the Ansariyeh coastal mountains east of the ports of Latakia and Jabla had a similar socioeconomic profile as the Shiites of Jabal Amil. They were a tribally organized and clan-based mountain peasantry. In the Latakia region the spread of tobacco cultivation in the seventeenth and eighteenth centuries provided the basis for the emergence of feudal-like families of Nusayri power-brokers who (like their hill and mountain counterparts elsewhere) vied for political advantage and sought lucrative tax farms. Nusayri clan and tribal identities became clearly identifiable as political forces by the eighteenth century, perhaps in response to the higher stakes that emerged with the growth of tobacco cultivation and its income. In time the appellation 'Nusayri' was abandoned as pejorative, and it was replaced with the term Alawite that emphasized the religious tradition's reverence for Ali, Muhammad's son-in-law. (The older terms Mutawila and Nusayri are only used today as dismissive labels in sectarian polemics.)

Despite the exploitative nature of the urban dominance in rural areas, peasants' abandonment of vulnerable villages may have had less to do with landholders' and tax farmers' overexploitation, and more with unrest, banditry and insecurity. In much of Syria, migrations from the Anaza tribes that occurred throughout the eighteenth century sowed uncertainty in those cultivable regions that were exposed to Bedouin raids. The Anaza influx led to the collapse of older arrangements or understandings with Bedouins that had assured at least a modicum of predictability in relations between 'the desert and the sown.' Although the Anaza migration was not as much of a factor in the more northern region of Aleppo, there too Ottoman weakness in the later eighteenth century opened the way for Kurdish and Turco-man tribal self-aggrandizement at the expense of more exposed settled cultivators. By the later eighteenth century the urban authorities often were unable to guarantee or offer security for open or exposed villages. The Ottoman government faced renewed military challenges from Russia, and the sultanate's diversion of resources and attention to the north contributed to imperial inefficacy in Syria. Weakening of the Porte's coercive powers meant that in some places, ill-disciplined bands of mercenary horsemen went into business for themselves rather than serve their nominal Ottoman masters, creating new uncertainties for cultivators, merchants and travelers.

COASTAL FLUORESCENCE: THE RISE OF ACRE

Regionalism remained an endemic factor of political life in eighteenth-century Syria. Adding to the political challenges of the time was an open contest for power between forces of the interior – generally grouped around Damascus – and forces of the coast. The shift in coastal fortunes was caused in part by new revenues available to coastal-based interests who stood to directly benefit from trade with France, a development that aided the emergence of a new regional power center at Acre.

In the middle decades of the century the aforementioned Zahir al-Umar – an Arab merchant with tribal connections and armed followers – established himself as the major tax farmer in the Galilee region, based first at Tiberias and subsequently at Acre. He formed alliances with other rural chiefs and sheikhs to become a strong regional player in hill country factional struggles. Zahir was quick to take advantage of French merchants' demand for Galilean cotton, establishing a monopoly that gave him a lucrative source of income to supplement income from taxes and tribute that came to him as the region's tax farmer. He began to rebuild Acre, a former Crusader port that had dwindled to little more than a village (albeit one that hosted French merchants). The security of his rule encouraged peasant cultivators, who expanded their cotton production and generally remembered him later as a just ruler who had been reasonable in his demands and expectations, and who had given them security in return for their loyalty and cooperation.

At the peak of his power (coinciding with an acute moment of Ottoman weakness at Damascus, 1774), Zahir came close to gaining formal recognition as the governor of the Ottomans' proximate coastal province, headquartered at Sidon. But with his mercantile background and political ties to anti-Azm 'localist' interests in Damascus (reinforced by personal ties through his first marriage to the daughter of a Damascene sharif), Zahir was seen as a threat to the pro-Azm forces in the city. They supported his regional adversaries based at Nablus, a town in the Palestinian hills south of Galilee. (Zahir tried repeatedly to subdue Nablus, but never succeeded.)

At the end of his career Zahir's descent was rapid. During the Ottoman–Russian war of 1768–74, Zahir had aligned himself with an ambitious Mamluk from Egypt named Ali Bey al-Kabir (d. 1773). Ali Bey hoped to carve out a sphere of influence in Syria for his Egypt-based rule, at the expense of Damascus and of the sultanate more generally. Once the war concluded, and the Russian fleet withdrew from the East Mediterranean, Istanbul resolved to deal with Zahir's opportunistic political behavior. The Porte orchestrated the aged Zahir's downfall and death in 1775, mobilizing local political and factional resources and exploiting a split between Zahir and one of his sons.

Despite this inglorious end, Zahir had enjoyed a long career (spanning roughly 50 years), and the conditions that allowed him to develop a regional power base at Acre from the 1740s did not end with his death. A Bosnian Mamluk named Ahmad al-Jazzar (d. 1804) took his place. Jazzar was an Ottoman loyalist who had been trained in Egypt, and had distinguished himself as an implacable and resourceful soldier during a peripatetic military career. His sobriquet Jazzar, 'butcher,' was originally not a term of opprobrium but of admiration, given to him by those who admired his ruthlessness.

Jazzar was named governor of Sidon, though his actual base was at Acre, and he maintained his hold on the office until his death. In the intervening years Jazzar also was often named governor of Damascus concurrently, though he usually did not reside there and would administer Damascus through a deputy. Acre continued to rise as a regional power center in its own right in the decades after the 1770s, overshadowing Damascus for a time. This is remarkable given that Acre had been an insignificant settlement just a few decades before. Crucial shifts were occurring in the economic and political relationships of the Syrian lands, as new international trade patterns took root and enabled a change in political fortunes that benefited the heretofore marginal coast.

Acre rapidly grew, sustained at first by the monopoly systems that Zahir had introduced and that Jazzar continued, as the port profited from first the cotton trade and after that the grain trade (including grain from the region south of Damascus, exported via Acre). Both Zahir and Jazzar used the talents of Greek Catholic and Jewish mercantile and scribal families to organize their administrations and oversee their affairs. Zahir was served by the Greek Catholic Ibrahim Sabbagh, who hailed from a merchant family on the coast of Lebanon. Jazzar promoted Haim Farhi, scion of a well-connected Damascene Jewish banking family. Owing to the patronage they enjoyed, both of these non-Muslim Syrians became powerful figures. According to the French consul in Acre, writing in 1772:

> The merchants of Acre are today nothing but the employees of Ibrahim al-Sabbagh, to whom they loan their names. He has seized all useful branches of trade and leaves them nothing but the sad satisfaction to go through the motions and to appear to strike many deals while, in fact, they only work for him.[17]

Sabbagh died in the same year as his patron Zahir in 1775. In time another non-Muslim, Haim Farhi, rose to a comparable position of power in the reign of Jazzar. Farhi was a financier from a famous Damascene Jewish family, and Jazzar brought him to Acre during the Jazzar's second governorship of Damascus in the early 1790s. Farhi rose to prominence quickly in Jazzar's administration. Farhi's status was enhanced further during the era of Jazzar's successor, one of

Jazzar's own Mamluks named Suleiman Pasha (Sidon/Acre governor 1804–19). A French consul wrote: '[T]here is a Jew here who in the name of Sulayman Pasha is the only owner, seller, and buyer; […] he pays not the least attention to the capitulations.'[18] Another French consular dispatch identified Haim as the real power in Suleiman Pasha's domain, oddly invoking a Venetian analogy to describe the political structure at Acre:

> Syria from Latakia down to Gaza is a republic with a senate consisting of freed men [i.e., manumitted Mamluks] who hold all the positions. It is under the control of the Jew Haim Farhi, who governs it despotically in the name of Sulayman Pasha, a Mamluk, who is its doge ['duke,' title of the ruler of Venice].[19]

The ascent first of Sabbagh, and then of Farhi, anticipate changes that soon would be afoot in the relationship of non-Muslims to Muslims in Ottoman Syria. Both men were clients of their powerful Muslim patrons, but the increasing importance of European powers to the politics and economic life of Syria meant that, within a generation or two, Christian and Jewish powerbrokers would have the option of breaking free of Muslim patronage altogether in favor of patronage offered by European consulates. This development would throw the inherited and generally accepted framework of Muslim-*dhimmi* patron–client relations into flux, with serious implications for inter-communal comity.

Acre's buildings were renewed and enhanced. As its population grew by in-migration, Christians (mostly Greek Catholics) came to form a majority of its population in the later eighteenth century. Newly built churches marked this Christian surge. With the rise of Haim Farhi there was also an in-migration of Damascene Jews. Today the most striking material traces of Jazzar's reign are Acre's fortified walls (which withstood Napoleon Bonaparte's 1799 siege), and Jazzar's Ottoman-style mosque built to assert his political and cultural legitimacy within an Ottoman milieu.

Jazzar subdued the Mutawila Shiite clans in Jabal Amil, who had been among Zahir's main allies, but he never established uncontested dominion in the Druze mountain region north of Jabal Amil and east of Sidon and Beirut. Instead Jazzar played factional politics there, attempting to wield influence indirectly by supporting one or another faction of the Shihab family who had succeeded the Maans as hereditary claimants to the mountain's Druze emirate. (In imperial Ottoman eyes, the Druze emirate was merely a glorified tax farm. Subsequently, however, Lebanese nationalists would interpret it as the foundation stone of a distinct Lebanese state.)

Jazzar and his two successors never brought the small port town of Beirut under their firm hegemony, a situation that made Beirut attractive to merchants. Beirut's reputation as a merchant-friendly port contributed to its rise as a mercantile center as Acre's star began to fade in the 1820s.

The growth of wealth and political power in Acre and its region during Jazzar's reign was one sign that Damascus's regional position was under pressure. Another indicator of the pressures facing Damascus was the rise of the Saudi-led Wahhabi movement, an ideological challenge to the Ottoman state that accompanied the Anaza tribal migration into Syria. Wahhabis claimed that Ottoman Islam was corrupt, and they criticized in particular Sufism, visitation to shrines and veneration of saints. Since Damascus had many such shrines, and it was the jumping-off point for the annual pilgrimage caravan, the city was particularly sensitive to the Wahhabis and their threat to the sultanate's prestige in the Muslim holy cities. (In fact the Wahhabis seized Mecca and Medina in 1803 and held them until an Egyptian expedition acting in the sultan's name drove them out ten years later.) Christian and Jewish elites lost ground in subsequent years, due to Muslims' anxieties arising from the combination of the mounting Wahhabi challenge, Bonaparte's invasion of Egypt in 1798 followed by his siege of Acre the following year, and growing fears about the sultanate's general weakness.

After some of his own Mamluks rebelled against him in 1790, Jazzar became paranoid and suspicious. He purged or executed those of his associates whom he thought were accumulating too much power – including some of his non-Muslim clients, allies and administrators. Thereafter among Christian chroniclers Jazzar fully deserved his 'butcher' sobriquet. Jazzar intervened in factional contests in Mount Lebanon, trying to turn the paramount lord of the mountain, Emir Bashir II al-Shihab, into a political client. But he was never able to achieve clear or untrammeled supremacy in the 'Druze mountain', or in Beirut or in Tripoli. Nevertheless he battled with Damascus for influence in the northern coastal province of Tripoli. (The aforementioned Barbar Agha – the Tripoli Janissary fond of collecting bags full of non-compliant Nusayri peasants' heads – was Jazzar's ally.)

Before the French invasion of Egypt in 1798, Jazzar had acted imperiously with respect to resident French merchants, causing them to abandon Acre as their major base of operations. During the Napoleonic Wars, France's merchant presence in the Levant dwindled further, due to Britain's blockade of French-dominated continental Europe. Even before this, French interest in Galilean cotton was declining as new sources of supply were opening up in North America. But Acre stayed afloat financially under Jazzar and his successors during the Napoleonic Wars, by exporting wheat via British or British-flagged ships in the Mediterranean. French merchants returned to the Levant with the conclusion of the Napoleonic Wars, but the determination of Jazzar's successors to maintain their monopoly system on unfavorable terms for Mediterranean merchants caused buyers and sellers to look for a port where circumstances were less onerous and more open. Beirut was attractive, lying as it did on the borders of control between the governors of Sidon (i.e., of Acre) and the princes of the 'Druze mountain' – Mount Lebanon. Jazzar's successors could not impose their monopolies in Beirut even when Acre nominally governed the town, and the Druze princes were eager to see Beirut port (and its revenues) develop. Beirut also started to become a base for American and British Protestant missionaries, who first set up shop there and in the city's mountain hinterland in the 1820s. Acre faded, and the Egyptian invasion of 1831 put an end to its short 80-year ascendancy.

Henceforth Syria's coast-interior rivalry would unfold within a new paradigm, that of modern statehood, and of the country's deepening integration into a European-dominated world economy.

THE 'LONG' EIGHTEENTH CENTURY

The 'long' eighteenth century connects Syria's early Ottoman period, when the land and its peoples adjusted to life in a new framework of sultanate and land-based empire, to the 'short' nineteenth century when Syria and the Ottoman Empire entered the irresistible orbit of industrial Europe. The long eighteenth century established patterns of regional rivalries and of urban–rural tensions that later would shape Syrians' experiences in the final Ottoman decades.

In the eighteenth century, regionalism was reflected in competition among different power centers to defend their interests or assert their local hegemony. Examples include the disparity in fortunes of Aleppo and Damascus, and the struggles for political and economic positioning between Damascus and the coast. Although Aleppo remained a significant center, it lost its former preeminence in the international transit trade. Damascus was ascendant for a time, as its governors became commanders of the pilgrimage caravan (also a major commercial event), and the city attracted trade from Baghdad. A new rivalry between the interior and the coast broke out, marked most dramatically by the rise of Acre under Zahir al-Umar and Ahmad al-Jazzar, developments made possible by the growing influence and importance of primary-products seaborne trade with Europe and the Mediterranean.

A sharp dichotomy is also visible between the interests and outlooks of urban and rural populations. The story of Barbar Agha's bagfuls-of-heads policies in the

Nusayri hinterland of Tripoli is one illustration, and the Shiite Rukaynis' disdain for the forces of the sultanate, who the Rukaynis insultingly likened to the armies of Pharaoh, is another.

These tensions between urban and rural populations were deepened by cultural and confessional differences. Urban areas were bastions of literary life and religious-cultural institutions, while rural areas were home to rustic peoples practicing forms of religion that were deeply rooted in the natural world and less connected to the authority of scripture or of the *ulama*. This added a layer of potential cultural hostility to the material divisions represented by the urban/rural dichotomy, multiplied all the more when the rustic rural population did not identify with Sunni orthodoxy in even a nominal sense. This was the case of the powerful though factionalized Druze, and of the less powerful but equally factionalized Nusayris.

An additional source of potential urban and rural differentiation and tension was linked to the tribal organization of many rural peoples, and the potential challenges that powerful tribal peoples posed to urban mercantile and agricultural interests. Such tensions are illustrated by the ability of tribally organized Kurds and Turcomans to harass or disrupt trade in the region of Aleppo, and of Anaza Bedouin tribes to threaten the security of trans-desert trade and pilgrimage routes.

In rapidly changing times the formerly stable relationship between Muslims and non-Muslims (Christians and Jews) became unsettled. The meteoric ascendancy of Greek Catholics in Zahir al-Umar's Acre is one indication of this, along with Christians' and Jews' precipitous loss of position after they had been clients and associates of Jazzar and his successors. The new economic and social forces at play – the rise of European trade and the growing importance of financial connections to European markets – created new opportunities for non-Muslim urban communities. Formally they still were *dhimmis*, protected and subordinate non-Muslim populations, but these wider transformations had the potential to create new perils as old norms faded and new ones had yet to be defined or to crystallize.

An invading Egyptian army entered Syria in 1831, abruptly introducing modern statehood into the country. The Egyptian administration's work was subsequently carried on by the Ottomans after Istanbul regained control. The sudden, and in some cases traumatic, imposition of new forms of state authority would be overlaid atop Syria's inherited dichotomies and tensions. These tensions would be pushed to a boiling point before the modern state in time triumphed – politically, militarily and culturally.

3

SYRIA BETWEEN EUROPE AND
THE OTTOMANS, 1820s–1900s

BLOODSHED IN DAMASCUS

On 10 July 1860, during a typically hot summer's afternoon in Damascus, the Syrian-born American vice-consul, Mikhail Mishaqa, was at home taking a siesta. Mishaqa was a self-trained medical practitioner and convert to Protestantism (from Greek Catholicism) whose family had long been in scribal service to the emirs of Mount Lebanon.[1] He was rudely awakened from his nap by cries and shouts that 'the Muslims of the city had risen up against the Christians.'[2]

Inter-confessional tensions had been growing in Syria. Damascenes followed the news of ongoing bloody battles between Maronite Christians and Druze in nearby Mount Lebanon. Christian refugees streamed to the city, bringing with them tales of woe. Rumors that Druzes were advancing on the city set people on edge. Damascus had a long history of inter-religious comity, but the regional environment was deteriorating rapidly. The growing strength of the European Christian powers fed popular Muslim resentments. Muslim elites who hoped to reverse recent reformist trends in Istanbul were looking for a dramatic way to register their opposition. In Mishaqa's account, the Ottoman governor of Damascus gave backhanded support to the anti-Christian uprising. When mobs invaded Mishaqa's house in the Christian quarter, he convinced them that because he was a vice-consul he should be allowed to take a message to one of the local military commanders. He narrowly escaped with his life, but his fleeing family was taken from him. 'I began to think of my family,' he later wrote,

> and what had happened to each of them […]. I didn't even know if the house had remained unburned for them to take shelter in […]. I didn't know what had happened to them, especially my injured daughter, who wouldn't know

how to bandage her wound [...]. Such thoughts kept me from thinking about the agony of my own wounds.[3]

Though as fortune would have it Mishaqa's family survived, the Christian quarter was left in ruins. Once the violence had run its course, thousands were dead (the exact number is unknown), and nearly all houses in the quarter were burned.[4] Survivors such as Mishaqa owed their lives to the intervention of Muslim notables (some with their own armed followers) who offered Christians safe haven and protection where the civil and military authorities did not. The events of July 1860 were the capstone of traumas caused by rapid changes in Ottoman Syria in the nineteenth century. Old relationships were overturned, new ideas of community and authority came to the fore, and by the time of World War I in 1914, Syrians had lived for many decades under a new type of authority: the modern state.

THE GREEK REVOLT AND OTTOMAN CRISIS

The weakness of the old Ottoman state been driven home in an undeniable way during the Greek Revolt which began in 1821. Short-term causes included onerous Ottoman exactions and demands on cultivators in the Peloponnese, to pay for Istanbul's suppression of a rebellious Albanian vassal further north. However, longer-term causes included growing ethnic Greek dissatisfaction with Ottoman rule in general, combined with new currents of national identity articulated by Greek intellectuals, political figures and merchants. In March 1821 Greek irregulars marshaled outside of the Ottoman garrisoned district town of Kalamata. A Greek commander later recounted:

As we went along all the Greeks showed the greatest enthusiasm; they came out and met us everywhere, carrying the sacred icons, with the priests chanting supplications and thanksgivings to God. Once I could not forbear weeping, on account of the ardour which I beheld. So we went on, followed by the crowds. When we came to the bridge of Kalamata, we exchanged greetings, and I marched forward.[5]

The Turkish defenders of Kalamata were outnumbered, and when they surrendered the Greek insurgents massacred them. Thus began a bloody and brutal uprising that ended in Greek independence, and did lasting damage to old Ottoman governing arrangements.

Lent justification by the new idea of nationalism, the Greek Revolt threatened a basic foundation of the old order. As a dynasty presiding over a multi-ethnic, multi-religious subject population, the Ottomans had since the fifteenth century relied on an alliance between the throne and the Greek Orthodox Church as one part of their governing formula. Aristocratic ethnic Greek families (known as the Phanariots after their Istanbul neighborhood) were part of the eighteenth-century empire's governing arrangements. Phanariots served as vassal princes in territories that later became Romania, and they worked as scribes, interpreters and emissaries for the sultanate in Istanbul. In many respects the Phanariot Greeks had been the Ottomans' 'foreign ministry' for dealings with Christian European states. The Greek Revolt, a constellation of ethnic Greek mercantile interests, ambitious politicians and disgruntled Christian peasants, challenged one of the core institutional arrangements of the old-style empire.

To the sultan's embarrassment, Ottoman forces including the Janissaries were not able to suppress Greek peasant rebels in rough hill country who had risen against their Muslim overlords. The sultan, Mahmud II (r. 1808–39), quashed a Janissary rebellion and abolished the obstreperous Janissaries in 1826, but he could not replace them immediately with an effective force. Therefore he called on his autonomous but avowedly loyal Egyptian governor Muhammad Ali Pasha to help out in Greece with the Pasha's new-style Egyptian army, modeled on the army of France. The Egyptians had some success, but European powers destroyed the combined Egyptian–Ottoman fleet at Navarino in 1827. Muhammad Ali blamed Ottoman incompetence for this setback, and demanded the governorship of Syria. The sultan refused.

THE EGYPTIANS INTRODUCE MODERN STATEHOOD

In November 1831, some 30,000 Egyptian soldiers advanced into Ottoman Palestine, and by the summer of the following year they had conquered the whole of Syria. The invasion was ordered by the ruler of Egypt, Muhammad Ali Pasha, and was commanded by his son Ibrahim Pasha. A governor of Albanian origin, Muhammad Ali Pasha believed that the sultan had not rewarded him for the Egyptian army's assistance to Ottoman forces against rebels in Greece (1827). Furthermore, Muhammad Ali resented the governor of Acre, Abdallah Pasha, who was harboring thousands of Egyptians who had fled their homes to evade Muhammad Ali's harsh policies of conscription and economic monopoly.

The Egyptians advanced rapidly into Palestine, bypassed Acre's strong fortifications and marched up the coast to Latakia, before pausing to consolidate their hold.

The siege of Acre from November 1831 to May 1832 was the hardest-fought battle of the coastal campaign. In the summer of 1832 Ibrahim Pasha's forces defeated imperial Ottoman armies that had mustered inland around Homs in a vain, last-ditch effort to stop him. The Egyptian conquest opened a nine-year period of rule that abruptly confronted Syria's inhabitants with a modern state.

On the face of it the 1831 invasion was a repetition of the earlier one undertaken from Egypt by another rebellious Ottoman vassal 60 years before, when the Mamluk Ali Bey al-Kabir moved on Damascus in alliance with Zahir al-Umar in 1771. But Muhammad Ali's government and army were qualitatively different from those of his Mamluk predecessor and, crucially, Muhammad Ali's administration represented the first appearance of modern statehood in the Ottoman region. He had built up a bureaucratized central authority with the intent and ability to assert a monopoly of force, *not* to share it with local paramilitaries and intermediaries. Muhammad Ali's administration made demands of its people as individuals, not merely as members of collective groups.

Muhammad Ali had become governor of Egypt in 1805, exploiting unsettled conditions after an Ottoman–British alliance forced the surrender of the occupying French army (1801). After beating back attempts by Mamluks to reclaim their former preeminence (and massacring a number of them at an infamous 'banquet' in Cairo's citadel in 1812), Muhammad Ali centralized power in Cairo, all the while presenting himself as a loyal vassal to his suzerain the Ottoman sultan. Indeed it was Muhammad Ali's Egyptian army that freed Mecca and Medina from Wahhabi control (1813), restoring symbols of Ottoman authority in the Muslim holy cities. Within Egypt he abolished tax farms, pensioned off tax farmers and ensured that all revenue accrued to his officials directly. Muhammad Ali's administration drafted Egyptian peasants in unprecedented numbers to construct public works in far-flung regions of the country, at great loss of life.

Finally, in the 1820s, he implemented a policy of military conscription that forced villagers to supply quotas of men for army service; the first time such a degree of state control had been asserted in the Middle East. Egyptian men were issued government identification cards to better control their movements and to stymie anyone trying to evade the military draft. In the meantime, Muhammad Ali raised revenues not only through more efficient taxation (that is, with less leakage to intermediaries such as the cashiered tax farmers), but also through encouragement of a new crop, Jumel cotton, destined for the English market at the time of the Industrial Revolution. He sent student delegations to France (which under the restored Bourbon monarchy was a friendly power) to study the arts and sciences of modern Europe, to apply these lessons to his army and its medical service, and to make his bureaucracy more effective.

Muhammad Ali's army was trained in modern tactics, and it was different from the ill-disciplined Janissaries and Mamluks that had preceded them. During the siege of Acre, Ibrahim Pasha exhorted the infantry under his command to remember and to use the battlefield tactics in which they had been drilled:

> We remind and alert you that once you receive orders of attack hold your rifles tight in your hands and storm your targets like fire [...]. Do not fear the enemy, because if they come with swords, then your bayonets will be longer; and if they come with muskets, then the continuous volleys that you have been trained to perform over the past eleven years will make every one of you count as ten of the enemy soldiers.[6]

When the Egyptian army conquered Syria, it therefore represented a new type of state authority that was distinctly modern. In contrast to Ottoman-style statehood, Muhammad Ali's administration was an autocratic, bureaucratized authority with a modern-trained conscript army at its disposal. This army nearly defeated the Ottoman sultanate itself in Anatolia, until halted in 1833 by international diplomatic intervention. Britain and Russia, especially, did not wish to see the Ottoman sultanate replaced by Muhammad Ali's more effective and pro-French regime.

The Egyptians remained in Syria until 1840, and throughout these years the Syrian lands still were nominally part of the Ottoman Empire as Muhammad Ali did not declare outright independence. The suzerainty of the sultanate provided a legitimizing framework for claimants to power in the Muslim domains of the Ottoman Empire, Muhammad Ali included. But he acted independently of Istanbul. He claimed the title of 'khedive' (a Persian word denoting high royal rank), a claim that the Ottoman sultanate did not concede at the time. As far as Istanbul was concerned, Muhammad Ali was a provincial governor who had morphed from a loyalist into a highly problematic rebel exploiting the sultanate's weakened and distracted situation. For nine years Muhammad Ali's capable son, Ibrahim Pasha (d. 1848), was Syria's day-to-day ruler.

Looking to expand government revenues, Muhammad Ali and Ibrahim encouraged European consuls, merchants and missionaries to take up residence in Syria, and expand their activities there. Eager for new markets to fuel industrial expansion, the British in particular leaped at the chance to enhance their representation, joining the French who already had a substantial political and diplomatic presence. Foreign merchants and consuls, as well as Protestant missionaries, made Beirut their center of operations, beginning that East Mediterranean port's rapid growth. New forms of governance were reflected in the creation of local administrative councils, and in a pledge of civic or legal equality for Christians and Jews alongside Muslims. Ibrahim Pasha's goal was to make the administration master of all who lived in Syria, without showing institutional favoritism toward the Muslim majority. He introduced a new poll tax on the Muslim population. For many unhappy Muslim subjects, this poll tax resembled the poll tax (*jizya*) that Christians and Jews traditionally paid as a token of their *dhimmi* status.

Despite gestures toward civic equality, the Egyptian regime did not speak the language of 'citizenship.' But while such a concept had no meaning in a militarized autocracy, the regime did impose itself in new ways on the population. No longer was 'the state' content to be a distant authority, separated from the subject population by semi-autonomous intermediaries. More and more it was an interventionist one that inserted itself into people's lives and made direct demands on them. Ibrahim's policies of taxation, conscription and disarmament provoked an insurrection in Palestine in 1834, which the Egyptian army firmly suppressed. While the government's policy of disarming the population was intrusive, Ibrahim Pasha exempted the Christian emir of Mount Lebanon and his armed, mostly Christian, followers in a bid to win the support of Emir Bashir II al-Shihab (r. 1789–1840).

The Egyptian period is generally credited with bringing order to the Syrian countryside, allowing for the repopulation of abandoned villages and the extension of cultivation. Ibrahim's administration viewed the settlement of pastoral nomads as a necessary step in establish of a modern-style administration. This attitude toward settlement of nomads would be shared by subsequent administrative modernizers including the Ottomans, the colonial French and twentieth-century Syrian nationalists.

Not all of Ibrahim's measures succeeded. The more powerful pastoral nomads who engaged in camel rearing and provided caravan security resisted agricultural settlement. According to one contemporary source, Ibrahim Pasha told Bedouin sheikhs near Karak in Transjordan in 1834,

> that if they were his subjects, they should bring their arms to him and stop wandering from place to place with their tents, and settle down and build houses like other Arabs, and plant vines and olives and become civilized. [But] they laughed and replied that they would surely die if they were to remain in one place for two months.[7]

Ibrahim had more success in the reliably watered northern and eastern hinterlands of Aleppo, where natural conditions for settled cultivation were better. He required merchants and notables of the city to advance capital for land reclamation and to share produce with cultivators. Muslim and Christian merchants and notables, as well as officers in the Egyptian army, were made responsible for reclaiming designated lands in return for tax breaks. Tax breaks and sharecropping arrangements encouraged semi-nomadic or sheepherding Bedouins to cultivate newly capitalized lands. Where cultivators could not be persuaded to settle, Ibrahim Pasha's officers compelled local peasants to move from their original villages to the new lands. Ibrahim's major motivation was to ensure provisioning for the large Egyptian army, whose strength ranged from 40,000 to 80,000 in Syria during the 1830s. Military conscription created labor shortages in some regions, but the prioritization given to land reclamation around Aleppo shielded the population there from conscription.

A growth in foreign trade accompanied Egyptian rule in Syria, as European and allied non-Muslim merchants expanded their activities. Christians of Aleppo, who were predominantly Catholic by this time, grew especially confident and began to throw off the public diffidence that long had defined relationships between Muslim rulers and their non-Muslim subjects. Catholics had benefited from pioneering French educational missions in the Syrian lands, and as a community they were becoming well connected and wealthy through merchant activities that encompassed Syrian–European and Syrian–Egyptian trade. Syrian Catholics' confidence in the 1830s arose in part from the happy fact that their overseas patron, France, was on friendly terms with Muhammad Ali's administration.

But the Egyptian regime's unpopularity created opportunities for the Ottomans and their British allies to foment unrest. Alongside conscription and forced disarmament, Ibrahim Pasha's universal poll tax caused great unhappiness among Muslims. The tax symbolically diminished Muslims' heretofore unchallenged superior status in a multi-religious society. Although Egyptian rule in Syria had been good for British trade, Britain feared that the Egyptian authorities were preparing to impose a monopoly system in Syria that would restrict British and British-connected merchants' activities. Moreover, Britain looked askance at Muhammad Ali's good relations with France. So Britain sided with Istanbul when a renewed Ottoman–Egyptian war broke out in 1839–40. The Ottoman army was inferior to Egypt's, but direct British and Austrian military intervention, combined with Syrian revolts against Egyptian rule, forced Muhammad Ali to sue for terms. The Egyptian army withdrew from Syria and would not return for another 118 years.

The Egyptian era in Syria, though short-lived, upended earlier power balances. It introduced modern statehood to Syria, challenged inherited assumptions about Christians' and Jews' subordinate status vis-à-vis Muslims, and opened the door to European political and economic inroads into the country. These developments would light the fuse of inter-confessional strife as the returning Ottomans attempted their own modern state-building project.

THE OTTOMANS RETURN AND TANZIMAT REFORMS

Having ousted Muhammad Ali from Syria with British and Austrian help, the Ottomans reasserted their authority in the country starting in 1840. The empire was in the early stages of a centralizing reform project that was still more of an aspiration than an achievement. On the eve of the Ottomans' reconquest of Syria a new sultan, Abdulmejid I (1839–61), issued a reform decree called the Tanzimat (1839) that set out an updated vision for Ottoman governance. The Tanzimat decree represented a victory for reform-minded officials, and it also was meant for international (especially British) consumption at a time when the Ottomans desperately needed Britain's help. Reformist Ottoman officials wished to present their state as a modern, nineteenth-century monarchy that should take its place among the recognized great powers in the post-Napoleonic world. The Tanzimat decree pledged to root out corruption and abuses, to govern with justice in accordance with the precepts of the sharia, to guarantee security of property, and to treat all Ottoman subjects equally whatever their religion. Thus the sultanate renounced its theoretically absolute power in favor of a system where state authority would be constrained by predictable legal norms and by judicial equality.

As part of the Ottoman alliance with London that allowed the empire to withstand the challenge of Muhammad Ali's Egypt, Istanbul had agreed to a free trade treaty with Britain (1838). In the midst of England's pioneering industrial revolution, the British government looked to expand international markets for manufactured goods (and to cheapen the price of raw material imports) by removing barriers to international trade. Under the terms of the 1838 treaty, whose provisions soon were extended to include all of the Ottoman Empire's major trading partners, imports were subjected to low tariffs. Once imported, foreign goods would not have to pay internal taxes (which had typically been charged when a merchant's wares entered a new town), and Ottoman government monopolies were banned (making raw materials cheaper and more accessible to foreign merchants).

Because European merchants mistrusted the Ottomans' ubiquitous sharia courts, believing that as foreigners and as (usually) Christians they would not receive fair hearings in commercial disputes with Muslims, the European powers pressed for special commercial courts to hear cases involving their interests and subjects.

The creation of special commercial courts, and the growing influence of European consulates, meant that local partners of European merchants (usually Ottoman Christians, sometimes Ottoman Jews) would receive benefits and extraterritorial privileges that flowed from the older Capitulations agreements.

When Ottoman rule returned to Syria in 1840 Syrians therefore entered a world of new uncertainties. Many opponents of Egyptian rule wanted a restoration of what they remembered as the *status quo ante*. This was true, for instance, of Druze lords in Mount Lebanon who had been exiled by the Egyptians' erstwhile ally, Emir Bashir. Local paramilitaries and their commanders the *aghas* – who until 1826 had enjoyed the status of Janissaries – were wary of centralization efforts that might sideline them and their privileges. Muslim notables sought to use the new institutions of the Tanzimat to entrench themselves in government and to protect their local interests. Emerging Christian elites, connected to European trade and consulates, wished to build on the symbols of civic equality that Egyptian rule had introduced and that the Ottomans' Tanzimat decree implicitly promised.

The Ottomans reconfigured local administrative arrangements, most notably with the introduction of formally constituted advisory councils in different towns. Depending on a town's demography, its council included Christian and Jewish representation. Free trade provisions were applied to Syria, and foreign goods as well as foreigners (merchants, missionaries and consuls) became ubiquitous. The inflow of foreign manufactures put indigenous or local handicrafts under pressure. Landlords or merchants able to benefit from the increased international demand for Syria's raw materials saw a road to riches. Likewise, elites among Christians and Jews, positioned now as business partners of European interests, accumulated wealth and concomitant political influence within their communities. Christian elites especially developed patron–client ties with European consulates, superseding the older importance of Christian clientage to powerful Muslim patrons. In time, rural areas were brought under more systematic central government (and therefore urban) control through military campaigns undertaken by elements of the new-style Ottoman army, backed up by paramilitaries (now called *bashibazouks*) who filled the gap left by the disbanding of the old Janissary-mercenary military systems.

INTER-COMMUNAL TENSIONS AND VIOLENCE

An early outcome of these changes was increasing inter-communal tension in mid-century Syria. These tensions signaled an unsettling of older arrangements that had, for better or for worse, been touchstones of stability or continuity in people's lives.

Mount Lebanon was a focal point of such tensions, although these were also felt in the administrative centers of Aleppo and Damascus.

Early in the era of Emir Bashir II al-Shihab in Mount Lebanon, political factions had been defined along feudal and family lines. Powerful mountain lords marshaled coalitions of allies and clients to contest for power and resources (tax farms) against factional rivals. These factional alliances were cross-confessional, and they did not define themselves as *religious* 'factions.' But during the era of Egyptian rule this changed and Emir Bashir allied with the invading Egyptians. He helped to put down an anti-Egyptian revolt led by Druze sheikhs, who were driven into exile forfeiting their lands and properties. Bashir, for his part, relied more and more on the Christian peasantry of Mount Lebanon and the Maronite Christian church for support, and even converted from Sunnism (the Shihabs' original faith) to Maronite Christianity. Therefore Bashir's factional forces were becoming predominantly Christian, and Christian identity was evoked in order to strengthen Bashir and to mobilize his supporters. While the Egyptian administration disarmed much of the Syrian population, they left Bashir's Christians alone. Mount Lebanon's Christians had developed into an armed political faction in a way that was new. After the Ottomans returned, and British pressure forced Emir Bashir II to abdicate, the Druze sheikhs whom he had exiled demanded the restitution of their forfeited properties. This led to tensions and clashes between supporters of the Druze leaders and the Christians who had been empowered by Bashir.

Confessional differences deepened with the intervention of European powers on behalf of their local clients. French governments identified the Catholic Maronites as their most important clients in the East Mediterranean, building on political contacts and religious ties that French officials and missionaries had developed since the seventeenth century. Looking to offset French inroads, the British befriended and supported the Druze sheikhs. 'Support' in this instance meant political intervention on behalf of their clients, and flows of weapons and money. British and French patronage of rival sides fueled internecine violence between Druzes and Christians over issues of land and of power. What developed in Mount Lebanon after 1840 was a crystallization of Maronites and Druzes as political factions, backed by rival European sponsors.

Although the post-1840 Ottomans initially attempted to impose a unitary territorial form of administration in Mount Lebanon, the local factions plus their European allies pushed back fearing that Ottoman plans would compromise their interests. The upshot was a series of elaborate administrative reorganizations, overseen by France and Britain, which took Druze and Maronite confessional identities as bases for territorial and governance arrangements. This set precedents that later would identify Lebanon as a land where political life rested on religious or communal identities. But in the shorter term, the mid-century Mount Lebanon story was one part of a phenomenon of European intervention in Syrian politics in a manner that inflamed sectarian or religious tensions.

Alongside European interventions, the industrial revolution and free trade policies in Syria had a deleterious impact. The inflow of mass-produced foreign (especially British) textiles under free trade provisions undercut the Ottomans' protectionist guild system that long had regulated urban manufactures. The guild system limited the numbers of people who could enter a particular trade, and ensured a protected market where producers and manufacturers at different stages of production would receive living wages and meet a standard of quality. However, this protected system could not withstand the flood of cheaper foreign imports, and the guild system began to break down.

Artisans most immediately affected were weavers and ancillary producers in the textile sector. Taken altogether these were the single largest group of manufacturers in all major Syrian cities and towns. The impact in a major weaving center like Damascus was to depress wages and introduce new uncertainties into people's livelihoods. As this uncertainty spread, well-positioned Christian elites (merchants, and protégés of foreign consuls) prospered. These Christian elites' connections with the foreign consuls gave them access to new forms of political power outside of the old Muslim-*dhimmi* patronage system. The Ottoman Tanzimat's promise of civic equality encouraged Christians to behave more forthrightly in public, exemplified by public processions, ringing of church bells, and disregarding sumptuary laws that dictated what kinds of clothing non-Muslims could wear in public.

Economic uncertainty and artisans' impoverishment combined with public displays of Christian prosperity and empowerment to generate inter-communal tensions that were ripe for exploitation. Some Ottoman administrative and local military figures had misgivings about the Tanzimat's administrative innovations, fearing that the new institutions (provincial councils, a modern-trained and staffed army) might deprive them of their powerbroker status. The *ulama* also raised objections. Along with expressing concern about the status of Muslims in general, *ulama* resented Istanbul's attempts to reduce their role in *waqf* endowment administration by creating a central mechanism to manage and administer endowments.

The new tensions were reflected in outbursts of anti-Christian violence in both Aleppo and Damascus. In the former the troubles occurred amidst escalating tensions associated with uncertainties of Ottoman political restoration and reform, and a new assertiveness by the city's Greek Catholic population. Up until the 1840s the Porte had resisted recognizing Greek Catholics as a separate community, on account of opposition from the Greek Orthodox patriarchate, which resented the loss of parishioners and properties to Catholicism. But in the 1840s the sultanate's attitude changed. The influence of the Greek Orthodox patriarchate had been diminished by the Greek Revolt, making the Porte less solicitous of the patriarchate's wishes. In addition, Greek Catholics lobbied hard for sultanic recognition, and were supported in these efforts by French diplomatic intervention. In 1848 the Porte recognized the Greek Catholics or Melkites as a separate and officially constituted religious community or *millet*. The triumphant Melkite patriarch returned to Aleppo in 1849 amidst widespread public celebrations. Bolstered by official recognition, and encouraged by the Tanzimat pledge of legal equality for Ottoman subjects of all religions, the generally prosperous and ascendant Greek Catholics of Aleppo threw off their erstwhile circumspection. New and larger churches were planned and begun.

Aleppo Muslims who worried about the new-style Ottoman state that was developing now had easily accessible symbols of this new order, in the form of Christian populations, places and properties. The spark that set off the Aleppo violence was a rumor that the government was about to implement military conscription in Aleppo. Muslim rioters sacked and burned Christian churches, shops and homes. Many of the perpetrators were linked to the former (but now disbanded) Janissaries. In their statement of grievances they declared their loyalty to the sultan and to Islam, and they called for a restoration of the respect and status that they (as Janissaries) once had enjoyed. They also called for the cancellation of a recently introduced property tax. Regarding Christians, the rioters demanded that they should revert to the public modesty and social-legal deference that had been the pre-Tanzimat norm.

Though property damage was extensive, a relatively small number of Christians (around 20) were killed. Most of the victims and torched properties were from the wealthy extramural Christian quarter of Jdaideh. Christians who lived in intramural quarters among Muslims appear to have been sheltered or protected not only by European consuls but also by Muslim neighbors. Interpreting the violence as a challenge to state authority, the Ottomans sent an army to impose control on Aleppo and punish the perpetrators. The attacking army used artillery that killed more people (Muslims) and inflicted more damage than the original rioters had.

By the time of the Damascus violence ten years later, the European presence in Syria had grown as a consequence of the Crimean War (1853–6). This war, sparked by arguments over access to holy sites in Palestine, pitted the Ottoman Empire, Britain and France against Russia. During the 1853–6 war British purchasing agents sought Syrian supplies to provision their armies in the Crimea. The Porte's deepening dependence on its European (especially British) allies was reflected in a new Tanzimat reform decree (1856) that both reiterated and explicitly endorsed the principle of equality before the law for all Ottoman subjects and appeared to mark a formal end of Muslim political and legal hegemony. When the 1856 decree was read publicly to a group of Muslim notables in Damascus, one of the kadis present recalled their reactions: 'All the Muslims became ashen faced and they asked God Most High that he glorify the faith and grant victory to the Muslims.'[8] Bloody battles between Druzes and Maronites in Mount Lebanon from 1858–60 added to the general unease. First the Greek Revolt, then Aleppo, then Mount Lebanon – violent conflicts in the Ottoman Empire increasingly took sectarian or confessional form, as the sultanate struggled to find a workable formula for modern rule, and as more powerful European states intervened in Ottoman and Syrian affairs to support their particular clients and interests. In this tense and uncertain atmosphere, Christian refugees poured into Damascus in the late spring of 1860 bringing with them tales of the Mount Lebanon clashes. Adding to Damascenes' unease were rumors of vengeful and loot-seeking Druzes converging on the city from the west (Lebanon) and the south (Houran). A small incident could spark a conflagration, and it did.

In July 1860, Muslim adolescents were arrested for scrawling crosses in public thoroughfares, and then mocking the Christian symbols. Crowds of the youths' coreligionists gathered demanding that they be freed. Angry voices urged Muslims to attack Christians in retribution for all that had gone awry in recent years. The bloodletting in Mount Lebanon and closer to Damascus in Wadi al-Taym (today in south-east Lebanon) was the kindling and eight days of violence against local Christians the result. Villagers and Druzes from outside the city abetted the mayhem, while local authorities looked on passively or helplessly. Military commanders stood aside as vengeful mobs and renegade soldiers burned Damascus's Christian quarter, looted property and killed thousands. The fear and chaos of those days is captured in a hasty note written by a British missionary in the Christian quarter addressed to the British consul in the Muslim quarter (whose premises were guarded and unharmed). The missionary, Smylie Robinson, described the unfolding disaster:

> For the last two hours and a half, the street past my house has presented a most terrible scene, first the rush and running of men armed, unarmed, boys, women, shouts, imprecations on the infidel Christians, cries of 'kill them, butcher them, plunder, burn, leave not one, not a house, not anything: Fear not the soldiers, fear nothing, the soldiers will not meddle with you.' [...] they were right. Nobody has interfered.[9]

Some Muslim notables intervened to limit the damage and give refuge to frightened local Christians and Europeans. However, the bulk of the Muslim elite in Damascus (as in Aleppo ten years before) subsequently argued that Christians had brought these misfortunes upon themselves through their alleged greed and arrogance. A few years after the events, the Muslim notable and future *naqib al-ashraf*, Abu'l-Su'ud al-Hasibi, recalled Muslims' grievances:

> Every Christian had some relative who had acquired a foreign nationality, in most cases the French. Whoever had a claim against a Muslim would delegate it to one of these foreign nationals. If a Christian quarreled with a Muslim, regardless who the latter may be, he would say: 'I am the subject of such-and-such a Power.' This assertion often proved to be false. Rather, [the Christian in question] would be protected by a relative or friend [who had acquired the foreign nationality].[10]

Al-Hasibi also sought to exonerate Muslim elites from any responsibility for the violence:

> Druzes, Nusayris, Jews, Mitwalis, Rafidis, wanderers, worshippers of sun and moon, Yazidis, Arabs and [people] of every community known in Syria and accustomed to misdeeds gathered from every part and corner to join the rabble of Damascus. The latter were not known for mischief before this incident [...]. My father said of them: 'These lowly people have no talent except for showing disrespect [to social superiors].' [...] Honorable citizens were not informed [about the mischief planned], and had no presentiment of it.[11]

REVERBERATIONS OF INTER-COMMUNAL VIOLENCE

At the end of July an Ottoman imperial army arrived to punish the perpetrators. Common people and soldiers found guilty of participation in violence were executed, while notables found complicit were exiled or imprisoned. Muslim notables decried the unfairness of Ottoman measures, including arrests, imprisonment, executions and the imposition of a collective fine on the city's Muslims to indemnify victimized Christians.

The Ottomans' urban order in Syria appeared to be fraying, even though the violence was not repeated in the burgeoning port of Beirut, or in secondary Syrian centers like Tripoli, Sidon, Homs and Hama where local notables intervened to contain tensions and forestall outbreaks. Beirut by this time had become a 'special case', a center of European interests and preponderantly Christian urbanism in Ottoman Syria. In the other towns, which were secondary ports or agricultural and manufacturing centers, European protégés had lower profiles than in Aleppo and Damascus, and tensions arising from novel forms of Christian self-assertion were less in evidence. But the collapse of long-standing inter-communal comity in Damascus was a major shock, and its reverberations were felt beyond Syria. The French government, acting in its self-appointed role as the protector of the Ottoman Empire's Christians, dispatched a force to Beirut. The Istanbul authorities, who desperately wanted to forestall deeper European intervention in the Ottomans' internal affairs, saw the violence as a challenge to state authority that needed to be put down decisively lest European powers use it as a pretext for further interventions. The official response was an unmistakable message from the Ottoman government that the old, pre-Tanzimat way of exercising and negotiating power had ended.

Istanbul's perspective was that if the Ottoman Empire were to retain its independence and sovereignty in the perilous circumstances of the later nineteenth century, it needed forcefully to assert its authority against those who threatened to undermine it. Urban notables in Damascus whom Istanbul blamed for the 1860 violence were punished and lost access to power and patronage. Loyalists took their places and became, in their turn, emblematic of late-Ottoman notability. Loyalty to the Ottoman state brought rewards, and Ottoman subjects elsewhere in Syria observed and learned. Henceforward urban notables concluded that their best interests lay in becoming part of the Ottoman project of state building rather than being obstacles to or opponents of it.

Ultimately the Ottoman government forestalled these threats to its Syrian authority. Though it had to concede some ground in Mount Lebanon, via creation of the internationally guaranteed autonomous district (called the Mutasarrifiyya) in 1861, Ottoman sovereignty was preserved in other Syrian centers. Urban notables were co-opted, figuring that their interests and positions were better defended inside the reinvigorated empire. Otherwise, they risked the perils of Ottoman fragmentation and likely European takeover.

Syrian Christians, who immediately after 1860 might have hoped for international guarantees beyond the geographically confined boundaries of Mount Lebanon, soon were seeking instead to find a secure place within the renovated empire. This evolution of attitudes is demonstrated in the writings of Mikhail Mishaqa in a memorandum to the US consul in Beirut written shortly after the events. His clear purpose was to encourage international intervention on Christians' behalf (as in fact did occur in Mount Lebanon):

> As for the Christians, they considered the Tanzimat reforms of the state to be effective and valid. Many of the young men, who had not known the injustice of the past, believed that the equality of subjects was clearly set out in the government's orders, and that the courts and government employees were in violation of these orders. They [Christians] had left behind the conditions of slavery and began to insult the Muslim when he insulted them and complained to the government when [the Muslim] struck them, exclaiming out loud 'we are your equals.' If a Muslim owed [Christians] a debt, they would submit a complaint and demand his imprisonment. They began to exercise their freedom in their choice of clothes [i.e., disregarding former dress codes to distinguish Muslims from non-Muslims] and life-style, demonstrating their emancipation from the bonds of slavery.[12]

Yet by the time he wrote his memoirs 13 years later in 1873, Mishaqa had adjusted his presentation of the violence's background. Now he blamed 'ignorant Christians' for provoking Muslims. His shift in tone demonstrates Mishaqa's recognition that Syrians' fortunes would for the foreseeable future unfold within an Ottoman political framework.

> As the Empire began to implement reforms and equality among its subjects regardless of their religious affiliation, the ignorant Christians went too far in their interpretation of equality, and thought that the small did not have to submit to the great, and the low did not have to respect the high. Indeed they thought that humble Christians were on a par with exalted Muslims. They did not want to understand that, just as equality was based on regulations and legal rights, the people of stature had to maintain their proper dignity before whatever community, especially when it came to Christians vis-à-vis Muslims.[13]

By this later date Mishaqa was acknowledging the endurance of Ottoman rule in Syria. After the traumatic events of 1860, the Ottoman state developed and embedded modern state institutions in the country. From this point onward, Syrian Arab elites would adapt to modern statehood rather than try to resist it.

REESTABLISHING OTTOMAN POWER IN SYRIA POST-1860

The Ottomans constructed a new type of cultural hegemony in Syria's cities during the last decades of the empire's existence, binding urban elites to the interests and institutions of modern statehood. Debates over the nature of the state had been settled in favor of a modern administrative model. A new land code in 1858 opened the way for registration of extensive lands in the hands of individuals, a procedure that overwhelmingly favored people with ties to the administration, incentivizing cooperation with it. In 1864 a new provinces law established the framework of provincial and district administration that offered ambitious loyalists opportunities to join the burgeoning civil service and to move upward in its ranks. This framework remained in place until the end of the empire, and was adapted by the governments that followed the end of Ottoman rule. A constitution introduced in 1876 (but suspended in 1878) established the principle of parliamentary representation according to province or district, which offered an additional way for Ottoman loyalists to integrate into the state. Even though the constitution and parliament were suspended for 30 years (1878–1908), the growth of municipal and provincial governments in the meantime offered other entryways to government service. The imperial government intervened more regularly in various aspects of life, including education and the provisioning of agricultural credits (which mainly benefited big landowners). Government initiatives in education grew out of concerns that non-Muslims were gaining advantages from the introduction of modern schools by foreign-inspired missionary and benevolent societies, and that the Muslim subjects of the state needed effective schools of their own.

Disastrous Ottoman defeats and new territorial losses in the Balkans, as the upshot of a war with Russia in 1878, shook Syrian Muslims' confidence. These developments sparked popular protests against conscription in Damascus and encouraged nervous Syrian notables to think about alternatives to the Ottoman state should it be totally lost. However, the stabilization of the state from 1879 onward reestablished the centrality of Ottoman loyalty – Ottomanism – to the political identities of urban Syrians. The reigning sultan, Abdulhamid II (r. 1876–1909), cultivated support among Arab notables. He emphasized the common bond of Islam and the identification of the Ottoman sultanate with a modern caliphate. He opened schools that offered Syrians and Arabs more generally promotion in the Ottoman system. Elite schools in provincial capitals including Damascus and Aleppo prepared graduates for high-ranking posts. Usually they came from well-to-do and well-connected families. Ottoman military schools, on the other hand, offered career opportunities for Syrians and other Arabs of modest means by giving them the chance to join the Ottoman army as officers.

Evidence for cultural identification with the modern Ottoman state is found in the decorations of houses that were built in Damascus in the later Ottoman decades.

The interiors of well-to-do families' homes were lavishly adorned with pictorial scenes, including those that evoked images of Istanbul as an imperial capital, and celebrated such triumphs as the first visit to Damascus (in 1912) of an airplane belonging to the fledgling Ottoman air force. Abdulhamid attempted to project an image of dynamic Ottoman–Islamic modernism, through such achievements as the opening of a telegraph line to Mecca (still memorialized today in Damascus by a monument erected in Marja Square), and the construction of railroads connecting the various Syrian–Ottoman cities together. The Hejaz Railroad held pride of place. It started in Damascus and went south to Medina, with a branch line to Haifa in Palestine. Other railroads (built with French capital) connected Damascus to Beirut, and both of these cities to Homs, Hama and Aleppo where the railroad met Anatolian lines that ran to Istanbul and that were projected to run eastward to Iraq (the so-called 'Berlin to Baghdad railway'). Public works projects (tramways, gas lighting, water works, electrification) in major cities – usually built by European companies – allowed urban Syrians to see themselves as part of a project of Ottoman modernity.

A paradoxical feature of Abdulhamid's autocracy was that, while it gave Arab landed notables a sense of participating in state-building modernization, it alienated many of the 'new men' who were needed to run the modern state and participate in public institutions. Graduates of modern schools who filled the ranks of the bureaucracy, who staffed the new schools, who worked in technical and professional fields and who developed the new crafts of journalism in the public sphere created by the press, chafed under the sultan's autocratic rule. Abdulhamid brought in press censorship and created the region's first modern network of police informants and spies.

Nevertheless many decades later, after the vicissitudes of French colonialism and the disappointments of national independence, urban Syrians looked back nostalgically at the later Ottoman period as a kind of 'golden age.' Despite nationalists' characterization of the era as one of alien 'Turkish' rule, the last Ottoman decades came eventually to be understood as a repository of 'heritage,' representing a lost integrity and innocence. In the 1990s and 2000s publications and television serials wistfully evoked society in late Ottoman times. The virtues and verities of 'true' or 'authentic' pre-colonial Syria were identified with the Ottoman years, a project of nostalgic memory-construction that juxtaposed awkwardly with vehement nationalist political condemnation of Ottoman rule.

The late-Ottoman experiment in promoting modern statehood and a modern political identity created a shared language of statehood and citizenship, at least in urban Syria. Elites and notables whose predecessors had been intermediaries between urban populations and imperial rulers became, in the final Ottoman decades, officials, civil servants and army officers who saw the Ottoman sultanate as a suitable expression of modern statehood – indeed, as the last remaining independent Sunni Muslim state of any consequence. Although non-Muslims could not aspire to the same kind of 'insider' status as Muslims, the urban and educated among Christians and Jews took their Ottoman citizenship seriously. Many non-Muslims found fulfillment as 'modern people' in the professions, some in private practice and others as members of specialized bureaucratic departments or military units. This consensus around the symbol of the sultanate began to fray in the years immediately prior to World War I. But it was only during the war that urban Syrians' bond with the Ottoman state broke down.

THE RECONQUEST OF RURAL AREAS

Consistent with the Ottoman government's goal of asserting state authority throughout its territories, the last Ottoman decades saw Istanbul's reconquest of autonomous and indirectly administered rural areas, incorporating them into formalized bureaucratic structures backed up with a year-round permanent presence of government administrators, garrisons and police posts. Typically residents of the rural districts had paid taxes or tribute to urban-based authorities. But aside from experiencing tax collection visits and punitive raids, rural districts had not been subject to ongoing centralized oversight. The old Ottoman state simply did not have the means or resources to establish such a presence, preferring instead to work through tribal or clan-based intermediaries. But now Istanbul wished to bring rural populations into the state as subjects who could be counted, taxed, enumerated and (when needed) conscripted.

Part of this drive to rural incorporation was impelled by economic or market forces. Merchants and landowners seeking to expand their domestic markets wanted to incorporate new communities into their circuits of trade and production. They did this in alliance with government bureaucrats, who viewed the growth of rural peoples' commercial ties with towns, and the reduction of rural autarkies and autonomies, as part and parcel of modern state building. Commercial agricultural estates appeared around Aleppo, in the vicinity of Hama, and in the plains of Palestine. New opportunities combined with greater rural security encouraged extensive, settled agriculture in lands that earlier would have been dual-use agricultural and grazing lands under nomadic tribal or clan auspices. These newly opened commercial lands usually were registered in the names of well-connected local officials or merchants, who recruited sharecropping cultivators to work them. Sharecropping cultivators came from semi-nomadic Bedouins, or already settled peasants seeking access to more land, or mountain peasants fleeing poverty and/ or clan and tribal divisions in their native districts. In places military campaigns brought recalcitrant rural strongmen to heel. This happened in the Palestinian hills in the 1850s, the Ansariyeh mountains in 1870, and against Druzes on the edges of the Houran wheat-growing region south of Damascus in 1862.

Assertion of state authority in rural districts did not necessarily remove the local strongmen from positions of influence. Typically the Ottomans sought to turn them into pro-Ottoman rural administrators. In Houran the Druze Atrash clan previously had been targets of an Ottoman military campaign. But after 1862 they agreed to align themselves with the government, and to assist Damascus's efforts to collect revenues from peasants and pastoralists and establish safe passage through their region. But some rural clans never regained the pivotal positions they once enjoyed. An example is the Abu Ghosh, whose eponymous village straddled the Jaffa to Jerusalem road (actually a caravan track) in Palestine. Recognized by the Porte as local powerbrokers, Abu Ghosh strongmen levied tolls and fees for safe passage. But once government-provided security (and modern roads suitable for wheeled traffic) became the norms of reformed Ottoman rule, the Abu Ghosh's older type of rural 'security' (or protection racket) was treated as a usurpation of state authority and they were suppressed.

In yet other places the extension of regular bureaucratic order was achieved by co-opting local populations, for instance in the region of Transjordan. Here the Ottomans established their first regular government office in 1867 in a town called Salt. The establishment of a land registry office encouraged people of Salt (who had long practiced private ownership in accordance with provisions of customary and sharia law) to obtain new documentation attesting to their legal title. Key Bedouin chieftains of the region, sensing how the wind was blowing, joined the scramble to obtain land titles, and they became owners in name and in law of lands that until then had been tribal domains for cultivation and animal husbandry. The expansion of commercial relations and of agricultural markets encouraged landowners to extend dry farming to new lands where annual rainfall allowed it. Seeking partners in the expansion of grain cultivation, tribal sheikhs and other Transjordanian landowners relied on credit from merchants and moneylenders in Jerusalem and Damascus. Owners imported farm labor from the region of Nablus, where hill peasants – now 'pacified' and brought into the widening circles of commerce and trade – were experiencing population growth and land shortages. Such pressures encouraged Nablus hill peasants to look farther afield for tenancy or sharecropping work, first migrating on a seasonal basis and later moving permanently to Transjordan where they cultivated the new estates.

As far as the state bureaucracy and its social allies were concerned, these developments represented a 'virtuous circle.' Government authority spread, becoming tangible in administrative offices and military outposts, and facilitated the growth of agricultural commercialization and capital flows from city to country. This further reinforced a demand or need for the state and its institutions. In places such as Amman (Transjordan) and Salamiyya (east of Homs), the Ottomans arranged for the settlement of newly migrated communities in order to extend the frontier of cultivation eastward. In Amman the community settled were Muslim Circassians (1878), who were refugees who had fled Russian conquest of their homeland on the eastern shores of the Black Sea. In Salamiyya the new settlers were Ismailis, a longtime Syrian community whose original villages in the Ansariyeh mountains had become unviable, constrained as they were by limited resources and by hostile and more powerful Alawite neighbors. (The Circassian legacy remains a marker of identity in modern Amman, Jordan and Salamiyya today is the principal Ismaili population center in Syria.)

The combination of spreading commercial agriculture and population pressure on hill lands was the background to two other Syrian migrations with significant later impacts. One migration was from Mount Lebanon, by now (1861–1915) an autonomous district adjoining the province of Syria (Damascus). In Mount Lebanon a Christian peasantry, unable to sustain themselves in land-poor villages, started emigrating in large numbers overseas, principally to the Americas. Abroad they formed the Syrian communities of the late nineteenth and early twentieth centuries (where the nomenclature 'Syrian' survived, even after the formal and final separation of Lebanon from Syria in 1920). About one-third of the émigrés returned to their villages in Lebanon, bringing with them new wealth, new tastes and new perspectives or outlooks. A lively Arabic press developed in the lands of emigration. One of the longest lasting was the New York Arabic-language paper *al-Huda* (est. 1898). In the pages of émigré newspapers ideas of modernity and of Syrian and Lebanese identity were advocated, discussed and debated. In time this émigré discourse developed strands of Lebanese and Syrian nationalism that were distinct from (but sometimes overlapped with) equally new ideas of Arab political identity, forming the seeds of what eventually became Arab nationalism.

The Ansariyeh mountains west of Homs and Hama were another region where migration out of mountain lands occurred in response to economic push and pull factors. Large landed estates appeared in the rain-fed hinterlands of these lowland cities, responding to the same demand for grain that extended cultivation in the new lands of Transjordan and that made the wheat lands of the Houran a source of enrichment for Damascus grain merchants. As the market for Homs and Hama's agricultural products grew, military chiefs and urban notables who already had claims to the taxation and revenues of the Homs–Hama hinterland became landowners in a full legal sense, under terms of the 1858 Ottoman land code. Labor for these new lands was supplied by, among others, Alawite (previously known as Nusayri) peasants who descended from their mountains to cultivate the new farms.

Here a commercial dynamic became overlaid with a confessional one. Landed elites were well-connected Sunnis and many of the sharecropping peasants were Alawites. Alawite chieftain families, who had been local powerbrokers in their own right in the pre-Tanzimat era, were more and more reduced to minor functionaries in the increasingly pervasive and ubiquitous Ottoman administrative system. After the Ottomans crushed autonomous or independent Alawite chieftains in a brief military campaign in 1870, their mountains were impoverished and population outflow rose. A Russian consular official in the port of Latakia wrote in 1870, 'the condition of the Nusayri districts is very sad and unhappy. For them, there is neither justice nor security.'[14] Ten years later, Muhammad Agha al-Barazi led a follow-up campaign against rebellious peasants. As a reward for his victory he received many villages and became district governor of Hama. The Barazi family became a leading landholding-administrative family in central Syria and Hama especially. Members of the family would play an important political and economic role in the subsequent era of French colonialism and in the early independence years.[15]

Though the government established an ongoing presence in the Ansariyeh mountains, the region's infrastructure lagged behind those of neighboring regions, and the communities there (principally Alawites) came to be regarded as among the most marginalized in late-Ottoman Syria. This situation would in time offer the post-Ottoman colonial power, France, an opportunity to play on Sunni versus Alawite social tensions and confessional identities for political gain. Rivalries stoked by French colonial policy in turn bequeathed to independent Syria social, confessional and political antagonisms that had significant consequences in the region of Hama especially.

One area where commercialization, state intrusion and formation of private property rights promoted rural conflict was in Houran. This grain producing region, 'the breadbasket of Damascus,' was where the connections to *aghas* of the old local Janissary corps and merchants of Damascus had characterized the 'localist' faction in Azm-ruled and early-Tanzimat Damascus. Now, in the later nineteenth century, ties between the Damascus grain merchants, rural paramilitary families and the grain producing peasantry took on new dimensions with the extension of cultivation and improvement in communications. Reverberations were especially felt in a portion of Houran called the Jabal Druze, the 'Druze mountain' (confusingly, a name formerly applied to Mount Lebanon, where Druze lords had once been the most powerful political figures).

Houran's Jabal Druze was a volcanic highland region inhabited mostly by members of the Druze faith, a community that originally had arisen in Mount Lebanon. Druzes had migrated to the Houran highlands in the eighteenth century. There they cultivated the land and defended their turf in a social organization that emphasized clan and tribal identities and loyalties. By the 1870s prominent families were keen to strengthen and consolidate their positions. The context was a growing integration of the Jabal Druze into wider commercial circuits, and Ottoman pressures that threatened to reduce the historic autonomy to which the semi-feudal leading families had grown accustomed. All of this occurred alongside Ottoman campaigns to bring Houran more firmly under central control, a process that bequeathed on it the sobriquet 'Houran *al-damiya*,' or 'Bloody Houran.'

The leading Druze families asserted quasi-feudal privileges, working to create in Jabal Druze the kind of 'feudal' structures that had only recently been dismantled (in favor of a landlord-merchant alliance and regional autonomy) in Mount Lebanon. Pressures that the Druze leading families put on their peasant tenants provoked a widespread anti-feudal uprising (1889–90), that resulted in the Atrash and other Druze chieftains calling on the Ottoman state to bail them out. The Ottoman authorities in Damascus did so, in a way that curbed the most provocative excesses of feudal exploitation while simultaneously strengthening the legal and institutional positions of the leading families, who now cooperated out of necessity with the Ottoman administration. Some Druze notables, like other elite rural families brought into the Ottoman system by conquest, co-optation or political necessity, found roles for themselves in this new state by supplying their sons for officer training in the Ottoman army.

The kinds of networks established by rural elites in the Ottoman officer training schools, plus (in Damascus) the connections forged between rural elites and the urban state apparatus, proved resilient. Some of these very same people, the networks they formed and the areas and communities from which they arose combined to support stubborn armed opposition to France as it attempted to establish or consolidate colonial control after the defeat of the Ottoman Empire in World War I.

SULTAN ABDULHAMID II AND OFFICIAL ISLAM

The Ottoman state also strove to inculcate a kind of quasi-national loyalty to the Ottoman sultanate in its population, particularly among Muslims after the definitive loss of most of the Empire's remaining Christian territories and populations in 1878. After that date the Ottoman sultan, Abdulhamid II, emphasized his claim to the universal caliphate and sought to rally domestic and international Muslim support around his throne as the last significant Sunni Muslim state in the world. The erstwhile Tanzimat ideals of civic equality for all Ottoman subjects regardless of their religion were not formally abandoned, but henceforth Ottoman state policy made no bones about the fact that if the empire were to survive it would need to rely on the symbols and tokens of Muslim identity. To this end, Abdulhamid's regime paid particularly close attention to the mostly Muslim Arabic-speaking regions of the diminished empire, including Syria.

In the race to modernize, Abdulhamid's government faced challenges from European powers. Moreover, the missionary or Christian schools that operated under foreigners' auspices gave non-Muslims an inside track on the acquisition of modern knowledge. Abdulhamid's regime no longer could let education be merely or mostly a matter of private concern, funded by endowments or *waqfs*. The state sought now to insert itself into public education in a new way.

In light of the insecurity felt by official Istanbul (insecurity borne of vulnerability and of well-founded fear that the Ottoman Empire was the target of stronger, avaricious foreign powers), the Porte asserted its control of Muslims' educational activities. Therefore the government discouraged grass-roots philanthropic attempts to establish modern Muslim schools. Abdulhamid's regime asserted a quasi-monopoly over Muslim modern education via state schools, where not only the modern sciences could be taught but also where an official form of Islam would be developed and inculcated. This was a hierarchical understanding of Islam that emphasized duty and obedience, and used the authority and prestige of selected loyalist Sufi leaders to inculcate the message. To this end, one of the principal propagandists for the pro-Abdulhamid policies of Islamic loyalty was a Rifaʻiyya Sufi sheikh from Aleppo named Abu al-Huda al-Sayyadi (d. 1909).

Educational officials in Istanbul believed that Muslim Syrians and other Muslim Arabic-speaking subjects of the empire needed to be socialized into this particular version of obedient, state-friendly Islam. Their outlook potentially put them at odds with Syrian Muslim thinkers who were seeking an intellectual revival of Islam through a renewal of critical enquiry rather than through the recitation of loyalist formulas. This policy also placed Abdulhamid's state in an uncomfortable, potentially condescending position toward subject communities who were Muslim in a broad sense but whose particular traditions lay outside of the discourse of learned Sunnism and the Ottomans' privileged Hanafi rite. Such communities in Syria would include the Druzes and the Alawites. So on the one hand rural elites, including Druzes and Alawites, could and would be trained as Ottoman officers, inculcated with a sense of loyalty to the state and dynasty in ways that promoted a modern sense of patriotism and quasi-nationalism, based on religion rather than ethnicity. But on the other hand there was at the same time a sense among Ottoman officials that officialdom had a kind of 'civilizing mission' among the more benighted of their Arab Muslim subjects, whether the civilizational deficit was expressed in terms of unorthodox beliefs or rural tribal loyalties.

The Ottoman state-building effort was successful up to a point, but in the period prior to World War I the various tensions and contradictions inherent in this process were not resolved – and perhaps were irresolvable. The modern state made demands of and had expectations of its citizenry that were quite new and unprecedented, and that marked an epistemological break with older forms of imperial or dynastic control that had not particularly cared what people thought. The old Ottoman sultanate had taken multiplicities of loyalties and identities for granted, rather than seeing them as potential 'problems' in the quest to build a modern, state-oriented and politically mobilized society.

THE MODERN STATE: URBAN–RURAL DIFFERENCES

The combined processes of state formation and affirmation of private property rights had less traumatic or transformative effects in urban areas than in rural ones. In the market garden and green belt lands around urban areas, complex webs of private property rights and a legal-judicial state regulatory apparatus had long been in place. In the irrigated and well-defined garden areas in the vicinity of various cities, Tanzimat legal and administrative changes were introduced without significant ruptures in socio-legal continuity. Likewise, the Ottomans' effort to codify the sharia and to create a kind of civil law (called *majalla*) derived from the sharia brought a greater sense of regularity and homogenization into civic legal matters, but these did not mark a sharp break in daily practice. Codification of sharia and customary principles did, however, create a blueprint for a uniform civil code, coexisting alongside older religious codes that more and more were restricted to matters of personal status (marriage, divorce, inheritance, etc.). In the immediate aftermath of the Ottoman Empire, the *majalla* civil code and the personal-status religious courts were inherited by the new colonial-era states along with the bulk of the late Ottoman legal apparatus.

Simply put, after 1860 especially, the cities of Syria adapted to the new institutions and assertions of the modern state. It helped that Ottoman policy aimed to incorporate Syrian (and other Arab urban) elites into the state structures. Syria's urban elites and professional classes gained the experience of working in and identifying with modern state institutions. Civil services positions such as mayors and city councils, inspectors of education and of agriculture, chief engineers, and so forth were open to Syrians with the right training and connections. Briefly after 1876, and a few years longer from 1908 to 1914, Syrian elites also engaged with parliamentary representation through a two-stage electoral process to select representatives for the Ottoman parliament. Syria's urban elites identified with the idea of the modern state, and saw the civil service and political and military institutions as appropriate reflections of their modern political identities. After the Ottoman Empire had passed into history, they would seek to construct a Syrian state, and to develop a sense of Syrian patriotism and nationalism, along the statist lines that they had experienced and worked with during the last Ottoman decades.

The rural areas, on the other hand, experienced the modern state in a more adversarial way. Even when rural elites were co-opted (through inducements or defeats) into modern state structures, the memory of antagonism to a distant if not hostile urban-centered state power continued to linger in the rural areas. When this combined with landlord exploitation (where landlords were supported by the state) or communal/ sectarian differences (where 'heterodox' Muslim rural communities found themselves subject to a predominantly Sunni identified urban power), there was little love lost for the modern state as it came to be understood during the late-Ottoman and colonial eras. The bases of post-Ottoman Syrian nationhood were riven by different memories, historical experiences and outlooks among various groups or segments within the Syrian population. The modern state had arrived in Syria, in some instances exacerbating social differentiation and older urban–rural tensions.

4

THE IDEA OF SYRIA AND WORLD WAR I

'THE CLARION OF SYRIA'

In the aftermath of the 1860 bloodshed in Damascus, the Beirut Protestant edu-
cator and writer Butrus al-Bustani published a series of broadsheets entitled *Nafir
Suriyya* (*The Clarion of Syria*). Its heading proclaimed (in a phrase attributed to
Muhammad) 'Love of Homeland is Part of Faith,' and Bustani's pen name was
'Lover of the Nation.' He called on Syrians to look deeply into themselves and to
root out the sources of discord and inter-communal violence in order to build a
community worthy of their nationhood. In *Nafir Suriyya*'s second issue (8 October
1860) he exhorted:

> O sons of the nation, you drink the same water, breathe the same air.
> The language you speak is one, the soil you step on is one, your habits, cul-
> ture, and interests are one […]. [T]he time will come when you will awaken
> from this […] slumber, and realize the significance of my advice and your
> public interest.[1]

The idea of 'Syria' became part of the pre-World War I public discourse. To be
sure, older localized identities continued to matter. These were understood to be
regional, local, clan and tribal. Confessional identity (Muslim, Christian, Jewish,
rustic 'heterodox') was not problematized and was still taken for granted. But
new ideas and concepts emerged alongside these, sometimes complementing
older identities or sometimes challenging them. The issue of political–cultural
identity was put on the table as the modern (Ottoman) state redefined relationships between the state and its subjects/citizens. Issues of identity also emerged
as new means of communications and transport broke down local particularisms
and forced Syrians to confront new realities of wider commercial and geographic

horizons. These debates unfolded within an Ottoman–Syrian world that would be shattered beyond repair during World War I.

NEW HORIZONS

People had always traveled: merchants, pilgrims, pastoralists all were aware of lands outside of their immediate locales. But the growing power of European consuls and protégés, on the one hand, and the new demands of the Ottoman state for loyalty, support and participation on the other hand put a new set of questions on the table. What did it mean to be Muslim and Ottoman, Christian and Damascene, Jewish and Syrian? The concept of 'Syria' itself began to be advocated by intellectuals and educators who sought to find a basis for common political and civic identity among people of various faiths, especially after the appalling inter-communal bloodshed of 1860.

The Maronite–Druze violence in Mount Lebanon might be incorrectly dismissed or cordoned off as 'traditional feuding among mountain people' (in fact it was *not* 'traditional,' as explained earlier). But the violence in Damascus (as well as the earlier outbreak of Muslim–Christian rancor in Aleppo) could not so easily be shrugged off or distanced. After all, the cities were the heart of the political communities that had developed in Ottoman Syria. Civic peace and order had broken down. If (according to intellectuals and thinkers) people of the Syrian lands were to get along, a way was needed to transcend this newly developed and dangerous Christian–Muslim polarization. The older, pre-Tanzimat Ottoman way of accommodating diversity by working with local communities of various kinds through intermediaries no longer sufficed.

Whereas Ottoman elites promoted a concept of 'Ottomanism' – loyalty to the Ottoman dynasty and homeland – some Syrian intellectuals posited the idea of 'Syria' as a discrete homeland within the Ottoman Empire. If 'Syrians' could discover and nurture what they had in common, then a way forward from bloody religious divisions seemed possible. Moreover, if Syrians were to become a modern people, capable of engaging creatively and equally with the forces of the modern (typically read as 'European') world, they would need to find a basis of identification and action that did not split them asunder because of religious divisions. The advent of new schools – missionary schools and private schools modeled on the modern education offered in missionary schools – created an 'enlightened' elite who self-consciously saw themselves as modern, and as responsible for nurturing a new understanding of Syrian identity.

What did Syrians have in common? First, the Arabic language, and second, attachment to the Syrian homeland. How was the Syrian homeland to be defined? They took the older Arabic-literary understanding of Bilad al-Sham and used the old/new word Syria as an equivalent. The word Syria had not been in common use locally since the era of Byzantine rule in the country more than one thousand years before. However, the word remained in use in Christian Europe, and also survived among Syria's Jacobite Christians who called themselves Suryani (known today as Syrian Orthodox). With the increasing European cultural influence in the nineteenth century, 'Syria' gained currency among the modern educated. The local use or understanding of the word got a major boost when the modernizing Ottoman government itself renamed the province of Damascus as the province of Syria in 1865.

Advocates of the Syrian idea were initially Christians, joined in time by modern-educated Muslims who likewise sought a locus for a specific patriotism more limited than the transnational religious community but wider than their local city. Syria advocates worked to define a common identity – Muslim, Christian and (potentially) Jewish – rooted in the land of Syria, the Arabic language, and a sense of a shared history and culture in the country.

The new literary genre of the historical novel introduced to the reading public a fresh way of thinking about the past. Historical novels' emphasis differed from older Muslim and Christian chronicles of dynasty and religious community. Now, through novels, Arabic readers could imagine that they were the heirs of a drama that stretched back to antiquity and that celebrated the heroes of old. One early novel (1871) was *Zenobia*, written by Beirut journalist Salim al-Bustani (Butrus al-Bustani's son). *Zenobia*'s protagonist was the Roman-era queen of Palmyra, whose name novelist Bustani invoked as a symbol of deeply rooted Syrian identity and heroic Syrian womanhood.

Improvements in communications and the development of early mass media encouraged Syrians to consider questions of identity in a new context. Distances were shrinking. Previously Damascus and Aleppo had been separated by nine days' journey, and Damascus and Beirut by two to three days over well-trodden but rough roads. By the end of the nineteenth century, though, railroads ensured that Beirut and Damascus were just nine hours apart, and when the railroad reached Aleppo in 1912 the trip between it and Damascus took less than two days. Even before the construction of the Beirut–Damascus railroad, a modern carriage road had opened in 1863, cementing Beirut's role as the principal port for central and southern Syria. The Beirut–Damascus carriage road was built by French capital, as were the subsequent rail lines. So now it was easier to visualize or imagine

Syria, because officials, merchants, and other travelers could speedily traverse the country in relative ease and comfort unlike the laborious caravan-driven overland journeys of yesteryear.

NEW IDEAS: THE MODERN PRESS AND PUBLISHING

Modern communications and the press further molded public consciousness. News and information traveled at lightning speed with the opening of a telegraph line between Beirut and Damascus (1861) and between Damascus and Istanbul (1863). Newspapers and periodicals reported on political news, on science and technology, and on arts and culture. In Sultan Abdulhamid's time the Syrian press was subject to censorship, but nevertheless the press created a common field of discourse for those who engaged with the print culture.

The first privately owned paper in Damascus was *Dimashq* ('Damascus'), a bilingual Turkish–Arabic publication founded in 1879 and owned by Ahmad Izzat al-Abid (d. 1924), who previously had worked on the Syrian province's official newspaper. An ambitious man, Abid was a devoted Abdulhamid loyalist who eventually rose to become one of the most powerful and wealthy men in Syria. *Dimashq* (1879–87) established itself as an early forum for the discussion of public issues including science and culture. It offered an alternative to the *ulama*, who prior to modern printing had been the principal producers of learned discourse.

The first independent newspaper in Aleppo was *al-Shahba* ('The Grey,' a sobriquet of the city), a unilingual short-lived Arabic paper established in 1877 during a brief moment of press freedom in the first Ottoman constitutional period (1876–8). Its editors included Abd al-Rahman al-Kawakibi (d. 1902), a young Islamic legal scholar and scion of a prominent *ulama* family. Appearing as it did at the dawn of the periodical press in Syria, Kawakibi felt it necessary to explain *al-Shahba*'s mission:

> Our paper has permission from the Sublime Porte to produce this literary paper so as to disseminate political news and local occurrences in a timely fashion. It will include as well a word or two about politics and also scientific and literary articles. Beyond this it will have investigations and studies to expand the public circle of knowledge and civilized literary exchanges. It will discover the secrets behind matters, enliven the thinking of the community, assist the state in local political actions and cry out when the local authorities infringe on the rights of society.[2]

Al-Shahba advocated administrative reform, and the selective incorporation of Western achievements within an overall context of cultural conservatism.

Twenty years later a magazine appeared in Aleppo, *al-Shudhur* ('Pieces'), edited by a French-educated Christian intellectual Abd al-Masih al-Antaki. Like *al-Shahba* its tone was didactic, but Antaki (unlike *al-Shahba*) saw modern Europe and particularly France as a model for an idealized concept of modernity – middle class, 'rational,' and largely free of internal contradictions and tensions.

Beirut and Cairo were the major centers of Arab intellectual and cultural life in the later nineteenth century, once modern publishing became the coin or the currency of cultural production. In Beirut, where Salim Bustani published his novel *Zenobia*, he also pioneered the genre of the Arabic short story. In Cairo, Syrian émigré Jurji Zeidan (d. 1914) popularized the historical novel genre, and modeled a new, direct prose style that appealed to a growing reading audience. After the first modern Arabic play (conceptualized as 'theater') was produced in Beirut in the 1850s, an aspiring Damascene playwright, Abu Khalil al-Qabbani (d. 1902), opened his own theater in Damascus. Frustrated by the cultural conservatism of his hometown (critics complained that Qabbani's writing was 'heretical'), he emigrated to Egypt where he built a successful career. From his Egyptian base Qabbani would tour Syria with his troupe.

Syrians in Egypt used the relative freedom afforded them in Cairo to write in wide-ranging and critical ways about their ancestral land. A women's press (edited and managed mostly by expatriate Syrian Christians) developed in Egypt during the 1890s where questions of women's role in society and of the proper structure of the modern family were discussed and debated. In Syria itself, upper-class women organized women-only salons for literary and cultural discussions. These were precursors to the formation of benevolent associations that, in time, served as launch pads for post-World War I women's associations.

Muslim advocates of religious reform, critical of the hierarchical and authoritarian values propagated by Abdulhamid, also took opportunities to express themselves freely in British-ruled Egypt. One of these was the aforementioned Aleppo writer and former *al-Shahba* editor Kawakibi. As a journalist, reformer and civil servant in Aleppo he ran afoul of the authorities, but his prominent lineage gave him a certain degree of protection. In 1898 he moved to Cairo where he could write with fewer restrictions. There he published books that critiqued Abdulhamid and the Ottoman Empire. Combining knowledge and skills from his background in traditional Islamic education and the modern press, Kawakibi condemned Sultan Abdulhamid's autocracy and questioned the Ottoman dynasty's claim to the caliphate. Despotism, Kawakibi said, had contributed to Islam's present-day weakness and stood in the way of the faith's revival and reform. Kawakibi championed what was by then a popular argument among Arabophone Muslim writers: Arabs had been associated with Islam in its early, formative days, and therefore Arabs had a special role to play in the future of Islam. From this starting-point Kawakibi issued a call for an Arab caliphate in preference to the Ottoman dynasty's claims. (Kawakibi's partisans believe that his mysterious death in 1902 was a result of poisoning by Sultan Abdulhamid's agents, an allegation never proven however.)

The evocation of early Islam was part and parcel of the Salafiyya intellectual movement that characterized the discourse of Arab Muslim religious reformers in the late nineteenth and early twentieth centuries. It was not quite 'nationalism,' but by consciously evoking an Arab ethno-cultural identity that was central to the project of Islamic reform, al-Kawakibi and his co-thinkers laid the groundwork for the eventual articulation of an Arab nationalism that would overlap and intersect with ideas of Syrian patriotism.

THE YOUNG TURKS

When a military rebellion in Macedonia forced Abdulhamid to restore the constitution in 1908, this 'revolution' undertaken by a group of military men and their bureaucratic allies, collectively known as the Young Turks, triggered widespread rejoicing in the major Syrian centers. The reformists' dream of an Ottoman nation formed out of a brotherhood (since formal politics was still an all-male activity) of its peoples briefly seemed attainable, until harsh realities showed otherwise.

For the moment, though, men of the new middle class flocked to the banner of the Committee of Union and Progress. The CUP was the Young Turks' political organization that emerged after 1908 to promote Ottomanist goals of modern citizenship expressed through political representation. Especially after a failed counter-coup of Abdulhamid loyalists in 1909, advocates of the CUP (called Unionists) worked to purge the government of Abdulhamid's conservative supporters. Yet Abdulhamid's political success in Syria had been built on his alliance with Arab landed notables attracted to the ideological symbols of the sultanate, caliphate and Islam. At a time when the empire faced severe international challenges including wars and invasions, the Unionists could not long continue undercutting a social group who were a bulwark of state power in Syria. So while non-Muslims and liberal Muslims in Syria initially supported the Unionists as advocates of liberal Ottoman citizenship, the Committee of Union and Progress was by 1912 re-inscribing Islam and Islamic rhetoric into its political platform.

Unfolding events blunted efforts by non-Muslims to integrate fully into the Ottoman constitutional state. In Aleppo, where the city's significant Arab Catholic and Armenian communities had initially identified with the constitutional movement, a newly appointed Unionist governor in 1910 adopted an oppositional stance to the city's Muslim landed notables where the Jabiris and allied families dominated local politics and administration. Yet in due course it was the Jabiris and their allies who triumphed. By the time of the 1912 parliamentary elections the Unionists had adopted Islamic rhetoric and were seeking to co-opt erstwhile Abdulhamid loyalists as government supporters. The landed notables had, in the meantime, demonstrated their political skills and adjusted to the new constitutional political environment. They used their wealth, position, and control of Muslim patronage and organizational networks to make themselves indispensable to the embattled Committee of Union and Progress. Perhaps the odds against 'equal Ottoman citizenship' were too steep, given the balance of political forces in the empire and its perilous international environment. (Austria annexed Ottoman Bosnia–Herzegovina in 1908, Italy invaded Ottoman Libya in 1911, and Ottoman Macedonia was partitioned by Serbia, Bulgaria and Greece in the Balkan Wars of 1912–13.)

DEBATES AROUND SYRIA AND SYRIAN IDENTITY IN THE MODERN WORLD

The restoration of the Ottoman constitution in 1908, and the forced abdication of Abdulhamid the following year, opened up a short-lived period of relative press freedom in Ottoman Syria. During the intense and drama-filled years between 1908 and the outbreak of World War I in 1914, the Arabic press was the fulcrum for the expression of ideas that had been developing and circulating during the previous decades. The Damascene Muhammad Kurd Ali (d. 1953) had founded his monthly journal *al-Muqtabas* in Cairo in 1906, but after the restoration of the Ottoman constitution he moved it to his hometown. Kurd Ali would become one of the best-known writers of his era, and *al-Muqtabas* one of Damascus's most important reviews. In its pages Kurd Ali emphasized the need for Arab reform and regeneration. He advocated a genre of modern Arabic poetry dubbed Neoclassical, which sought to revive and evoke the literary achievements of what more and more Arabs saw as their medieval 'golden age.' Kurd Ali employed the newly developed concept of 'civilizations' to compare Arabs and the West. Like most reformists Kurd Ali accepted the concept of contemporary Arabs' 'decadence.' The cause, he said, was their submission to authority (cf. al-Kawakibi), their subordination of reason, and their reliance on 'imitation' rather than on critical thought. In some of his writing Kurd Ali racialized the Ottomans as 'Tatars' and argued that they were inherently incapable of reason, and that the Arabic language was vastly more suited to civilization than Turkish. In contrast to the Muslim literati of earlier generations, he saw Istanbul as a symbol of backwardness rather than of Muslim modernity. (Later, during World War I, Kurd Ali expressed support for the Ottoman war effort and softened his prewar anti-Turkish stance.)

Kurd Ali reaffirmed what had become by this time the standard Muslim reformists' position, that decadence was not caused by Islam itself, but by defective understandings of it. Islam properly understood, he asserted, is progressive and fully compatible with modern life. Like the Christian Aleppine al-Antaki, Kurd Ali idealized Paris as a symbol of Western civilization at its most refined. An optimist in the prewar period, Kurd Ali looked to create a synthesis of Western and Eastern civilizations. He saw Japan and Egypt as two possible syntheses-in-progress. They were, in his estimation, modern Western-style states that had nevertheless retained their 'Eastern' cultures.

The paradox for Muslim reformists like Kurd Ali was the threat posed by the West. He found European imperialism abhorrent and he was critical of the foreign schools in the Arab East that did not use Arabic. Kurd Ali hoped that Muslims would be able to strengthen and rediscover their cultural heritage while catching up with Christians in terms of economic and entrepreneurial acumen. He was critical of the Syrian social structure where large tracts of land were in the hands of a few rich owners, to the detriment of peasants and agricultural progress.

Kurd Ali's was a middle-class, reformist vision that argued for an Arab–Muslim revival that would draw on a proper understanding of Islam and a synthesis between Arab and Western civilizations. In that sense his viewpoint overlapped with the views of those who wanted to reform and Arabize Islam, on the one hand, and who wanted to adopt a Western (French or Parisian) model of modernity, on the other. Reformists and Salafists looked to *al-Muqtabas* and other like-minded papers to present and debate their viewpoints, which put them at odds with Damascus's conservative landholding-bureaucratic elites. An ideological current of conservatism rose up to speak back to the reformists, especially after the forced abdication of the conservatives' patron Sultan Abdulhamid in 1909. The principal Damascene vehicle for the articulation of the conservative world-view was the newspaper *al-Haqa'iq* ('Truths').

What these press debates had in common was an obsession or preoccupation with modernity. The modern world was inescapable. The very institutions that allowed for a widely circulated press to exist were evidence of that. For nearly all writers the basic issue this posed was how to be effective actors in a European-dominated modern world, while also being 'true to oneself.' But this begged the question of what that 'self' was or ought to be (Arab? Muslim? Syrian? Ottoman? Some or all of the above?). The Ottoman Empire was still a fact, and for most Arab writers its existence was more or less taken for granted. Few foresaw that the empire would entirely cease to exist. (A handful of mainly Christian writers who hoped for direct European intervention were the exceptions.) Within this overall Ottoman 'given,' however, how was community to be defined and how could Syrians/Arabs/Muslims/Christians work effectively in modern circumstances? Different trends crystallized around these questions.

For some Muslims the answer was to identify with a modernist discourse of Islam, and to find in 'true Islam' the same virtues and strengths which had allowed the Europeans to become masters of the globe. So whether European success was attributed to reason, or to science, or to constitutionalism, Muslim reformers argued that Islam, when 'properly understood,' contained these principles. Some who thought in this way regarded the Ottoman Empire as the modern state that would assist Muslims in realizing these principles. Others saw the Ottoman status quo as an obstacle, and although they did not want to do away with the Ottoman political framework altogether they wished to see a more overtly modernist or reformist approach to the faith, in contrast to the official religion that had been propagated by Abdulhamid and his allies.

Whether they were reformist Salafis or pro-Abdulhamid conservatives, Muslim writers and activists saw their home region Syria as one of the countries within the Ottoman Empire, a country that had a proud Islamic history, and that culturally and linguistically was linked to Arabs and to Arabic, which were after all foundational elements of Islam. This tendency represented a kind of 'Muslim Syrian patriotism' – not quite nationalism inasmuch as the Ottoman sultanate (however flawed or contested) was assumed to be the political vehicle for this particular identity.

Among Christians who participated in this mass media discourse and the 'new public sphere,' issues of identity were understood in a different way. Many, to be sure, were Ottoman loyalists who saw the sultanate as the modern state to which they belonged, and within which their aspirations ought to be realized. But there was no prima facie sense of deference to the Ottoman 'fact' on Islamic loyalist grounds – rather, those Christians who acknowledged and accepted the sultanate generally did so on pragmatic grounds, hoping over time to strengthen those elements of the more recent Ottoman statehood tradition that emphasized 'equality of all citizens/subjects before the law.' Christian writers focused on questions of homeland and community at the sub-empire level.

For modernists, earlier generations' identification with a local place and a wider (in principle, universal) religious tradition was no longer enough – at once too wide-ranging and too parochial to be of much use in a world where 'homelands' mattered. To be an Orthodox Christian of Damascus or a Catholic Christian of Aleppo was at once too undifferentiated (Orthodox and Catholics were found in many different countries), and too specific (Damascus and Aleppo were glorious, etc. but they were just individual cities – not homelands or countries in the modern sense). Therefore the homeland as an intermediate space of belonging was embraced as a way of making the universal more specific and the parochial more cosmopolitan. For many, 'Syria' was the homeland idea that resonated.

This Syria was not clearly defined – it was larger than the Ottoman province of Syria (which did not include the coast north and south of Beirut), and might include only a part of the Ottoman province of Aleppo. Still, for those who advocated and identified with it, Syria was seen as a geographic and cultural unit whose history had a certain integrity and coherence. In cultural terms the Arabic language was considered to be a factor of unity in Syria, since both Muslims and Christians spoke the language. (Jews had an ambiguous place in this Syrianist discourse. Most Ottoman Jews identified politically with the empire, or communally with their faith, but the 'homeland' idea that resonated most strongly with those drawn to it was the 'Land of Israel' or Zionist idea. But at this early stage Ottoman Jews as part of a far-flung Ottoman and international community did not, in the main, adopt a Jewish *nationalist* point of view.)

The Syrian idea was an urban intellectual project, supported as well by large numbers of Syrian Christians who lived away from the country. The Syrian émigré community in Egypt had easy access to the megaphone of the periodical press. Other communities of Syrians lived in the Americas, where they published newspapers and formed associations that sought to strengthen ties to their hometowns and to advocate on behalf of the idea of Syria. Some Christian advocates of Syria hoped that France might play a role in bringing about Syrian self-government. Typically these kinds of sentiments were strongest among Catholics, since Orthodox Christians looked not to France but to the Russian Empire for patronage and support.

Early advocates of Syrian identity were urban, intellectual, and more Christian than Muslim. Nonetheless, Muslim and Christian Syrians could and did find common cause, especially after the restoration of the Ottoman constitution in 1908 and the renewal of parliamentary life in Istanbul. Christians' idea of Arabic as a 'national' language dovetailed with Muslims' emphasis on Arabic as their language of religion and heritage. Muslim and Christian Arabists took action together to strengthen the use of Arabic in the Ottoman Empire after the old Arab aristocracy temporarily fell from favor following the deposition of Abdulhamid. However, Christians (usually Catholics) who advocated the separation of Syria from the Ottoman Empire pulled in a different direction from Muslims who sought, in general, to reform and strengthen the Ottoman Empire and to reinforce Arabs' attachment to it.

The great majority of the population was not included at all in this early proto-nationalist discourse. Rural people and the lower classes of the cities largely remained outside of these ideological developments. The nationalist–reformist discourses of Syrianism, Arabism and Ottomanism went over their heads, if they noticed it at all. These populations' attachment to Arabic was not politicized. Primary loyalties continued to be local or tribal, oriented to clan and community. Among the Muslim majority, appeals to defend Islam when 'Islam was under attack' also fell on fertile ground.

Skeptical popular sentiments dovetailed with the rise of a self-consciously traditionalist discourse in some elements of the press. Because modernists argued that inherited norms and mores needed to be updated or rethought in the name of modernity, traditionalists developed positions designed to rebut modernist arguments and to assert a reified view of tradition. Typically these arguments revolved around women and the family. As modernists argued for monogamy and for women's education on utilitarian grounds (contending that the future of the nation/community is its children, and educated mothers are needed to raise appropriately conscientious sons, and polygamy does not promote healthy modern family values), traditionalists responded by criticizing these ideas as threatening the integrity of the family structure and the shape of public morality defined by religion. Religious conservatives, usually Muslims, typically advanced such viewpoints although there is no prima facie reason that conservative-minded Christians and Jews might not have adopted a similar discourse with respect to women (though not to polygamy). But the preponderance of modernist discourse among educated Christians and Jews means that the most vigorous representatives of traditionalist discourse were Muslims. Also, the alacrity with which educated Christians and Jews embraced a vision of the 'modern' family structure became an element in their self-understanding as 'modern' people.

Among Muslims, though, the modernist versus traditionalist debate was contentious and prolonged. Both sides cited religious values, 'properly understood,' in support of their respective positions. What came to be called traditionalist discourse was not truly traditional, in the sense that now its defenders were self-consciously attempting to define an outlook and a social order against a rival vision (or rival visions) that were making inroads among many of the educated. The legal and social practices of an earlier era had been taken for granted, as legitimate, timeworn and 'natural,' within whose parameters legal interpreters might argue or find accommodations in the name of public welfare or public interest. The new traditionalists of the early twentieth century (and beyond) were consciously dealing with an ideological and social challenge to norms that no longer were taken for granted.

SYRIA IN WORLD WAR I

These various debates would have developed in certain ways had World War I not intervened to overturn completely the earlier contexts in which they unfolded. Unresolved issues included inter-communal relations, concepts of homeland, the role and proper interpretation of religion in the modern era, the relationship of the rural majority to these concepts, overarching political identities and loyalties, and the challenge posed by the dominant European colonial powers. All of these were in play in 1914. There is no counterfactual way to know how they might have developed without the collapse of the Ottoman Empire in World War I. As it happened, the future of Syria and the entire Middle East was shaped by the experience of the war. The Ottoman Empire and the peoples within it entered into a dark tunnel, and survivors emerged from it four traumatic years later with old options cut off, new ones beckoning, society-wide traumas to absorb, and victorious imperial powers bent on remaking the postwar environment to suit their interests.

There is no reason to believe that Syria would have emerged as a quasi-national political vehicle in the Ottoman Empire had the latter been spared defeat in the war. Pre-1914 Syria was at one and the same time a cultural assertion, a romantic idea, and an Ottoman province with Damascus at its center (but a province with no coastline, and with Aleppo and Jerusalem/Palestine excluded from the province's boundaries). During the war the Ottoman military commander, Jemal Pasha, treated Greater Syria (from Aleppo to Palestine) as one unit, but this was a wartime exigency and not necessarily a blueprint for the postwar era. In the end historical contingency created the modern state of Syria, along with the other states of the post-Ottoman Fertile Crescent.

During the war Syria's people and their society experienced shock and upheaval unlike any they could recall. The demands of mobilization for total war were unique, novel, and devastating. The experience is remembered in the Syrian lands as the *safarbarlik* – a word originally denoting Ottoman military conscription, but that came also to connote the food shortages, famine and flight that overwhelmed people as they struggled to survive. The hardships of conscription had a knock on effect, inasmuch as fewer hands were available to grow food. The state seized animals and chopped down trees to feed the war machine. Locusts destroyed crops in Palestine in 1915, and drought devastated the Aleppo breadbasket in 1917. A French and British naval blockade of the Syrian coast prevented food shipments from making up for deficits in production. Desperate women sold their bodies for crusts of bread. Up to half a million Syrians died of famine and illness.[3] Poor distribution meant that people in certain parts of the country (especially Mount Lebanon, but not only there) literally starved to death. Contemporary reports of cannibalism were rife, and the rumors spread rapidly. A wartime eyewitness in Beirut recorded the gruesome scene:

> I saw a carriage with hands extended from the back so I looked closer and found out that these were the corpses of women and children who had succumbed to the famine. The city of Beirut had assigned these carriages for the living to roam around and pick up the dead people who had succumbed in the streets to dispose of them.[4]

Wary of the loyalty of its Syrian Arab conscripts, Ottoman army units in which these conscripts served were marched far away to serve on distant fronts (Gallipoli and Anatolia/Russia), meaning that most of the regular Ottoman troops in Syria were unhappy and sullen Turkish draftees. In addition to destitute and internally displaced populations, Syria experienced the impact of the state-organized Armenian Genocide (1915), in which Ottoman Armenians were marched from their lands and homes in Anatolia to marshaling centers in Aleppo and Syrian Mesopotamia, with over one million dying or being killed along the way. This tragedy left thousands of bedraggled, destitute and orphaned survivors in the Syrian lands. (Some Bedouins in Mesopotamia took pity on orphaned Armenian children and adopted them, raising them as their own.)

During the war, Syrians who had been advocates of administrative decentralization and 'Arab rights' within the Ottoman Empire were arrested and tried, and many of them were hanged. The prosecution accused them (not incorrectly) of having been in contact with consulates of enemy powers, but at the time of these prewar contacts Britain and France had not been enemy states. So for those Syrians and other Arabs who had hoped that the Ottoman Empire could be further reformed to become a kind of dual monarchy or decentralized structure with clearly defined Arab rights, the upheavals, trials and executions of World War I put paid to this imagined future.

Nonetheless, along with the Arab conscripts who had little choice in the matter, many Arab officials and administrators (Syrians among them) remained loyal to the government until the end. It was still, in their minds, 'their' state, one to which they owed allegiance, and one which was the last bulwark of Muslim or local independence against the ambitions of expansionist European powers. This explains Muhammad Kurd Ali's cooperation with Jemal Pasha. Kurd Ali closed *al-Muqtabas* and agreed to edit a pro-Ottoman, pro-German wartime newspaper in Damascus called *al-Sharq* ('The Orient'). For Kurd Ali and his co-thinkers, the Ottoman state (including the symbol of the caliphate) was the last, best defense against European colonial expansion. During the war Kurd Ali expressed hope that afterwards, more Arabs would learn Turkish and more Turks would learn Arabic. 'This is inevitable,' he wrote in 1916, 'for Arabic is the tongue of Islam and is immersed in the history of Muslims, while Turkish is the language of politics and administration.'[5] For pro-Ottomans, the alliance with Christian Germany was a pragmatic concession to the realities of power, made easier to defend because Germany had not demonstrated any appetite for territorial expansion in the Ottoman–Arab lands.

The attempt of Sharif Hussein of Mecca to rally Arabs to the anti-Ottoman cause with a British-sponsored 'Arab Revolt' (dramatically depicted in the famous movie *Lawrence of Arabia*) attracted some Arab Ottoman army officers (including those captured as British prisoners of war), and some Arab tribes (often motivated by gold rather than ideology). However, most Arab army officers continued to serve in the Ottoman ranks, and tribes in Transjordan were standoffish at least until it became clear that the British–Hussein alliance had gained the upper hand. In the neighboring region of Iraq, Arab tribes served as effective auxiliaries in the Ottoman forces, and assisted in early Ottoman victories against an overextended British-commanded (but largely Indian-manned) expeditionary force.

Exhausted and bled white by four years of total war, beset by drought and disease and deprived of essential supplies from its collapsing German ally, the Ottoman leadership threw in the towel in October 1918. Ottoman armies in Syria, commanded at that point by General Mustafa Kemal (the future Ataturk), withdrew from the country bringing an end to 400 years of nearly continuous Ottoman rule.

THE NEW ORDER AND MODERN STATEHOOD

The years after 1831 saw the beginnings and consolidation of a 'new order' in Syria that endured until World War I. The foundations of modern statehood were laid in these decades. Milestones along this way were the implementation of the Ottoman

Land Code (1858) which sought to register land in the names of its owners, as well as to clarify different land categories and to assert state rights over land that did not have individual or *waqf* ownership. Another significant administrative milestone was the implementation of the new provinces law in 1864, which established a hierarchical system of provincial administration (modeled on that of France) to designate responsibilities and responsible officials at the provincial, district and village levels. A uniform civil code, the *majalla*, was introduced. These initiatives survived the Ottoman Empire and were carried over, with some modifications, into the post-Ottoman Syrian states established by France after 1920.

What kind of state, or states, would appear in Syria after the demise of the Ottoman Empire was an open question. The Ottomans had attempted to build a modern administrative state in the lands of Syria, a country that had deeply rooted histories of regionalism, local particularism, urban–rural dichotomies and cultural-religious diversity. In the more recent period, inter-confessional tensions had led to traumatic violent incidents that spurred Ottoman reform and European political intervention in equal measure. At least it could be said of the Ottomans that they had been the legitimate authority in the eyes of most of the political class in Syria – the administrators, civil servants and military officers who formed the backbone of the modern state apparatus. But now, post-World War I, the Ottoman state was shattered beyond repair. The political legitimacy that it had claimed, and often enjoyed, would not automatically adhere to the Ottomans' successors. Modern statehood had been partially achieved, but modern nationhood hardly at all.

5
FRANCE AND THE CREATION OF
THE SYRIAN TERRITORIAL STATE

BIRTH OF A NATION?

On 24 August 1925 an insurgent force of more than one thousand armed men advanced on French-ruled Damascus. They were Druzes, Bedouins and peasants from the Houran and their leaders had prearranged with Damascus sympathizers to rendezvous with hundreds of armed horsemen coming out from the city. The goal was to extend into Damascus an uprising that had begun during the previous month in the Jabal Druze. The Damascenes were led by two former Ottoman army officers, and the rural insurgents by another former Ottoman officer and a senior member of the Atrash clan. Unfortunately for them, a French airplane detected the two groups' rendezvous and attacked them. The lone French plane was soon joined by others and the insurgents scattered under the withering aerial bombardment and machine gun fire.

This incident marked the beginnings of a widespread uprising. After their unhappy experience on August 24, insurgents adopted small-scale guerrilla tactics. A proclamation surreptitiously distributed in Damascus the previous night called on Syrians to rise up in the name of the nation:

> Syrians, remember your forefathers, your history, your heroes, your martyrs, and your national honor. Remember that the hand of God is with us and that the will of the people is the will of God. Remember that civilized nations that are united cannot be destroyed. The imperialists have stolen what is yours. They have laid hands on the very sources of your wealth and raised barriers that divided your indivisible homeland. They have separated the nation into separate sects and states. They have strangled freedom of religion, thought, conscience, speech and action. We are no longer even allowed to move about

freely in our own country. To arms! […]. The die is cast. Our war is a holy war […]. To arms! God is with us. Long live independent Syria![1]

The proclamation offered an expansive view of the Syrian nation, and was signed by Sultan al-Atrash, the principal figure in the Jabal Druze revolt.

Twelve years later, a nationalist administration had indeed been established in Damascus. Emboldened by an unratified treaty that they had recently negotiated with France, the Damascus nationalists asserted their domestic authority by sending a series of administrators to the remote Jazira. There, they encountered hostility from local populations of tribal Arabs, Kurds, Assyrians and Armenians who favored autonomy under French protection. Pro-nationalist tribal forces raided a large Christian village, Amuda, in July 1937 and massacred many of its inhabitants. This incident intensified autonomist, anti-nationalist feelings in the Jazira. In December autonomists kidnapped the newly appointed nationalist governor of the Jazira. Tensions continued to simmer, climaxing in spring 1939 when a 'war of the flags' broke out. Nationalists in Qamishli tried to festoon the city with Syrian flags, while autonomists tore the flags down, ground them in the dirt and urinated on them.

These contrasting developments from 1925 and the late 1930s underline the tensions and difficulties that vexed Syrians in the interwar period. Nationalists attempted to construct a collective identity and a nation state out of the post-Ottoman colonial reality. Other Syrians rejected the nationalists' vision of national identity and statehood, asserting that the nationalists' viewpoint reflected merely a sectional interest that masqueraded as a general sentiment. For their part, the French were eager to exploit and deepen political and social divisions inherited from the Ottoman era – especially sectarian, regional and urban–rural differences – for the purpose of entrenching France's role in the country.

FAISAL'S BRIEF INTERLUDE OF ARAB SELF-RULE IN SYRIA

The end of hostilities between the Ottoman Empire and the Allies in 1918 saw geographic Syria occupied by British and British-allied forces, including the army of the Arab Revolt. On the losing side, Arab conscripts from the defeated Ottoman armies made their way back home through a devastated and stricken landscape. Most people's concerns focused on survival and subsistence. Conscription, war and famine left women widowed, children orphaned, and farms and fields un- (or under-)tended. International relief efforts concentrated principally on identifying and assisting Armenian Christian survivors of the wartime Ottoman regime's genocide.

Syrians involved in political life faced an uncertain world. The Ottoman sultanate–caliphate, a fixture for 400 years, was gone. In the Syrian interior, Britain's ally Faisal, son of Sharif Hussein of Mecca, headed an Arab administration based at Damascus. Faisal and his supporters wished to consolidate an Arab administration and build an Arab state in Syria, but the established landowning power brokers of the major towns (most importantly Damascus and Aleppo) did not trust him. They feared marginalization by upstarts and outsiders (from the Hejaz and Palestine) who had betrayed the sultanate/caliphate and had pinned their flags to Faisal's (and Britain's) mast. Moreover, the notables of Aleppo did not want to see their proud city subordinated to Damascus. The Faisal administration's emphasis on Arab identity as the new currency of political legitimacy also posed particular problems for Aleppo. Though Aleppo was predominantly Arab, the city's political and economic role in Ottoman times made its population markedly multi-ethnic. The city's regional prominence had rested on alliances and understandings with extensive Kurdish and Turkish hinterlands.

Adding to the uncertainty was Syrians' knowledge that Britain had made commitments to its ally France regarding the allocation of territories and spheres of influence in former Ottoman lands. The Sykes–Picot agreement, negotiated among the Allies in 1916 and made public by the Bolsheviks after the Russian Revolution in November 1917, envisaged Syria, Lebanon and Mosul as French controlled. With the opening of the Paris Peace Conference in 1919, France pressed Britain to make good on its territorial promises. As a down payment toward this and to mollify its ally, Britain withdrew its forces from coastal Syria north of Palestine in November 1919, handing over their positions to French troops. British forces also withdrew from Damascus.

Faisal's followers in Syria grew nervous about the country's future. In summer 1919 an American delegation (the King–Crane Commission) visited the Syrian lands to ascertain public opinion and report back to the peace conference. Nearly everywhere they went the commissioners heard the same refrain: Syrians wanted independence, they rejected French tutelage, and they opposed Britain's promise to create a 'national home for the Jewish people' in Palestine, a pledge embodied in the Balfour Declaration of November 1917. Only in Mount Lebanon did established political leaders, representing the dominant Maronite Christian population, welcome the prospect of French rule.

To press their point, Syrian notables (including some who were critical of Faisal) organized the General Syrian Congress in Damascus in spring 1919.

In areas under Arab administration delegates were selected according to the old multi-tiered Ottoman electoral law. In regions under British administration (Palestine and the coast), delegates were respected figures from notable political families who supported Arab independence in Syria. The Congress positioned itself as the legal and political successor to the Ottoman parliament in the Syrian lands. The Congress worked to support Faisal, on the one hand, but also to constrain him when they feared he was prepared to make too many concessions to the European powers.

For his part, Faisal was a realist. He had lived many years in Istanbul, had been a member of the Ottoman parliament from the Hejaz, and during the war he was the principal point of contact between his father's Arab Revolt and British representatives. Visiting London in December 1918, Faisal conferred with another of Britain's allies, the pro-British Zionist leader Chaim Weizmann (d. 1952). The two men reached an accord where Faisal conditionally offered to accept the Jewish national home in Palestine if Syria received full and unfettered independence. Faisal hoped to enlist the Zionist movement's political and diplomatic support for Syrian independence, even if the price for this support would be acceptance of some kind of Jewish Palestine.

However, Faisal's attempt to form a diplomatic and political alliance with the Zionist movement was short-lived, as news of the Faisal–Weizmann accord outraged public opinion in Syria. Arab activists from Palestine were among Faisal's supporters, and Palestinian cities and districts were represented in the General Syrian Congress. Angling for Arab self-rule in Syria that would include their home regions, these delegates referred to Palestine as 'southern Syria.' The Faisal–Weizmann accord, and other examples of Faisal's willingness to bend to British (and later French) desiderata, added to popular mistrust of his administration.

Nevertheless, in the 1919–20 interregnum Faisal remained the most visible symbol of Arab self-rule in Syria and, in March 1920, the General Syrian Congress proclaimed Syria's independence with Faisal as king. This step was less an expression of support for Faisal personally as it was an effort to present the Allied powers with a political *fait accompli* in advance of scheduled Anglo–French meetings at San Remo, Italy to decide the final division of the Syrian lands.

But in the meantime, Faisal's Arab nationalist supporters encountered difficulty administering and controlling the country. For the established powerbrokers we met in previous chapters, slogans of Arab nationalism mattered less than practical questions of authority, control and patronage now that the sultanate was gone. Having been pillars of the old Ottoman establishment, they looked naturally askance at some of the Arab nationalist ideologues who were riding Faisal's administration to power. Urban landholding elites mobilized constituencies of sheikhs, merchants and artisans (in the cities) and villagers (in the countryside) to defend their interests. Popular slogans in Damascus and Aleppo roused shopkeepers, artisans and laborers around themes of 'homeland' (*watan*) and defense of Islam. The concept of *watan* was elastic: it might be ultra-local (one's city or region), or it might be some understanding of Syria as a country, or it might be a lingering concept of the sultanate, and its associations with the defense of Islam and of the moral order represented by Muslim rule. In contrast, the Arab nationalists' slogan 'religion belongs to God, the homeland belongs to all' did not evoke the same popular enthusiasm, understanding or acceptance.

In ethnically mixed Aleppo, the pro-Faisal press took pains to explain who among Aleppines could be regarded as an 'Arab,' by way of arguing that former compatriots and countrymen now regarded as 'Turks' should be removed from the city. In December 1918 a new official gazette named *Halab* ('Aleppo') announced 'a ruling concerning the Turks present in the city and we [the new Faisal-led administration] have advised them to register their names as soon as possible.'[2] The ruling or decree continued:

1. The Turks born in Aleppo and married with Arabs are not to leave these relationships.
2. The Turks with proprietary or trade relationships who have maintained a good demeanor during their stay in Aleppo are exempt from deportation.
3. Turkish civil servants and others who have none of these relationships nor a livelihood are to depart immediately and the Arab government will assist them and guarantee their safety.[3]

The Arab nationalist press also sought to inculcate among readers a new understanding of history, representing an early attempt to create a Syrian Arab historical consciousness that would define its local or regional Other as 'the Turk.' As part of this project, publicists invoked the authority of European Orientalists to prove or to demonstrate the worthiness of Arab identity. One such publicist in October 1919 wrote in *Halab*:

In a French book, I stumbled across a page from the history of Arab civilization and I wanted to translate it so the readers could be informed about the extent of the efforts which our grandfathers had expended in the advancement of science and knowledge, and of the great hand they had in the various arts and industry so that they could be an example to us in our modern life.

And so we should follow their example and their lead, and we should not be content only with taking pride in them.[4]

These kinds of efforts at ideological re-engineering were in their earliest and most preliminary phases during the unsettled 18 months of Faisal's administration. But circumstances soon conspired against Faisal and his supporters establishing political or ideological hegemony.

IMPOSITION OF FRENCH RULE

In April 1920 Britain and France agreed, at San Remo, on partition lines for the Syrian and Iraqi lands. Britain was to receive control of Iraq and Palestine, including Transjordan, while France was to receive control of Lebanon and Syria. Internal boundaries were up to France and Britain to define, but the lines of demarcation between French and British spheres created enduring southern borders for Lebanon and Syria, and the Syrian–Iraqi border as well. Within their respective spheres Britain created the countries of Palestine (1920), Transjordan (1921) and Iraq (1921). France created Lebanon (1920), while the remaining territories under French control eventually were consolidated into Syria (1936), except for the district of Iskanderun, which France ceded to Turkey in 1938–9.

The formal mechanism for the creation of these new states was the mandate system. France and Britain were to hold 'mandates' for these new states on behalf of the recently established League of Nations (1920). As mandatory powers, France and Britain were obliged to establish institutions of self-government and to assist these countries to achieve self-rule and eventual independence. The mandated territories were newly created colonial protectorates said to be transitional in nature. French and British policymakers assumed that, no matter how quickly or slowly these newly defined countries moved toward self-government, European powers' tutelage would continue. The full story of the various mandates belongs to general histories of the modern Middle East, but it is France's establishment of control in Syria that concerns us here.

With the San Remo partition agreement of April 1920, Great Britain in effect washed its hands of Faisal's administration in Damascus. While Britain urged France and Faisal to come to an accommodation, it was clear now that Britain would not intervene on Faisal's behalf against France. Aware of the weakness of his position, Faisal bent over backward to accommodate French demands. These included demobilization of his small army, acceptance of French advisors and stationing of French soldiers in the country. But popular opinion in unoccupied Syria was strongly against the French and their imperialism was already well known from Arabs' and Muslims' experiences in North Africa. Abdul-Qadir al-Jazairi (d. 1883), one of Damascus's prominent Muslim leaders in the nineteenth century, had even been a leader of Algerian resistance to French conquest in the 1830s and 1840s. Moreover, France had long been identified in the Levant with its support for Catholic Christians, deepening Muslim misgivings about being subordinated to a power known for supporting the expansion of Christian privileges in a predominantly Muslim land and empire. (Francophiles, in rebuttal, argued that France was merely protecting and defending the rights of religious minorities.) In the context of European imperial expansion, French policy fanned the flames of sectarian mistrust and discord.

It was one thing for the San Remo conference to proclaim that France would exercise a mandate for Syria; it was another thing for France to establish its authority. French control would have to be imposed by force. In July 1920 French units moved east toward Damascus from Lebanon. Faisal's diplomatic efforts to accede to French demands came to naught and he fled to British controlled Palestine. The French wanted nothing to do with Faisal (viewing him as a British agent), and they wanted to be rid of him. (As it happened, a year later Faisal resurfaced in Baghdad as the British-appointed king of Iraq.)

As French forces moved toward Damascus, Faisal's defense minister, Yusuf al-Azmeh, mustered columns of soldiers and militia and moved them westward to meet the foe at the battle of Maysaloun (with which this book began), where the superior French force broke Azmeh's forces and killed him. After Maysaloun the French continued their march eastward and occupied Damascus. With the assistance of conservative notables who had never trusted Faisal or his associates, France established a local administration.

French forces met more prolonged armed opposition in the north of the country. In the Ansariyeh mountains an Alawite leader, Sheikh Saleh al-Ali (d. 1950), led a resistance campaign. Although the French occupied Aleppo without a battle, they faced sustained resistance around the northern city and in the Zawiya mountains between Hama and Aleppo. An ex-Ottoman civil servant from the region, Ibrahim Hananu (d. 1935), led the northern resistance. The French also faced armed opposition in Anatolia (present-day Turkey) from nationalists led by former Ottoman general Mustafa Kemal ('Ataturk,' d. 1938). As of yet no border distinguished Turkey from northern Syria. Hananu collaborated with his former Ottoman colleagues in Kemal's movement to resist the extension of colonial Christian rule into predominantly Muslim lands that only two years before had been part of one and the same sultanate. The ideological appeals issued by the Hananu movement variously included Syrian patriotism, Arab nationalism and Ottoman–Muslim loyalism. In the minds of many, the fates of the Turkish and Syrian movements against France were intertwined.

These various ideological appeals reverberated differently among the diverse populations of Aleppo, the Zawiya region and the Ansariyeh mountains. Alawite rebel leader Saleh al-Ali made common cause with Hananu and showed public deference to notions of Syrian patriotism and self-government, but these abstractions were employed in service of local self-rule that would reflect the distinct social and tribal structure characteristic of the Alawites' mountain population. Although the numerous Catholic Christians of Aleppo city by and large welcomed French rule, the mostly Orthodox Christians of the Zawiya region (whose administrative center was Idlib) did not.[5] In general, Orthodox communities sought to strengthen ties to their Muslim compatriots in the name of Syrian and Arab identification. Meanwhile, Muslim leaders in the Zawiya hills acted to protect loyalist Christian communities, reflecting habits and attitudes that mixed old-style Ottoman patronage of non-Muslim communities with *noblesse oblige* (by which the more powerful leaders demonstrated their authority by asserting protection of potentially vulnerable communities). Syrian patriotism and nationalism were two of the ideas vying to establish themselves in the post-Ottoman ideological confusion, and Orthodox Christians had been among those most attracted and attuned to Syrianist ideas.

Consolidation of French control in Syria's north was assured only when France struck a deal in October 1921 with Mustafa Kemal's Turkish Anatolian movement and agreed to abandon France's claims to parts of Anatolia, in return for Kemal's withdrawal of support for Hananu and other anti-French Syrian militants. The line of demarcation between French and Turkish control placed the coastal district of Iskanderun in Syria. Further east, the new Turkish–Syrian frontier followed the existing path of the railway line that extended from north of Aleppo to the Tigris river. Except for the border at Iskanderun, subsequently (1939) revised in Turkey's favor, this demarcation established an enduring international frontier between Syria and Turkey. Aleppo permanently lost a large part of its historic Anatolian hinterland that once had included the now-Turkish city of Antep, renamed Gaziantep. With Mustafa Kemal preoccupied with establishing Turkey, the French in Syria could suppress militant opposition without fear of Turkish intervention or interference. As for Hananu and other northern Syrian rebels, they were forced to acknowledge that the dream of restoring some kind of Muslim/Ottoman rule in Syria and Turkey had fallen out of reach. Henceforth Hananu et al. would focus their energies and ambitions in the Syrian arena.

In the meantime, France extended symbols of its authority into Syria's vast east, the Jazira, a portion of Mesopotamia lying between the Euphrates river and the newly defined Iraq border. France did not bring the Jazira fully under its control until 1930. To achieve this the French cultivated alliances with Arab Bedouin chieftains, especially those from among the powerful Anaza tribes whose historic connections to kin across the newly drawn borders gave them disruptive potential. The French confirmed Anaza chieftains' privileges as autonomous local rulers, and set up a special administrative unit, the Contrôl Bedouin, to administer their affairs. A majority of the population in northern Jazira were Kurds, especially after the Turkish authorities suppressed a Kurdish uprising in Turkey (launched in the name of defending Islam) in 1926. France agreed to recognize the Kurds' clan and tribal leaders, and to protect their communities from Turkish incursions. Another significant group in the Jazira were Assyrian Christians, who resettled there under French auspices after being driven from their native villages (now across the border in Turkey) during World War I. The wartime Assyrian massacres were a kind of echo or reverberation of the Armenian Genocide. Syria's principal urban center for Assyrians was the new town of Qamishli, built up when the region's older administrative center (Nusaybin) ended up on the Turkish side of the newly demarcated border. The substance of French administration in the Jazira would need time to be fleshed out. Meanwhile, it was administered separately from other parts of the Syria mandate.[6]

CONSOLIDATION OF FRENCH RULE

Having established their control, the French went about setting up the Syrian administration. One of the first things they did was to expand the frontiers of Ottoman Lebanon, and they divided the remainder of the Syrian mandate into separate states. Early on there was one state centered at Damascus, another at Aleppo, a third in the Druze mountain, and the fourth in the Ansariyeh mountains. The French called the last one the Alawite state, but later they renamed it for its administrative center, the Mediterranean port of Latakia. The coastal district of Iskanderun and its largest city, Antioch, remained separate from the rest of Syria. The district's population had a narrow Arab majority but included a high proportion of ethnic Turks over whom Ankara claimed authority. Throughout the 1920s and 1930s France was sensitive to official Turkish interest in the district.

The separate Druze and Alawite states endured for most of the French Mandate years, and were not finally and definitively disbanded until 1942. Greater

Lebanon was designed as a Christian-dominated state controlling the coast west of Damascus, and extending down to the border with British Palestine. Lebanon became a permanent fixture on the Middle Eastern map with the proclamation of the Lebanese Republic (under French Mandate) in 1926. Afterward Lebanon's political and institutional developments were distinct from those in the remainder of France's mandated Syrian territories.

The French brought to Syria habits of colonial administration that they had developed in Morocco, where France had established a 'protectorate' in 1912. Some prominent French appointees to Syria were veterans of the Morocco administration, where the French sought to identify and to cultivate powerbrokers who would look to France to secure their positions against rivals. In this way the French administration in Morocco emphasized and encouraged loyalties defined as tribal or ethnic, but not 'national.'

French administrators in Syria took a similar approach. They patronized established political figures who were not diehard nationalists, and who stood to benefit from French support. An early pro-French figure was the Antiochene Subhi Barakat (d. 1939), designated the 'president' of French controlled Syria from 1922–5. Another enduring pro-French politician was Sheikh Taj al-Din al-Hasani (d. 1943), scion of an illustrious Damascene religious family who intermittently served as France's Syrian prime minister, and then president (where he died in office in 1943). Under terms of the mandate, figures such as Barakat and Hasani had little authority beyond the ability to reward their friends and supporters, but patronage power is mostly what they wanted anyway. Office-holding, for them, was less about national independence than it was about rewarding their friends, growing rich and besting their rivals. They were useful window dressing for France, allowing Paris to claim that it was fulfilling its mandate obligation to prepare the country for self-government under French guidance.

In the Alawite and Druze states, France built institutions around particular regional and religious identities aimed at strengthening these communities' sense of separateness, setting them against the inland centers of Damascus, Aleppo, Hama and Homs, which were strongholds of Syrian Arab nationalist sentiment. The particular identities associated with region, tribe and sect would (the French hoped) become institutionalized to forestall nationalists' insistence on the unity of the Syrian people and territories.

Christians in Aleppo were a particularly important local constituency for the French Mandate. Christian Armenians had long been a part of Aleppo's multicultural fabric, but now thousands of newly arrived Armenian refugees and survivors of the 1916 genocide were naturalized as Syrians and settled in a new purpose-built neighborhood. Moreover, the old and substantial Arabic-speaking Catholic community also supported French rule and voted mostly for pro-French candidates. In the mandate's early years elections were stage-managed affairs where pro-French forces would ensure that their supporters got to the polls and supported their candidates. Anti-French or nationalist forces mistrusted the French and were not yet ready, so soon after the colonial conquest, to lend legitimation to French rule by seriously investing in the polls.

THE GREAT SYRIAN REVOLT, 1925–7

Remarkably, the first major anti-French revolt to take on a national character originated in the Jabal Druze among the people and in the state that the French thought could be cultivated as loyal clients. France established the Jabal Druze administration in 1921 at Suweida, where a French delegate advised a Druze council. France's elevation of one Druze leader (a member of the Atrash family) to the governorship stoked internecine rivalries, in a setting where chiefly authority had historically been decentered and not concentrated in one person's hands. Sultan al-Atrash, a prominent member of the Atrash clan, a nationalist and an erstwhile supporter of Faisal, led sporadic Druze guerrilla resistance which the French suppressed by 1922. However, the resignation and then death of the French-appointed Druze governor in 1923, and the council's inability to come up with a consensus replacement, led to the appointment of a French officer as acting governor. He was Gabriel Carbillet (d. 1940), an impolitic man who in short order alienated a significant proportion of the Druze leadership during his nearly two years in office (September 1923–May 1925). The French authorities, in the meantime, continued to harass Sultan al-Atrash, whom they saw as the principal instigator of anti-French opinions among the Druzes.

In July 1925 Sultan al-Atrash launched a major revolt by besieging the French garrison at Suweida, and then defeating a relief column sent from Damascus. The rebellion quickly spread to the garden suburbs of Damascus, the Ghouta. There, militias loyal to the nationalist notable Nasib al-Bakri (d. 1966) seized control of the dense gardens, and wrested control of southern districts of Damascus from the French. These southern districts, especially Midan, had long been connected to the Houran grain trade, and Midan's merchants were associated with people of Houran and the Jabal Druze. Such urban–rural connections belied France's assumption that Syria's peoples were a 'mosaic' of discrete and unrelated parts who could be handily manipulated.

Meanwhile, in the center of the country at Hama, insurrectionists attempted to seize control of the city from French forces, but the insurgents were beaten back. In both Damascus and Hama, the insurgents were an amalgam of tribal allies plus popular militias drawn from mobilized peasantry and artisans. But the most important powerbrokers remained aloof from the guerrillas and, by doing nothing, made it easier for France to reassert control. Landholders were worried about the negative consequences of a sustained rebellion, both in terms of the economic disruption it would cause and the danger of a mobilized armed populace who might escape the framework of top-down patron–client ties.

The insurgent leader in Hama was a former Ottoman officer, Fawzi al-Qawuqji (d. 1977), who had subsequently served in (and then deserted from) a locally recruited and French-commanded military force. In the run-up to the Hama insurrection, Qawuqji thought he had garnered the support of a leading land-owning notable, Najib al-Barazi (d. 1967), but at a critical moment Barazi abandoned Qawuqji's uprising, ensuring its failure to seize Hama. (This Barazi was a descendant of the nineteenth-century military figure Muhammad Agha al-Barazi, the founder of the family's fortunes in Hama.) In Damascus the only landowning notable of consequence to take part in the rebellion was Nasib al-Bakri, who had been associated with the Arab Revolt and Faisal's post-World War I administration.

Significant ideological support for the revolt came from Damascene nationalists. In June 1925, one month before the outbreak of Sultan al-Atrash's uprising, a group led by medical doctor Abd al-Rahman Shahbandar (d. 1940) formed the People's Party, the first nationalist political party in French-ruled Syria. The People's Party called for the independence of Syria within its 'natural frontiers' (i.e., *not* those drawn by the French and British), and planned to contest local elections to offer an alternative to France's conservative allies and collaborators. Shahbandar came from a Damascene merchant family background. He was close to pro-Hashemite organizers (supporters of Sharif Hussein's dynasty) who worked in Transjordan and Egypt, and along with Sultan al-Atrash he was one of the leading figures in the 1925-7 Great Syrian Revolt, as it came to be known.

With the revolt unfolding against the still unsettled boundaries and understandings of the nation, rebels articulated a program that variously emphasized Syrian, Arab and Muslim identities. The creation of the People's Party, and the militant struggle of the 1925 uprising, marked the birth of Syrian Arab nationalism as a popular (or rather potentially popular) ideology.

France's response to the uprising was brutal. When rebels seized southern Damascus, French artillery and aircraft shelled and bombed the captured neighborhoods into submission on 18–19 October, causing widespread destruction and killing nearly 1,500 people. French forces publicly executed rebel prisoners and left their bodies on display to serve as a warning to others. Syrian nationalists protested to the League of Nations against France's harsh measures, but the League (dominated as it was by France's peer imperial powers) did not censure France.

The revolt's challenge to France was formidable. The colonial authorities had to bring additional troops to Syria to suppress it. As French military and political pressure wore down the rebels and cut off external sources of funding from nationalist sympathizers in neighboring lands, rebels pressured populations for donations in regions that they controlled or where they had a presence. What nationalists depicted as 'revolutionary taxes' were often experienced as demands for protection money or extortion from those on the receiving end. Reports of onerous rebel behavior fueled France's narrative that the mandate authority was fighting criminal gangs, not genuine national revolutionaries.

Propaganda wars notwithstanding, the larger political outcome of the 1925–7 revolt was that the French defeated the most militant opponents of their rule, and forced the rebel leadership (Sultan al-Atrash, Nasib al-Bakri, Abd al-Rahman Shahbandar, Fawzi al-Qawuqji) into exile. Landowning notables, many of them sympathetic to nationalism but not to armed militancy, hoped the French might now engage in an inclusionary political process. The revolt left 6,000 Syrians dead and 100,000 homeless.[7] The magnitude of the revolt rattled the French, who began to doubt the feasibility of ignoring and bypassing Syrian nationalists, reluctantly concluding they had at least to engage with their non-militant variety. So whereas the armed militants had been defeated, they had forced the colonizing power to reckon with Syrian nationalism.

THE NATIONAL BLOC AND 'HONORABLE COOPERATION'

In 1928 nationalist-oriented landowning notables and their political allies formed the National Bloc, which would be Syria's principal nationalist political organization for the remainder of French rule. The Bloc sought 'honorable cooperation' with France – to work with France in a way that was not collaborationist, to develop the national project in Syria and attain self-government and independence. For their part, while the French continued to support collaborationist political figures, Paris recognized as well the need to open a dialogue with the non-militant nationalists. To this end, France organized elections for a constituent assembly in 1928, and nationalists figured prominently in the elected assembly.

The constitution came into force in 1930, but only after France inserted a clause affirming its rights as a mandatory power. For the time being the separate Druze and Alawite states, as well as the Iskanderun district, were excluded from Syria's constitution, although the major inland cities plus the Jazira were brought in. Under the constitution's terms, a Syrian parliament was chosen in two turbulent rounds of elections in 1931 and 1932. Due to their political base in the inland cities, the National Bloc gained a majority of the seats. Pro-French or collaborationist candidates also won seats, alongside large numbers of non-affiliated rural representatives. Parliament opened in June 1932 with government leadership positions and cabinet posts shared between 'moderate' nationalists (who wanted to pursue dialogue with France) and overtly pro-French figures. The most coherent political faction was the National Bloc, whose leaders put at the top of their agenda negotiating a treaty with France.

The National Bloc was a coalition of landowning notables, often drawn from the same class and from some of the same families as those who had served the Ottoman Empire in its final decades. They were mostly from the major interior towns of Damascus and Aleppo, with supporting participation from Homs and Hama. The Bloc had a smaller presence in the former Alawite state (renamed Latakia in 1930), along with partisans in the Druze state and in Iskanderun district. But the Bloc dominated office-holding only in the truncated Syrian state. The group's leading figures in its early years included Hashim al-Atassi (d. 1960) from Homs, who formerly had been an Ottoman administrator and then became president of the General Syrian Congress during the short-lived Faisal era. Another significant personality was the Damascene Jamil Mardam Bey (d. 1960), a Paris-educated descendant of the illustrious sixteenth-century Ottoman governor of Damascus, La La Mustafa Pasha. The Mardam Beys owed their modern prominence to their administration of their ancestor's vast and wealthy endowment.

To create and maintain functional unity within the Bloc's ranks, the Damascus wing cooperated with prominent politicians from Aleppo. The doyen of Aleppo nationalists was former Ottoman official Ibrahim Hananu, Mustafa Kemal Ataturk's old ally, who had returned to Syria as part of a French amnesty in the wake of his earlier pro-Ottoman, pro-Turkish anti-French guerrilla campaign. Hananu was joined by Saadallah Jabiri (d. 1947), scion of the old Aleppo family who became the northern city's most prominent nationalist leader after Hananu's death in 1935. The prominence of Atassi, Mardam Bey, Hananu and Jabiri underscores the debt that nationalist Syria owed to its Ottoman past.

The National Bloc mostly froze out partisans of the Hashemite family such as the still-exiled Abd al-Rahman Shahbandar. He was close to Abdullah of Transjordan, a British-appointed Hashemite ruler who by this time (the early 1930s) had lost his former luster as a symbol of Arab nationalism. In any case, the National Bloc's interest in Arab nationalism was more rhetorical and instrumental than anything else. The Bloc's priority was to gain self-rule for Syria and reduce French preroga- tives, and its partisans viewed it as the legitimate embodiment of the Syrian nation.

Being largely composed of landowners the National Bloc leaders were by no means social revolutionaries. Potentially social-revolutionary aspects of Syrian nationalism – armed and mobilized Syrian peasants and artisans – had been sidelined by the repression of the 1925–7 revolt. Instead, the Bloc's landowner- politicians behaved according to habits that they and their class had acquired in the later Ottoman decades. They were intermediaries or go-betweens, using their social influence and patronage power to link client populations to governmental authority. This made the National Bloc socially conservative, with their primary goals political rather than social or economic.

Remarkably, the Bloc was actually able to monopolize nationalist political space in Syria as the decade continued, even in the midst of the severe crises posed by the effects of the Great Depression. Popular dissatisfaction with material conditions was channeled into anti-French sentiment, not directed against the landowner- politicians' privileges, and it is doubtless that French policies (especially Paris's insistence on tying the Syrian currency to the depreciating French franc) deepened the country's woes. Dissident movements that arose in the Syrian body politic – most notably a form of radical nationalism associated with the League of National Action (est. ca. 1932) – were for the most part absorbed and co-opted into the National Bloc's political networks. By the end of the 1930s, the Bloc was itself becoming more politically radical because of the meager results that 'honorable cooperation' with France had yielded.

What Jamil Mardam Bey and his associates wanted from 'honorable coopera- tion' was a treaty with France comparable to the one that Great Britain had signed with the Iraqi government in 1930. The Anglo–Iraqi Treaty of 1930 brought the Iraq mandate to a formal end in 1932, symbolized by that country's admission into the League of Nations, albeit ensuring continued British preeminence in Iraq. Baghdad would align its foreign policy with Britain's, foreign (including British) ownership of Iraq's resources and infrastructure would be respected, and British armed forces would continue to be based on Iraqi territory. But Iraq would become fully sover- eign in internal matters and its armed forces would be under Iraqi command.

Mardam Bey and the National Bloc sought to achieve similar results for Syria. In their view, just like Iraq with Britain, independent Syria would recognize a spe- cial position for France and would align itself internationally with French interests.

However, France would have to give up its oversight role and cede full internal authority to the national Syrian government. After many false starts, the National Bloc negotiated an agreement along these lines with France in 1936. The successful round of negotiations were preceded by a seven-week general strike from January to March 1936. The strike demonstrated the National Bloc's urban support and it pressured France to change its policies. Negotiations were facilitated by the temporary ascendance of a left-wing government in Paris, the Popular Front, which grouped socialists and communists in the cabinet. As part of the Franco–Syrian Treaty, France agreed to dissolve the coastal Latakia state and the Druze state, so that independent Syria would include all of the French mandated territories except the Iskanderun district and Lebanon.

During negotiations, the National Bloc unsuccessfully argued that Iskanderun should be folded into Syria. With the Franco–Syrian Treaty now foreseeing the end of the formal French Mandate, Turkey insisted on having a direct political role in the district. As for Lebanon, the National Bloc accepted the Lebanese frontiers drawn by France, a significant milestone toward finalizing a distinct and separate Lebanese state. In return, the Bloc gained from France accession to Syria of the Latakia and Druze regions.

The Syrian parliament ratified the treaty despite criticism from radical nationalists that it gave too much to France. In the period afterward, Mardam Bey's government found itself in a bind since France's reluctance to ratify the treaty left him politically exposed. In repeated pleas to Paris to ratify the treaty, Mardam Bey and the National Bloc leadership made additional concessions, further undermining their nationalist authority and strengthening Mardam Bey's critics. Chief among these, and the man best positioned to take over the political space that Mardam Bey forfeited, was a wealthy radical nationalist, Shukri al-Quwatli (d. 1967), who would become independent Syria's first president.

The son of Damascene merchants and landowners, Istanbul-educated Quwatli had been a member of the Arab nationalist society al-Fatat during World War I. He was an official during Faisal's administration, and he spent the early mandate years in exile working with the Cairo-based Syria–Palestine Congress on behalf of (Greater) Syrian independence. Amnestied in 1930, Quwatli returned to Syria and used his family's fruit orchards around Damascus to develop the Syrian Conserves Company (1932). This was around the same time that he became active in National Bloc politics. Quwatli became a pole around which opposition to Mardam Bey's relative moderation gathered. Over time Quwatli co-opted into his wing of the National Bloc mostly middle-class activists who at first organized outside of the Bloc when they formed the League of National Action in 1932. The League was made up of modern-educated men, graduates of government and professional schools, as opposed to older-style religious schools. They included lawyers, professionals, journalists and school graduates, usually of middling background and 'modernist' in outlook, who were not part of urban patron–client relationships and the traditional or 'backward' social forms that undergirded the authority of National Bloc figures in the older quarters of Syria's towns. Instead, members of the League formed an association based on ideology. By conviction they were radical pan-Arabists, in contrast to the Syria-centrism of the National Bloc. They did not wish to see France retain any political, economic or military rights in independent Syria, in contrast to the dwindling notion of 'honorable cooperation.' From within the National Bloc, Shukri al-Quwatli harnessed radical nationalists' energies and ideological commitments to build support for his Bloc faction. Quwatli's star rose as Mardam Bey's reputation declined.

France's cession of the Iskanderun district to a Turkish puppet administration in 1938, finalized by the district's annexation to Turkey in 1939, struck a further major blow to Mardam Bey's national reputation. France acceded to Turkey's annexation of Iskanderun because of growing international tensions in the East Mediterranean between France and Italy, whose fascist leader Benito Mussolini sought to extend Rome's influence. France did not wish to see Turkey become an enemy again as it had been during World War I.

Turks were a large minority in the district of Iskanderun. Because of the support they received from the Ankara government, they were well organized and well funded compared to the non-Turkish majority and they could make life difficult for the French. The Arabs of Iskanderun district, on the other hand, were more numerous than the Turks but they were less coherent as a political force. There was no sovereign Syrian government to support them. The Mardam Bey administration in Damascus was under French Mandate and it had no formal authority in the district. Moreover the Arabs of Iskanderun (unlike the Turks) were religiously heterogeneous (Sunnis, Alawites and Christians), meaning that the bond of religious solidarity could not be easily invoked on the Arab side. ('Secular' Turkish identity, by contrast, was rooted in a firm substratum of Sunni Muslim communal ties.)

The most prominent Arab activist in Iskanderun was a young French-trained Alawite lawyer named Zaki al-Arsuzi (d. 1968). Ideologically Arsuzi was affiliated with the League of National Action, potentially putting an additional obstacle (if there were not enough already) in front of obtaining even crumbs of support from the feeble Mardam Bey administration. With the acquiescence of the League of Nations, France connived to create an 'independent' state in Iskanderun (renamed Hatay) under local Turkish rule, which was but a brief prelude to the territory's annexation to Turkey proper. About 50,000 Arab and Armenian residents fled to Syrian territory, not wishing to live in Turkish Hatay. The reputation of the Mardam Bey government hit rock bottom.

Along with the pan-Arab League of National Action, another ideological current that pressed on the National Bloc came from Islamic movements rooted in the popular quarters of the cities. Emphasizing the Islamic dimensions of Syrian identity and society, these movements appealed to merchants, *ulama* and artisans tied to the domestic markets and manufactures of Syria's towns. During the mandate various Islamic associations grew up in the interior cities, often led by *ulama*. They emphasized Muslim morals, Islamic identity and the centrality of Islam to public life. They insisted that the National Bloc not retreat from a defense of Muslims' rights, and they sought reassurances about the leading role of Islam. Major issues around which they mobilized were the supremacy of Islamic law, French control of education (particularly as this affected Muslim girls), and the public deportment of Muslim girls and women ('veiling' versus 'unveiling'). When in 1939 the French introduced legal changes that weakened the centrality of sharia, Islamic associations helped to mobilize a popular backlash that gave the beleaguered Mardam Bey an opportunity to resign the premiership as a 'hero' after he embraced the Islamic movements' position and refused to implement the changes.

The emergence of the League of National Action and the Islamic associations anticipated Syria's future political conflicts. Within a few years, currents identified with Zaki al-Arsuzi and the League of National Action would develop into the Baath party (1947), and the Islamic associations would form the basis of the Syrian Muslim Brotherhood (1945).

THE NATIONAL BLOC AND THE DIVERSITY OF SYRIA'S POPULATION

The National Bloc's relationship to Syria's non-Muslim religious communities was ambiguous. On the one hand, nationalist Christians were represented at the highest levels of the Bloc, most notably Faris al-Khoury (d. 1962). He was a Beirut-educated Protestant lawyer who had represented Damascus in the Ottoman parliament, joined the Arab nationalist society al-Fatat during the war, was one of Abd al-Rahman Shahbandar's associates in the People's Party, and later became prominent in the National Bloc. In addition to his previous political experience, part of Khoury's preeminence stemmed from his role as one of Syria's pioneering industrialists and, in 1930 and in partnership with nationalist-oriented landowners and merchants, he had co-founded the National Cement Company.[8]

Khoury was emblematic of Syria's nationalist Christians (mostly Greek Ortho-dox), who expressed devotion to the idea of the Syrian nation and sought to build political alliances with their Muslim fellow countrymen. In the sensitive politics of the colonial era, nationalist-oriented Christians were careful not to bind their interests closely to the patronage of France. While Christians in Anatolia and the Balkans had developed national identities that deepened their sense of separation from Muslim Turks, a comparable dynamic had not universally taken hold in Syria. To the extent that Syrian intellectuals and activists had worked to develop a sense of Syrian Arab nationalism as ideological glue for a new political formation, national-ist Orthodox and Protestant Christians mostly embraced that identity.

Like many Syrian Protestants, Khoury's family were converts from Greek Orthodoxy. In the nineteenth century, Arabic-speaking Orthodox Christians had rebelled against their Greek-speaking hierarchy, and the patriarchate of Antioch (actually based at Damascus) had become an emphatically Arabic-speaking church. Moreover, Arabic-speaking Orthodox Christians were a significant demographic presence in different parts of geographic Syria, and so to the extent that they conceived their communal identity in spatial terms, 'Syria' offered a good fit. The Bloc's goal of independence and self-government was congruent with nation-alist Christian sensibilities. So too was the Arab dimension of the Bloc's discourse, understood as representing a cultural affiliation rather than as a synonym or cover for transnational Muslim identity.

However, the National Bloc's relationship with Syria's Catholics was more fraught. This was especially significant in the city of Aleppo, where 35 percent of the population was Christian, the bulk of them Catholic. For the most part Aleppo's Catholics were not Latin rite. Instead, they were Eastern churches that had accepted the primacy of Rome while keeping their distinct liturgies and identities. Two of the most important were the Greek Catholics (Orthodox rite) and the Syriac Catholics (Syrian Orthodox or 'Jacobite' rite). When these communities embraced Catholicism in the Ottoman era, they began to distinguish themselves culturally and educationally from their erstwhile coreligionists – the Greek Orthodox and the Syrian Orthodox – since Catholic identity brought them into the orbit of France. French education, francophilia, French culture, and a sense of being a socially emancipated and 'modern' population became hallmarks of Aleppo Catholics' self-understanding.

Aleppo's Catholics were strongly represented in the liberal professions such as journalism, law and medicine. In the post-1908 Ottoman constitutional period, their leading lights proclaimed loyalty to the Ottoman sultanate as a constitutional framework that grouped together different religions and ethnicities. Fathallah

Qastun, the Catholic editor of an Ottoman-era Arabic newspaper in Aleppo, wrote in 1910:

> Indeed we have established schools in all the corners of the kingdom, even villages have places of learning to instruct children in the basics of reading, writing, and arithmetic, moreover we have taken from the Europeans the cultivation of women [...]. We are nearing the summit of modern civilization, Europeans are amazed by our enterprise and our vigor [...] so much so that some have bowed their heads as if to say: he who wishes to attain real civilization let him follow the example of the Ottomans.[9]

When the Ottoman state disappeared after 1918, Catholics were wary of the short-lived Faisal regime and of the pro-nationalist political bloc identified with Ibrahim Hananu and his allies. The same Fathallah Qastun, who in 1910 had praised the Ottomans, recalled in 1921 the relief that he felt when French forces replaced Faisal's Arab administration in Aleppo in 1920:

> [Faisal's supporters] spread lies that France and the French were the enemies of religion and civilization, but they did not deceive with their lies anyone except primitive tribesmen and naïve people [...]. [V]oices of joy and welcome greeted the beloved French soldiers and their commander [...], who spread out over Aleppo like the waves of the sea. As they entered, no blood was spilled, and they prevented a reign of terror. This established good feelings and confidence in Aleppo.[10]

A prominent exception to Catholics' overall pro-French political orientation was the French-educated lawyer Edmond Rabbath (d. 1991), who wrote eloquently about the Syrian national cause and who became closely associated with Aleppo nationalist Saadallah al-Jabiri. But for the most part Catholics of Aleppo developed institutions and loyalties during the mandate that were distinct from those associated with the National Bloc. In addition to voting for pro-French candidates, they organized a scouting movement (Scouts de France) and a paramilitary movement (the White Badge) that stood in counterpoint to the nationalist-affiliated Arab Scouts and the Bloc's youthful paramilitaries, the Steel Shirts. (Both the White Badge and the Steel Shirts were inspired by the then-current iconography of European fascism.) These organizations sought to mobilize uniformed middle-class youths into disciplined mass movements espousing and expressing national-communal consciousness. When in the 1940s France departed Syria, and the National Bloc (followed later by more radical nationalists) came to the fore, Aleppo's Catholics were politically marginalized. Nationalists suspected them of being insufficiently patriotic at best and French 'collaborators' at worst.

Another distinct element in Aleppo who stood aloof from the National Bloc were the city's Armenians, and they too developed their own institutions and sought to preserve a distinct cultural identity. To the extent that Syrian nationalism as an idea prescribed or advocated greater homogeneity among the country's population, Armenians looked askance at it. In turn, Bloc partisans and grass-roots Muslim activists often thought of Catholics and Armenians alike as 'outsiders' to the imagined national-communal body politic.

As for the Druzes, they were more easily integrated into the symbolism of Syrian national identity. At first they could point to their role in the 1925–7 Great Syrian Revolt and to the towering figure of Sultan al-Atrash as a militant early pioneer of the Syrian national movement. Yet following the suppression of the revolt, French authorities cultivated a constituency among rival Druze chiefly families, who grew accustomed to working within the revived administrative structure of the Druze state. The National Bloc, as an urban-based movement, sought cooperation with Druze notables. However, predominantly rural Druzes were not Bloc 'insiders' with access to its power structures and patronage systems. Urban nationalists would have occasion to question Druzes' fealty to the urbanites' vision of the Syrian nation, based as the urbanites' vision was on urban (and mostly Sunni Muslim) hegemony over Syria's national politics and identities.

Alawites posed another question mark in terms of how they would fit into the kind of Syrian identity associated with the National Bloc. The French successfully appealed to Alawite clan and tribal leaders in terms of drawing them into the administrative apparatus of the Alawite/Latakia state. Up until the mid-twentieth century Alawites were primarily a population of the mountains and interior plains, while major coastal towns (Latakia, Tartous, Jabla) were predominantly Sunni and Greek Orthodox Christian. The National Bloc had its supporters among the Alawite/Latakia state's coastal residents, but even many of this population saw advantages in working within the local structures that the French had established. When, as an upshot of the 1936 Franco–Syrian Treaty negotiations, France agreed to incorporate Latakia into Syria, pro-French forces there petitioned Paris against this move. In 1939, on the eve of World War II when France had abandoned the Franco–Syrian Treaty of 1936, Paris reversed itself and restored the Latakia state.

During these years a political–religious movement emerged among the Alawite population led by a charismatic shepherd named Suleiman al-Murshid (d. 1946). By the 1930s, Murshid had become a wealthy and influential man who commanded a movement loyal to him as a prophet and political leader. With the absorption of Latakia into Syria in 1936, Murshid was elected to the Syrian parliament. He supported Mardam Bey's treaty with France, but after the Mardam Bey government's resignation in 1939 and the subsequent re-separation of Latakia from Syria, Murshid became an advocate of Alawite/coastal self-rule ('separatism') and he worked closely with the French. He resisted efforts by the National Bloc to forge a unitary post-colonial independent Syria. Instead Murshid wished to preserve his autonomous authority in the name of protecting the distinct features and identity of the coastal region in general and of the Alawites in particular. His status as a charismatic religio-political leader threatened the nationalists and discomfited his rivals among Alawite notables. The National Bloc-led independent state of Syria convicted Murshid of criminal charges and executed him in 1946.

During the era of 'honorable cooperation,' and then resuming after 1941, the National Bloc had difficulty asserting its political authority in the Jazira region. Here, the combination of local Arab and Kurdish tribal identities and mostly pro-French Christian populations meant that the kind of urban-based Syrian Arab nationalism that seemed a good fit for Damascus and (with some historical amnesia) in Aleppo did not predominate in Syria's east. The Jazira had long been part of Mesopotamian demographic structures and economic relationships. Now, the newly drawn Iraqi–Syrian border bisected these. The French established and reinforced border outposts facing Turkey and Iraq, but saying that these territories were now part of 'Syria' and giving substance to that assertion were two different things. Tribal populations might cooperate with the National Bloc (or with the French), or they might not, depending on their understanding of their interests. In general, the most powerful tribal chieftains kept the Bloc at a distance, and resisted attempts to put them under Damascus's authority. Assyrian Christians, whether in towns like Qamishli or settled in villages along the Khabur river, saw France as a guarantor of their status and viewed the National Bloc (and any 'national' Syrian government) as potentially hostile to their cultural identity and their well being. Many of the Kurds, like Christians, were recently arrived refugees from Turkey and they did not wish to subordinate their interests to Damascus-based nationalists who evidenced little knowledge of the region and its peoples.

During its period in government in the 1930s, the National Bloc struggled to have its jurisdiction in the Jazira recognized. After the Franco–Syrian Treaty in 1936, violence broke out in the Jazira in 1937 as the National Bloc tried to expand the authority of its administration into the region in the name of national unity. Spurred on by local French officials, an alliance between rural Kurds and urban Assyrian Christians agitated for regional autonomy under the protection of France.

Meanwhile, the National Bloc encouraged Arabs from the areas of Aleppo, Homs and Hama to move to the Jazira to enhance the region's Arab character. The Bloc government fired Kurdish and Assyrian government employees and replaced them with Arabs. In 1938 Jazira autonomists organized a boycott of National Bloc government offices in the region. The Damascus-centric Syrian identity promoted by the National Bloc was not a natural fit for populations who did not want to be subjected to a distant, alien and Arabizing regime in Damascus.

The National Bloc's hopes of inheriting and exercising political power in Syria would depend not only on controlling a government administration created by the colonial state, but also on the Bloc's relationship to the armed forces. During the mandate, France mostly relied on its own imperial troops – the Armée du Levant – to garrison the country and to suppress opposition. Alongside this they recruited an internal police force, the gendarmerie, whose most notorious units were staffed by ethnic Circassians. (As noted earlier, Circassians were a Muslim ethnic group originating in the Black Sea region who had been resettled in Syria in the aftermath of Tsarist Russia's bloody conquest of their Transcaucasian homeland in the nineteenth century.) But the core of what would become the Syrian and Lebanese armies was the Troupes Speciales du Levant, composed of soldiers and officers recruited from Syria and Lebanon. The French recruited the Troupes Speciales from the general population, but the combination of social prejudice against colonial military service among urban elites and French outreach to non-Sunni populations, meant that officer ranks of the Troupes Speciales had a high proportion of Alawites, Druzes, Ismailis and rural Sunnis. The National Bloc thought of the Troupes Speciales as a colonial tool, and the Bloc's leaders felt socially and politically distant from the institution that was to become the Syrian army. Confronted soon after independence with major regional crises, the independence-era Syrian leadership and the Syrian army would fail to address them effectively. Their combined failures would initiate a period of unrest and turmoil in the newly independent republic.

Therefore the articulation and definition of a Syrian national identity, tied as it was to the existence of an actual (albeit new and colonial) Syrian state, was beset with difficulties from the outset. Syria's long-standing ethnic, social and cultural diversity was an awkward fit for the new, post-World War I paradigm of political community embodied in the nation state. Along with the nation state paradigm came pressure to construct a national historical narrative that progressed inexorably to the nation state, and posited a common national identity. These efforts to construct a unified nation, which would be hard enough in the best of circumstances, were all the more daunting in the face of a French colonial administration whose practice was to emphasize and to deepen Syria's political and social differences.

EMERGENCE OF THE SYRIAN WOMEN'S MOVEMENT

Charitable societies associated with bourgeois and upper-class women developed into activist associations during and after World War I. A pioneer in these efforts was Nazik al-Abid (d. 1959), from a well-connected family of civil servants in Damascus. During the war she supported Faisal's Arab nationalist cause, and afterward she helped to organize an early version of the Syrian Red Cross (later, Red Crescent). An honorary officer in Faisal's hastily raised Syrian army, she was at the battle of Maysaloun against the French in July 1920. In Faisal-era Damascus she published a pioneering women's journal that advocated women's rights in the new Syria, emphatically including political rights. In February 1920, a few months before Maysaloun, Abid explained hopefully how giving a voice to women in her publication could advance the national cause:

> And even if a male writer and a female writer argue and fight about a subject, they will understand each other and they will arrive at truths worth expressing, and so lift this wretched nation from the ruin of misery to the peak of happiness.[11]

Some years later Abid was a co-founder of the Syrian and Lebanese Women's Association (1928). By that time she had moved to Beirut, where she married a feminist from Beirut's Muslim bourgeoisie, Muhammad Jamil Beyhum (d. 1978). Leadership of the Syrian Women's Association after that was most closely associated with Adila Beyhum al-Jazairi (d. 1975), born in Beirut to the same Beyhum family but married into the well-established Jazairis of Damascus. Unlike Abid and her co-thinkers, who had argued (in vain) for inclusion of women as full voting citizens in the mandate-era state, Jazairi believed that suffrage (political rights) would follow from improvements in women's social rights. Therefore she and her colleagues who came to dominate the Syrian women's movement argued that women should focus on 'patriotic motherhood' rather than immediate political rights. At a meeting of the international Eastern Women's Conference in Damascus in 1930, a Lebanese delegate explained:

> What is required for women to progress is that they become perfectly educated; this education is necessary for women as much as for children […]. Nothing more than ignorance blocks progress and the happiness of men and women. When women know how to raise children [sic!], they can demand from men their rights and take them in hand.[12]

Through demonstrations of their value and importance to the nation, advocates of 'patriotic motherhood' believed, women would be in a stronger position to press for political rights later. But the delegate's quoted statement inadvertently reveals why the Syrian Women's Association remained politically sidelined. By acknowledging that women in their majority were uneducated and asserting that they did not even know how to raise children (something Syrian women had, in fact, been doing for countless generations), the women's movement conceded high ground to advocates of patriarchal understandings of citizenship. Women would have to 'earn' the right to be considered full citizens through improving themselves, a concession that rendered men (whether colonists or nationalists) arbiters of women's worthiness for full citizenship.

Nazik al-Abid understood the perils of this position, but Jazairi's accommodating line may have been the only pragmatic way for bourgeois and middle-class women to carve out public spaces for themselves once the Great Syrian Revolt was suppressed and the 1930 constitution adopted. Women activists were fearful of being wrong-footed and caught in the middle of the nationalist versus colonialist binary of post-1928 politics. The earlier, Nahda-era openness to wide-ranging debates about the family, marriage, and women's roles in society became stifled in the polarized atmosphere of the colonial era. Women activists' apprehensions were illustrated by the strong negative male, nationalist and religious response to a published appeal by a Lebanese Druze woman in 1927 calling for Muslim women to have the freedom to unveil, that is, to dispense with the face covering that had been a hallmark of polite upper-class urban society in the Ottoman and early mandate eras. The author, Nazira Zain al-Din (d. 1976), was a judge's daughter who advanced Islamic reformist arguments that previously had been developed and used by Muslim feminists in Egypt. She cited Qur'anic sources and examples from early Islamic history to argue that severe restrictions on women's dress and public activities were not truly Islamic. As an argument for 'true' (modern-minded) Islam, Zain al-Din's viewpoint had the potential to appeal to some men of the nationalist camp (such as the Beirut feminist, and husband of Nazik al-Abid, Muhammad Jamil Beyhum). But Zain al-Din's tactical mistake was to appeal to 'the state,' meaning the French, to solicit government authority to improve women's legal status and obtain for them greater personal freedoms. She sent her book to the French High Commissioner with a public letter that appeared in newspapers:

> Permit me, excellence, to give you a copy of my book for your high appreciation, because no one would be more qualified than the Honorable Representative of France, Mother of all civilization, of liberty and all light,

to extend his strong hand to save the weakened Muslim woman and lift her from the dark abyss of slavery where she was arbitrarily plunged, contrary to the Book of God.[13]

Her appeal to the French High Commissioner was grist for the mill of social conservatives, whether they were populist Islamists or elite nationalists. They portrayed Zain al-Din's proposals as part of a colonial plot to undermine the family and to weaken society's values. Jazairi's more cautious approach of advocating patriotic motherhood tried to avoid the pitfall of ending up on the wrong side of a rhetorical war based on binary opposition between Syrian nationalism and French colonialism.

Women did not obtain voting rights until 1949, six years after Syria's declaration of independence and three years after France's final evacuation. Toward the end of the 1930s, Jazairi herself realized that women activists had painted themselves into a corner, as the National Bloc administration of Jamil Mardam Bey aligned with populist Islamic associations in a bid to regain some of his lost popularity after the failure of France to ratify the Franco–Syrian Treaty, and the takeover of Iskanderun by Turkey.

Nonetheless, taking the long view of what the Syrian national movement accomplished during the French Mandate era, women entered public life in a decisive way. Advocates of women's participation used the national movement and the anti-colonial struggle as wedges to open up space for their new roles, arguing that women were half the nation and that the nation could not be strong unless its women were educated and empowered. Eventually even conservative groups came to accept women's participation in public life and institutions, seeking however to impose restrictions or standards on women's dress, deportment and public behavior according to what they deemed to be 'Islamic.' Still, the stubborn problem remained: women became symbols of larger struggles, which opened up to them some room for maneuver while also maintaining patriarchal control and strictures. Activist women had difficulty escaping this conundrum.

HESITANT STEPS TOWARD A NATIONAL CULTURE

During the period of French rule, Syrian nationhood was a work-in-progress. The anti-colonial revolt of 1925–7 and the National Bloc's activities in the 1930s represented political efforts to achieve nationhood. By the same token, creating and articulating a national culture was also a challenge, and more difficult to distinguish from wider currents of Arab cultural production. Syrians in Ottoman times had played a major role in the modern Arab 'awakening' or Nahda through their contributions to literature and learning. After World War I, as Syria became a territorially defined country under colonial rule, the new challenge was to develop and define a modern Syrian culture that reflected the intelligentsia's aspirations for independent nationhood. Syrians had far fewer resources, and less room for maneuver, than did their peers in Egypt in the 1920s and 1930s. In many instances, it seemed that Syrians were either following Egyptians' lead, or simply being overwhelmed by Egyptian cultural output.

Damascus made a claim to being the arbiter of modern Arabic language use through the establishment of the Arab Academy in 1919. Modeled after the Académie française, its goal was to ensure proper Arabic usage in education and in printed mass media, by developing new vocabularies and ruling on grammatical usages to ensure that proper Arabic or high Arabic would not be watered down and corrupted by colloquial forms and modern loan-words. The writer and wartime Jemal Pasha-ally Muhammad Kurd Ali was the founding director, and he served in that capacity until his death in 1953. Because Damascus was the first Arab capital where a self-identified Arab nationalist administration came to power (Faisal's brief Syrian 'kingdom'), the Arab Academy and Damascus's historical association with the medieval Umayyad caliphs and their 'Arab kingdom' ensured that Syria would hold a prominent place in the development of a modern Arab cultural imagination.

The Neoclassical trend in Arabic poetry continued to predominate, but it was joined in these decades by a new Romantic trend in which Syrian émigrés participated. The Romanticists abandoned strict neoclassical meter, used more accessible language and offered greater scope for more personal expression. The Syria-based author who was the best-known exemplar of the Romantic trend was Omar Abu Risha (d. 1990). Born near Aleppo, he trained as a chemist in Britain, but worked as a librarian in Syria and later as a diplomat. He published his first volume of poetry in 1936, and his final collection appeared in 1971. Themes treated in his poetry were the highly personal ones of love, passion and heartbreak, but his writing also included references to social and political issues.[14]

The story of the interwar Arabic novel is mostly an Egyptian one, and Egypt remained the center for the development of this literary form. In contrast, the contribution of the Syrian publishing industry was modest. The first novel published in Syria, *Na'am* ('Yes') by the Aleppine Shakib al-Jabiri (d. 1996), appeared in 1937. An activist who supported the National Bloc, Jabiri was banished by the French in 1937 and he wrote the novel while studying chemistry in Geneva. It dealt with a familiar interwar theme of tensions between East and West as played out in personal lives and in wider society. Jabiri went on to play a cultural role in the 1940s and 1950s, and he also held a diplomatic position at one point.

Syria's nascent film industry was strangled at birth by a combination of French hostility and Egyptian commercial successes. There were only two Syria-produced films in the mandate era. The first was *Innocent Suspect* (1928), a story of thieves and brigands who threatened villages near Damascus during the Faisal era. Made just one year after the first Egyptian movie, it was a modest commercial success. Many of the same people produced a second film, *Under the Damascus Sky*, in 1934, which bankrupted its producers. The French forbade its public showing, claiming that the filmmakers had violated international copyright laws through their selection of music. Moreover, by this time the first Egyptian talkies were on the market, and cinema owners were more interested in screening these popular, commercially successful products. Cairo became the Hollywood of the Arab film industry, and Syrians who wished to work in film emigrated to Egypt. The pioneering Syrian films are remembered as efforts to create a national presence in the new cultural form, but not until the 1970s did Syrian film producers establish themselves as a distinctive voice in Arab and international cinema.

Egypt also became the preeminent center for recorded Arabic music, but in this domain Syrian cultural producers held their own. While singers and musicians who wished to gain wide popularity were drawn to Egypt and its recording and film studios, musicians who worked in Syria could continue to find employment and to develop their local traditions. Aleppo especially emerged as a creative musical center. From the mid-nineteenth to the mid-twentieth centuries, wealthy male merchants entertained guests with live music, and wealthy women hosted analogous women-only events. Aleppo's status as a multi-confessional and multi-ethnic cultural crossroads contributed to the richness of its music scene, as did the strong presence of Sufism in the city. Public venues for the performance of music began to develop in the 1930s. Later in the twentieth century, Aleppo would earn wide recognition as one of the major exemplars of classical or quality Arabic music. Nevertheless, on the whole during the interwar period of colonial rule, Syrian cultural producers labored in Egypt's shadow.

THE END OF THE FRENCH MANDATE

World War II brought the mandate to an earlier end than France would have wished. At the outset of the war (1939) the French declared martial law, suspended the constitution and restored the Druze and Latakia states. With France's defeat by Germany in 1940, Syria and Lebanon came under the administration of the collaborationist Vichy regime and as such German and Italian agents and military personnel had access to the countries' territory. After suppressing a pro-Axis coup in Iraq in May 1941, the British moved into Syria and Lebanon in June. They fought a brief war with the Vichy garrison, and then handed nominal authority over to their allies, the Free French of Charles de Gaulle (d. 1970). However, a condition of the handover was that the Free French pledge independence for Syria and Lebanon.

Constitutional life was restored, and the Druze and Alawite states reincorporated into Syria – this time for good – in 1942. After elections in 1943 the National Bloc re-emerged as the dominant political force. Now its major figure was Mardam Bey's critic Shukri al-Quwatli, who became president and navigated the path to independence.

Following his election victory, Quwatli sounded confident and optimistic. On 2 August 1943 he exulted:

> The country has now passed one of the preparatory stages for its free constitutional life and Parliament is now about to meet. Now are our hearts filled with tranquility, joy and assurance. Now throughout the provinces and towns the nation, as a body, has stood by the men it knows and who know it […]. Now the nation has given proof of the unity of its classes and its aims and now all doubts have been dissipated.[15]

Aleppo's Saadallah al-Jabiri and Damascus's Faris al-Khoury were successive prime ministers, and Mardam Bey (still a Bloc figure, but no longer its major leader) held various ministerial portfolios including foreign minister. Syria proclaimed its independence (and was recognized as such by the Allies) in 1943. It was a founding member of both the United Nations and the Arab League in 1945.

The French remained reluctant to disengage. Britain supported the National Bloc's demands for an unconditional end to the mandate, which left de Gaulle feeling that France had been unceremoniously and unfairly pushed out of its mandated territories so that Britain could fill the evacuated political space. After one last angry bombardment of Damascus in 1945, the French withdrew their remaining forces from Lebanon and Syria the following year, and handed control of the Troupes Speciales to Lebanese and Syrian command. With this, the French era ended. They left behind a state with arbitrary boundaries and with no consensus about nationhood. To the contrary, French policies had cultivated and exacerbated ethnic, regional and sectarian fault-lines.

The leadership of independent Syria – President Shukri al-Quwatli and the National Bloc administration – now were fully responsible for Syria's domestic and international policies. Multiple challenges soon overwhelmed them and condemned the country to a quarter century of political turmoil and instability.

6

CRISES OF INDEPENDENT STATEHOOD

THE ERA OF MILITARY COUPS

As Damascenes awoke on the morning of 30 March 1949, they discovered that the army had quietly taken power under cloak of night. Soldiers had arrested the president and prime minister, seized the radio station and the headquarters of the police and gendarmerie, and government ministers had been detained. Communications with the outside world were temporarily cut off. They key officers who organized the coup claimed that they had acted to save the nation from its corrupt or wrongheaded politicians, and that the new government would correct the errors of the recent past. Damascenes were to experience at least eight more such events. Revolving-door governments underscored Syria's chronic crises of independent statehood until a final coup in 1970 brought to an end an extraordinary period of political turmoil.

FRAGILE INDEPENDENCE

With the final withdrawal of French troops and the government's takeover of the armed forces in 1946, Syria became fully independent. But it was a fragile new state. Syria's newly demarcated frontiers had not existed for long, and before that (in pre-colonial, Ottoman times) Syria had been merely an idea. The country's fragility was a product of its history. It lacked the kind of institutionalization that benefited older and better-developed political nations. Syrians wishing to turn a novel national idea into a sovereign political structure had little transferable experience of responsible self-rule. The late Ottoman system of patronage and elected bodies (municipal councils, the fledgling parliament) was aimed at binding Syrian elites to an imperial system that was defunct after 1918. Though the French Mandate that followed was ostensibly designed to set the stage for self-government (perversely, by first destroying Faisal's existing Arab administration), France throughout the years of its mandate did not permit Syrians to wield any significant authority. Moreover, as we have seen, Syrians' sense of national community was highly uneven. Different communities related to the Syrian national idea in different ways, and some hardly related to it at all. Finally, the end of French and British rule in the Middle East left numerous unsettled colonial legacies and issues. These embroiled Syria in conflicts outside of its frontiers, and encouraged different factions in Syria to solicit external intervention in the country's internal affairs. Notably, a mere 12 years after attaining independence Syria ceased to be a sovereign state altogether. From 1958 to 1961 it was united with (in effect, annexed by) Egypt as part of the United Arab Republic.

Syria's first decade of independence saw some achievements. The development of light industry proceeded apace, emphasizing textiles, food, tobacco and construction materials. Industrial growth depended on domestic private capital and access to Arab markets. A predominantly agricultural country, independent Syria saw new private investments in agriculture, with the result that wheat and cotton cultivation expanded in the Jazira region especially. Rising yields brought food security and (with cotton) helped stimulate the development of a medium-scaled textile industry. Infrastructure improvements included construction of new roads and railways, and a major land reclamation scheme that drained swamps in the Ghab depression (middle Orontes valley, north of Hama). Introduction of water pumps and tractors increased cultivation in the Jazira, making it the country's new breadbasket. Education expanded and schools became more widely available, though they still served only a minority of the population. In the central regions of Homs and Hama, organized movements of peasants and workers campaigned for inclusion in the body politic, and for recognition of their collective rights as wage-earners and cultivators. Indeed if independent Syria had turned out to be a success story, these developments might today be interpreted as early steps toward creating a more productive economy and a more inclusive politics in the era of decolonization.

In the main however, Syria's immediate post-independence political history is one of tumult and fragmentation, marked by an absence of constitutional norms and a willingness of political actors to call on the help of external powers against internal rivals. The first post-independence elections were held in 1947 and the mandate-era National Bloc split into two. The Bloc had been more a collection of personalities than a party organization, and now it had lost the unifying glue of campaigning against the French. One of its spinoffs was the National Party, Damascus-based and little more than a personal vehicle for President Shukri al-Quwatli. The other was the People's Party, based in Aleppo and Homs and headed by the Aleppine Nazim al-Qudsi and his Homs allies, the landowning Atassi family who played a prominent role in the city's politics.[1]

The post-1945 People's Party represented northern interests and reflected Aleppo's historic links to Mesopotamia. The People's Party were mostly pro-Iraqi at a time when the Hashemite monarchy in Baghdad sought to extend its influence and authority into Syria. To counter the People's Party's pro-Hashemite stance, the Quwatli-led National Party looked to Egypt and Saudi Arabia for ballast. In terms of their actual programs there was little to differentiate the National Party from the People's Party: both represented merchant and landlord interests, and neither were attuned to the ideological ferment that soon would roil Syrian political life.

EMERGENCE OF IDEOLOGICAL PARTIES

The 1947 elections offered some indicators regarding ideological politics. The Muslim Brotherhood, established in 1945, elected a sympathizer in Damascus. Agrarian socialist organizer Akram al-Hourani (d. 1996) won a seat in Hama. But most of the parliament were independents who represented local, family or parochial interests. One of the elected independents who had a national vision and who would play a prominent role in Syrian politics up to 1963 was the Damascene industrialist and businessman Khalid al-Azm (d. 1965), a descendant of the Ottoman-era political family.

The Muslim Brotherhood grew out of the Islamic associations of the mandate era and unified them under its umbrella in 1945. Its founder in Syria was Homs-born Mustafa al-Sibai (d. 1965), dean of the Faculty of Islamic Jurisprudence at the University of Damascus. Like the associations that produced them, the Muslim Brotherhood were primarily an urban group, influential among the pious artisans, merchants and shopkeepers of the towns, especially the older and densely built-up historical neighborhoods. They were loosely affiliated with the Egyptian parent organization founded in 1928, and which Sibai had joined while studying in Egypt. The Brotherhood combined a reformist Islam (legal-scriptural, skeptical of populist Sufism) with an unbending belief in the normativity of Islam as a basis for social organization and political action. Like the country's other ideological movements, the Brotherhood viewed Syria as a local field of operation for a doctrine or an idea that transcended the borders of the newly established Syrian state.

The Muslim Brotherhood (like the Islamic associations before them) pressured the old-line nationalists, and criticized political elites for corruption or self-dealing, and for any signs of retreat from normative Islamic principles. Pressing for the

1 View of Aleppo from the south-west (photographed pre-1914). The medieval citadel looms in background and two sixteenth-century Ottoman mosques are identifiable by their pencil-shaped minarets. On left: the Adiliyya. On right: the Khusrowiyya.

2 Nawfara coffee house in Damascus (1938 photo). This café, in the shadow of the Umayyad Mosque, is still in business in the same location today.

3 Rural life: threshing wheat in a northern Syrian village (1930s photo).

4 General view of Damascus from above Salihiyya, nineteenth century.

5 Damascus courtyard house, late nineteenth–early twentieth century.

6 Pilgrims in Damascus on their return from Mecca. In the background is the Mahmal, symbol of the sultan's patronage and protection of the Mecca pilgrimage. Photograph from 1903.

7 French authorities publicly display corpses of slain rebels, Damascus 1925.

8 Ruined Damascus neighborhood after the French bombardment of October 1925. Courtesy of the Otrakji family collection.

9 Husni Zaim, author of the first military coup.

10   Nasser receiving a hero's welcome in Damascus, 1958, with Quwatli at his side.

11   Cult of personality: Hafez al-Assad's image looms over Damascus in 1999.

12   Bashar billboard, Damascus, 2006.

13   Government soldiers in rubble of the eighth-century Umayyad (Great) Mosque in
Aleppo, after capturing it from rebels in 2017.

interests of their urban Muslim constituencies, the Brotherhood would in due course come into conflict with Syria's other, secular, ideological movements.

Akram al-Hourani from Hama was born with a grudge against the big landowning families of his hometown. His father had stood against one of them in elections for the Ottoman parliament, and lost. The big landowning families lived opulently from the toil of others, and controlled local politics though patronage and fear. Descended from a family of Sufi sheikhs who had enjoyed a popular urban and rural following, the secular Hourani was trained as a lawyer. He was seized by the plight of peasant sharecroppers and campaigned for cultivators' empowerment. He aimed to curtail landlords' power, prerogatives and property ownership. His slogan was, 'Fetch the basket and the shovel for burying the Agha and the Bey'[2] (it rhymes in Arabic).

Hourani was initially affiliated with a radical nationalist party called the Syrian Social National Party (SSNP, est. 1932). It was a product of its time, influenced by fascist organizational forms and iconography (its emblem was, and is, a modified swastika). The SSNP emphasized the unity of the nation and the authority of its charismatic leader, a Lebanese–Brazilian teacher named Antoun Saadeh (d. 1949). The party's secular vision imagined Greater Syria as a distinct national homeland, and it attracted radical nationalists of the early independence era who did not wish to see Greater Syria lost or dissolved into a larger Arab or Islamic whole. Hourani, however, eventually left the SSNP and in 1950 he formally constituted his own political party and movement, under the name the Arab Socialist Party.

FAILURE IN PALESTINE

Quwatli and his National Party followers did not have much time to savor the fruits of power. Syria, like other newly independent Arab states, faced an urgent challenge in view of the chaotic end to Britain's Palestine mandate. In November 1947 the United Nations General Assembly voted to partition Palestine into a Jewish state and an Arab state, a resolution adopted over Arab objections. The Jewish national movement in Palestine had been nurtured by Britain in the interwar years. After World War II and the experience of Nazi Germany's genocide of Europe's Jews, both the US and the USSR supported Jewish statehood. In the wake of the partition resolution, the Jewish national movement (institutionalized in the mandate as the Jewish Agency) set out to establish a Jewish state in Palestine, a country whose majority population was Arab. From late 1947 to May 1948 Britain progressively withdrew from the country. In the meanwhile, Palestinian Jews and Arabs fought to seize positions that Britain evacuated. The Jewish Agency abandoned static defense and launched a war of movement in April 1948 to link up the parts of Palestine earmarked for the Jewish state. Their goal was to secure and expand the Jewish state's frontiers, and to relieve an Arab siege of Jewish neighborhoods in Jerusalem. These actions triggered the first substantial wave of Palestinian Arab refugees (the Nakba), and there would be more, ultimately numbering over 700,000.

Syria's engagement in Palestine occurred through the Arab League, of which Syria was a charter member.[3] Quwatli's main purpose regarding Palestine was to ensure that Abdullah, the Hashemite king of Jordan (formerly Transjordan), would not benefit from the end of the Palestine mandate. Quwatli's opponents in the People's Party looked to the Hashemites of Iraq for support, while their allies the Druze (and the legendary Sultan al-Atrash) looked to Jordan. Quwatli feared that Abdullah and the Druze would conspire to oust him and his government in the name of realizing the original 'Greater Syria' ambition of the 1918–20 period, when Abdullah's brother Faisal administered Damascus. Quwatli sought Arab state intervention in Palestine in order to block Abdullah. In this he was backed by Egypt and Saudi Arabia.

At Syria's instigation the Arab League sent a few thousand indifferently equipped volunteers into Palestine in the spring of 1948 to assist the local Palestinian Arabs, whose cause was widely supported in Syria. This intervention was presented to the Syrian public as an effort to 'save' Arab Palestine, and the volunteer unit was called the Arab Salvation Army. Its commander was the same Fawzi al-Qawuqji who had attempted to raise a revolt in Hama in 1925. For politically engaged Syrians, Palestine was a popular cause – a country that was Arab, mainly Muslim, and part of the notional 'natural Syria' which had been a geopolitical whole (under the Ottomans) within living memory. Quwatli hoped that the Arab Salvation Army could check Jewish advances and act as a counterweight to Abdullah of Jordan, whose territorial ambitions in Palestine and in Syria itself were no secret. The better-led, better-equipped and more effective Jewish forces routed local Palestinian militias and the Arab League volunteers, sparking the initial Palestinian refugee crisis. This failure led directly to the intervention of Arab state armies when the British mandate came to an official end on 15 May and the State of Israel was proclaimed. The intervening Arabs were working at cross purposes, and Arab states' motivations for military intervention were linked to their internecine rivalries. Syria's preoccupation remained Jordan. The Hashemite Kingdom, still closely tied to Britain, looked to implement partition by seizing the bulk of the territory earmarked for the Palestinian Arab state, while accepting the reality of the newborn Jewish state and leaving it alone. Quwatli and his prime minister, Jamil Mardam Bey, wished to defend their rule in Syria and to curtail Abdullah's ambitions.

Supported by a unanimous vote in parliament, Quwatli sent the small, poorly equipped and politically mistrusted Syrian army into action. Its contingent in Palestine numbered no more than 2,500 to 3,000 men. They entered northern Palestine and had little effect on the overall outcome of the first Arab–Israeli war (1948–9), which ended in a decisive Israeli victory. In the end, the Syrian army succeeded in holding on to three small pieces of former Palestine between the Sea of Galilee and Lake Hula when the armistice with Israel was signed in 1949.

Syrian Jews paid a high price for the Palestine conflict. Long established in Damascus and Aleppo, especially, Jews were indigenous to Syria where they lived and worked in the Arab cultural milieu. Some were descendants of Andalusian Jews who had been dispossessed and expelled from Spain in 1492 (the Sephardis), while others had Near Eastern roots that stretched back to antiquity (the Mizrahis). When linguistic identity came to the fore in the late nineteenth and early twentieth centuries, it became common to refer to them all as 'Arab Jews,' in much the same way that one might speak of 'Arab Christians.' But in the twentieth century, when Arab and Jewish nationalisms developed in opposition to one another in Palestine, Syrian and other Arab Jews found themselves in an increasingly perilous position. Muslim and Christian Arab nationalists regarded Jews with suspicion, as potential fifth columnists and 'Zionist agents.' Although one Jew was elected to parliament from Damascus in 1943 on Shukri al-Quwatli's list, Arab nationalists gave free vent to anti-Jewish sentiments as the conflict over Palestine intensified. In December 1947, after the UN vote to partition Palestine the month before, anti-Jewish violence and murders rocked Aleppo. Large numbers of Jews fled Syria in the immediate aftermath, and the once-thriving Jewish community of Aleppo rapidly dwindled.

The creation of Israel the following year worsened Syrian Jews' predicament. Looking to deflect popular anger away from its own failures, the Syrian government subjected Jews to onerous travel and other restrictions. For a time Jews were allowed to leave Syria (Lebanon, the US and Israel were top destinations), but only if they surrendered their property first. Although a few thousand Jews remained in Damascus and Aleppo, their communities were shadows of their former selves. In later years remaining Jews were forbidden to emigrate. If they traveled they had to leave close family members behind as hostages to travelers' return. In 1965 the discovery of an Israeli–Jewish spy in high government circles, a man with Syrian ancestry, deepened government surveillance and suspicion of remaining Jews. As Syria built up the apparatus of a police state in the late 1950s and beyond, Jewish life was closely monitored.

After the armistice agreements in 1949, Israel was established in three-quarters of Palestine, and 90 percent of the Arabs who had lived in the area that became

Israel were made refugees. Up to 100,000 of them took refuge in Syria. The failure of Arab arms overall, and popular anger at the 'corruption' of Quwatli and his associates who were blamed for the Syrian army's material shortages and lack of success, created a crisis of legitimacy in winter 1948–9. Quwatli compounded his political difficulties by using the army to subdue anti-government protests in November–December 1948, signaling to the officers their relative strength versus Quwatli's political weakness.

REVOLVING-DOOR COUPS

On 30 March Syria experienced the first of what would be many military coups when General Husni Zaim (d. 1949), in league with a number of other disgruntled officers, overthrew the shaky parliamentary regime and sent Quwatli into exile. Zaim was an officer from Aleppo who had started his career in the Ottoman army, defected to the Arab Revolt during World War I, served in the French-commanded Troupes Speciales, was cashiered for embezzlement by the Free French, and then brought back into the army and rose to be the Syrian army's Chief of Staff during the 1948–9 Arab–Israeli war. Before launching his coup, Zaim sounded out foreign embassies to assess their likely responses. There was no love lost between Quwatli and any of the French, British or Americans and so, receiving no international red lights, Zaim made his move.

US support for Zaim partially derived from Washington's inclination during the early Cold War era to see army rule in newly independent countries as an effective counterweight to the growth of communist and pro-Soviet sympathies. As disciplined, hierarchical organizations devoted to order, trained and supplied by former colonial powers, armies were depicted as 'agents of modernization' that could bring in reforms to reduce communism's appeal to restless and disaffected populations.

The Syrian army had been founded as a colonial force, its recruitment heavily weighted toward rural people and ethnic or religious minorities. With independence there had been a rush of recruitment into the Syrian army officer corps. Most of these new recruits had few ties to, or sympathies with, the old nationalist elite represented by the National Bloc and its spinoff parties, mostly coming from small-town, rural and religious-minority backgrounds. Well-to-do Sunni urban elites disdained military service, whereas capable and ambitious young men from non-elite, non-urban backgrounds saw the officer corps as a promising and patriotic path of upward social mobility. Even as early as 1949 then, the old nationalist leadership, represented by Quwatli, Mardam Bey et al., had few cards to play when confronted by widespread public disaffection and unhappiness in the ranks of military officers.

But the army was not ready to govern, at least not yet. With Syria's future in the balance, a power struggle erupted between pro-Iraq partisans (who ultimately sought union with Iraq, including the extension of Hashemite family rule to Syria) and partisans of continued Syrian independence. The pro-Iraqi, Aleppo-based People's Party had initially welcomed Quwatli's ouster, but when Zaim did not receive the kind of open-handed support he anticipated from Baghdad, he moved abruptly in the direction of Quwatli's old anti-Hashemite Arab allies, Egypt and Saudi Arabia. Behind this intra-Arab rivalry for influence in Syria stood Great Britain (sponsor of the Iraqi government) and the US (patron of Saudi Arabia, and seeking closer relations with Egypt where Britain was unpopular and resented). Zaim introduced a smattering of reforms, the most enduring of which was women's suffrage, and he approved a proposal that had been stalled in parliament to run an American oil pipeline from Saudi Arabia across Syrian territory to the Lebanese Mediterranean port of Sidon (the Tapline project).

The exercise of power went to Zaim's head, and soon he alienated the officers who had assisted him in the coup as well as wider currents of public opinion. In June 1949, Zaim manufactured a single-candidate election and assumed the office of president; he soaked up flattery from monarchs in Cairo and Riyadh; he made plans to set up a special foreign bodyguard of Yugoslav Muslims; he promoted himself to the military rank of marshal complete with a glittering baton, in all likelihood the most glittering baton that the Syrian army had ever seen. And beyond these personal vanity projects, he drew close to Turkey despite Syrians' still-raw memories of the loss of Iskanderun, he endorsed a US proposal for a regional pro-Western military pact, and he proposed an agreement with Israel that would have amounted to Syrian recognition of the Jewish state, with no obvious quid-pro-quo on Israel's part regarding outstanding issues of boundaries and Palestinian refugees.

Burning so many political bridges to nationalist opinion simultaneously, Zaim was vulnerable to a second coup in August 1949, supported by some of the same officers who had backed him the previous March. The frontman for this British-supported, Iraqi-engineered coup was Colonel Sami Hinnawi (d. 1950), who turned to the People's Party and other pro-Iraq elements for political support. In the course of the coup, an officer affiliated with the SSNP shot Zaim dead, in revenge for Zaim's extradition of SSNP founder Saadeh to Lebanon where he was executed after a hasty trial. (The Lebanese government wanted Saadeh because of a failed SSNP putsch attempt.)

Hinnawi organized elections for a constitutional assembly in November. The exiled Quwatli's National Party boycotted the polls, but the Aleppo-based People's Party stood for election and emerged as the dominant grouping. Immediate union with Iraq was not implemented, however, because the People's Party had reservations about becoming bound by treaty to Great Britain, which an Iraqi takeover of Syria at this point would have entailed. The People's Party and independents dominated the assembly, but three ideological parties won single seats. They were the Muslim Brotherhood, the radical Arab nationalist Baath (est. 1947), and the SSNP. The election of three ideological party representatives to the 1949 constitutional assembly was a harbinger of future trends. For the next few years, the ideological parties would play an increasingly important role in the politics of Syria, even though they never attained popular or parliamentary majorities.

Worried that Hinnawi and his allies were preparing to lead Syria into a union with Iraq, a group of nationalist army officers in turn overthrew him in December 1949. Col. Adib Shishakli (d. 1964), who would dominate Syrian politics for the next four years, led this third and final coup. He became Syria's first effective military ruler.

Shishakli was from Hama, had been in the Troupes Speciales, and served with distinction in the volunteer Arab League force that vainly attempted to stem the Jewish advance in Palestine in the spring of 1948. Earlier in the 1940s, Shishakli had been a member of the SSNP, and for a time Shishakli was closely allied with radical lawyer and politician Akram al-Hourani, also from Hama and also a member of the party. Shishakli had assisted Hinnawi's coup, apparently seeking revenge against Zaim for the latter's role in sending SSNP founder Saadeh to Lebanon for execution. However, Hinnawi's coup had been supported by Iraq, and Shishakli feared that Hinnawi and his pro-Iraq allies were prepared to sacrifice Syria's independence to Baghdad. These considerations formed the background to Shishakli's own coup.

Shishakli assumed the title and office of president only in the final months of his four-year ascendancy (July 1953–February 1954), although throughout he had the final say in Syrian governments by maintaining control of key ministries and the army through his protégés. Because the People's Party dominated the constitutional assembly, it continued to provide personnel for leading government ministries, but the armed forces now lay outside of the civilian cabinet's authority. The People's Party were pro-Iraqi, and had received help and support from the Iraqi government, but the party's advocacy of Syrian–Iraqi unity was stymied by the unpopularity of the Iraqi government among professed nationalists. Gradually the People's Party lost influence as Shishakli and his Hama-based allies, including Akram al-Hourani, kept Iraq unity plans at bay. Though like Hourani an early member of the SSNP, Shishakli after taking power sought to unify the army around him, not to turn the army into an instrument of the SSNP or any other party. Hourani, in the meantime, began to advocate for progressive social policies on an Arab, not merely Syrian national, level.

As the People's Party and the pro-Iraqi tendency that it represented declined in power and influence, Hourani consolidated a political base of his own by reviving his anti-landowner Arab Socialist Party in 1950. This was the context for the merger of his Arab Socialist Party with the Baath in 1952, automatically delivering to the unified grouping his rural base in the Hama region. Henceforth the full name of the merged organization would be (and remains to this day) the Arab Baath Socialist party.

Tensions grew between Shishakli and the army, on one hand, and the civilian politicians on the other. Public issues and disagreements focused mainly on the People's Party's ties to Iraq and its sponsor, Britain. Opposition to the People's Party, including royal Egypt, Saudi Arabia, Syria's ideological movements, and the exiled Quwatli's National Party, was resolved in favor of the army when Shishakli launched a second coup of his own in November 1951. Shishakli acted, for the time being, with the support of the army and Syria's ideological movements and parties (the Muslim Brotherhood, the Baath, Hourani's Socialists and the SSNP). Henceforth the civilian politicians had to live with the army as a political actor. The idea of the army 'returning to barracks' was far removed from the country's realities.

Shishakli ran Syria as a military dictatorship, though mostly from behind the scenes while his protégés acted as government front men. In conjunction with Hourani, he initiated a series of anti-landlord reforms. Enunciating a nationalist line, the government also announced restrictions on foreign institutions and schools. To quell potential opposition the Muslim Brotherhood was outlawed.

His origins in the Syrian nationalist SSNP notwithstanding, Shishakli drifted more and more toward an ideological Arabism. He wanted to leverage his base in the army to become master of the country's political situation, not to be a servant to one of the existing parties. On 25 August 1952, Shishakli announced the formation of a one-party model to be called the Arab Liberation Movement, declaring:

> The Arab Liberation Movement is not a new party to be added to the list of old parties to confuse the nation and divide its forces. It is a loyal and sincere attempt to regroup the good elements from all parties and all classes, to forge them into a single powerful bloc, fully capable of restoring the nation's confidence, and give the country a voice which is listened to and respected.[4]

Shishakli went on to assert that Syria was the epicenter of the Arab idea and would be in the vanguard of Arabs seeking to undo the corrupt leaders who had betrayed the Palestinians. To this end, Damascus radio became a propaganda instrument broadcast to neighboring Arab countries. Shishakli was anticipating some of the themes that would soon become the stock-in-trade of Gamal Abdul Nasser (d. 1970), who emerged from the Egyptian military coup of 1952 to become president of Egypt two years later. But Syria, unlike Egypt, was in no position to project any kind of power or authority outside of or beyond its frontiers.

Meanwhile, Shishakli became consumed with power and drifted away from his earlier backers. In December 1952 his General Staff announced the unearthing of a 'plot' against the regime and a crackdown on political opposition. This is the moment when the ideological parties who earlier had welcomed Shishakli's disbanding of the older parties became, themselves, potential victims of Shishakli's intelligence services. It marked a break between him and the Baath, which now included Hourani's Socialist wing. Eventually tensions would rise between Shishakli and the nationalist parties.

Michel Aflaq (d. 1989), the French-educated Damascene schoolteacher who had co-founded the Baath, commented retrospectively that Shishakli's devotion to Syrian sovereignty (against Iraqi ambitions) was hedged about with conditions:

> Although [Shishakli] opposed union with Iraq, he was deeply committed to the Saudis, the Egyptians, and the French, and his independence was just as limited. French spokesmen, in particular, spoke of Shishakli as the champion of Syrian integrity, but this was because he played their game opposing Baghdad and thus the British.[5]

Shishakli assumed the presidency in July 1953, and proclaimed his devotion to Arab nationalism. Opponents including the Baath accused him of flirting with Washington-sponsored defense plans that aimed to supplant the British-led Hashemite Arab bloc (Iraq and Jordan) with an American-led bloc that would include Egypt and Saudi Arabia. In July 1953 opposition parties and personalities held a secret meeting in the Atassi family's bastion of Homs to plot Shishakli's downfall. Taking part were representatives of the old-line National and People's Parties, the communists and the Baath. A significant geographic center of opposition to Shishakli was the Jabal Druze (officially renamed in the independence era as Jabal al-Arab, the 'Arab mountain'). The clan-based leadership in the Druze community had friendly ties to the Hashemites of Jordan, where veteran nationalist Sultan al-Atrash had taken refuge for a decade after the suppression of the 1925–7 anti-French revolt.

Shishakli saw the Druzes as a thorn in his side, and as obstacles to his program of authoritarian centralization. Doubting the loyalty of Druze army officers, he posted them to the remote Deir ez-Zor garrison near the Iraqi border. In Shishakli's era the Jabal Druze was starved of public investment as Syria's agriculture flourished in other regions. Non-Druze functionaries were assigned to administer the Jabal, and the government suppressed the region's lucrative hashish trade with Jordan. An Atrash-led anti-government uprising in January 1954 was fiercely suppressed by government troops and artillery. No longer could irregular forces challenge the government's army, whose size grew dramatically during Shishakli's rule.

The Egyptian military regime supported Shishakli against the Druzes, attributing unrest in the Jabal Druze to British and Hashemite machinations. Not for the last time, official Egyptian commentary used sectarian language to characterize events in Syria. Cairo radio declared:

> The Druzes are a sect. They are not Arab; they are not Arab in any way. The Druzes hate the Arabs. The Druzes have their own beliefs. They are servants of the British and Jews in Israel. The Druzes are traitors, enemies of Islam, friends of Israel.[6]

Whereas pan-Arab nationalists like the Baath insisted that Arab nationalism could bridge confessional differences by emphasizing culture and language as criteria of national inclusion, Cairo's commentary highlights other uses of pan-Arabism, as being equivalent to Arab-Sunni identity.

In February 1954 a military insurrection based in the Jabal Druze, Homs and Aleppo overthrew Shishakli. The anti-Shishakli military conspirators had Iraqi support and funding. His removal inaugurated a new era of political uncertainty. Parliamentary government was restored and the most democratic elections in the Arab world up to that time were held in September 1954. But the ensuing governments were precarious. The army officer corps was factionalized, and had grown accustomed to wielding political power. The public jousting of the political parties hid their more surreptitious struggle for political influence within the officer corps.

The 1954 elections revealed a new balance of public political forces in Syria. The traditional parties that had grown out of the National Bloc, namely Quwatli's National Party and the Aleppo–Homs based People's Party, declined. The Baath won a large number of seats, their merger with Hourani's party having handsomely paid off. Khalid al-Azm, an independent nationalist who was open to working with the communists, emerged at the head of a bloc of independents willing to follow his lead. The communists and the SSNP also won a single seat each. While the old politicians were not yet finished, they were no longer driving events. The ideological parties, boosted by their alliance with factions of the officer corps, were in the ascendant even though none could claim broad-based support across the length and breadth of Syria.

Political life in the following years was boisterous. Pent-up demands for workers' rights and national demands for higher revenues from the foreign (principally British) owned Iraq Petroleum Company were major internal issues. But overshadowing everything was Syria's growing entanglement in the US–Soviet Cold War. The shaky Syrian state, weak and internally divided, became the object of a fierce and highly polarizing struggle that centered around superpower rivalry and the issue of an alliance treaty called the Baghdad Pact.

SYRIA IN THE COLD WAR

In 1955 the US was growing increasingly alarmed at the USSR's diplomatic inroads in the Arab world. Both Syria and Egypt, dissatisfied with their erstwhile colonial arms suppliers France and Britain, respectively, purchased weapons from the Soviet bloc. In response, the US began to push for a pro-Western anti-Soviet alliance system in the Middle East whose Arab anchor would be Britain's most significant remaining Arab client state, Hashemite Iraq. Egyptian President Nasser interpreted the Baghdad Pact alliance proposal as an Anglo–American attempt to isolate Egypt and to curtail Cairo's regional influence.

Nasser had made Egypt part of the non-aligned movement established at Bandung, Indonesia in 1955. In the eyes of Nasser and his supporters, the US-backed Baghdad Pact was a symbol of neocolonialism, a replacement of direct colonial rule with new patterns of dependency on the Western powers. This Egyptian viewpoint resonated in Syria and captured the imaginations of large numbers of nationalists. Nasser's reputation soared after Egypt withstood a combined British, French and Israeli attack in October 1956 (the Suez War, or second Arab–Israeli war) aimed at overthrowing his government after Nasser's nationalization of the Suez Canal in July. Caught off guard by the tripartite attack, and embarrassed by a textbook case of old-style imperialism, the US joined with the USSR in demanding the withdrawal of the invading armies.

As Nasser's reputation rose, so too did the strength and visibility of Syria's communists. The growth of communist influence among the public and in parts of the army raised fears among the Baath that they risked being outflanked on the left and in response they tightened their affiliation to Nasser and Egypt. Nasser had formed a partnership with the USSR but on his own terms, demanding the dissolution of

Egypt's communist party. Egypt's regional reputation was enhanced after Bandung and especially after the Suez War. Fearing that Syria was on the road to 'going communist' (arms deals, economic agreements championed by Syrian communists and their most important non-communist ally, Khalid al-Azm), the US in 1957 tried in cooperation with Iraq to overthrow the Syrian government and ensure the triumph of pro-US, pro-Western forces in the country. These US efforts at subversion were part of a wider goal, enunciated in the 1957 Eisenhower Doctrine, of supporting Middle Eastern countries that faced threats from the USSR or from 'international communism.'

Tensions in Syria ramped up, fanning the flames of political paranoia, mistrust and recriminations. Syria had become a contested prize in the Cold War, and power struggles went on within the officer corps and among the political class. For a time the Baath and the communists were in alignment regarding policy. Fundamentally, though, the two were rivals appealing to similar constituencies, and the Baath drew closer to Nasser in a bid to bolster their position. Meanwhile the SSNP, fiercely anti-communist, had been implicated in the assassination of an important pro-Baath, pro-Nasser military figure in 1955. (He was Adnan al-Malki, who as a 'martyr' to the nation was buried in a tomb in a posh western neighborhood of Damascus, subsequently named after him.) Though ideologically at odds, the SSNP and the pro-British Iraqi monarchy made common cause to overturn the pro-Nasser and communist currents in Syria.

Events of the first decade of Syrian independence underscored the weaknesses of the Syrian state and the absence of a definitive sense of Syrian nationhood. Political personalities and parties appealed to outside powers to undermine their rivals. Civilian politicians and army officers mistrusted one another, and officers too were split into contesting factions who looked to sources outside of Syria for support. Though nation-building – the construction of a national economic infrastructure, and the incorporation of wider segments of the population into political life – scored some gains, these did not outweigh the centrifugal political and social forces that stymied the consolidation of a clear Syrian nationhood. And this was made worse still by Syria increasingly becoming seen as a pawn or a prize in regional and Cold War struggles and rivalries. In short, Syria enjoyed neither popular legitimacy nor was able to articulate and defend a national interest. Within a short time it would cease to exist altogether.

EGYPT ANNEXES SYRIA AGAIN: THE UNITED ARAB REPUBLIC

In this fraught environment veteran nationalist Shukri al-Quwatli returned to the presidency in 1955. As Syria's crises deepened, he presided over a military-driven

movement to deliver Syria into the hands of Nasser and Egypt, a remarkable surrender of sovereignty and independence that was supported especially by the Baath
and opposed by the communists. Syrian military officers took the initiative, leaving
Quwatli to play catch-up.

Though Syrian advocates of union wanted a federated state, Nasser was wary of
Syria's fractured political scene. While the newly proclaimed United Arab Republic
featured an appointed Syrian regional government, and Akram al-Hourani became
one of the UAR's vice presidents, the union was clearly on Nasser's terms. Egyptians
commanded most key government ministries. The state's capital was Cairo. Egypt
governed Syria through the security services, and the pro-Nasser head of Syria's
military intelligence, Abdel-Hamid al-Sarraj (d. 2013), dominated the Syrian scene.
Wary of Sarraj's ambitions, Nasser eventually brought him to Cairo and replaced
him in Syria in 1960 with an Egyptian loyalist, Vice President and General Abdel
Hakim Amer (d. 1967), who became in effect Nasser's plenipotentiary in Syria.

The UAR introduced Syrians to the twentieth-century police state, a legacy
that would mark the country from then on. Resenting their powerlessness, Syrian
civilian politicians who had advocated for union with Egypt broke with Nasser.
Hourani went his own way in 1959, and the Baath – deprived of any effective power
in a union they had championed – began to fragment. The UAR leadership in turn
suppressed all the old political parties. In doing this Nasser was simply repeating
the formula that he had implemented in Egypt: do away with the old, quarreling
and 'corrupt' political parties and replace them with a unitary one-party state that
(purportedly) would create national unity and promote the country's social and
economic development.

Nasser and his associates did not trust the politicized Syrian officer corps. Syrian
army officers with Baathist ties were transferred to Egypt where they could be closely
watched. A group of them in 1959 formed a clandestine Military Committee, which
in the following decade became an important instrument in Syrian political history.
One of its members was an air force officer named Hafez al-Assad (d. 2000). In the
meantime, though, the UAR reduced the number of Syrian officers in the unified
state's army, and transferred the Syrian military academies to Cairo.

To add insult to injury, Syria was treated as an economic colony of Egypt.
Egyptian goods were freely allowed into Syria but Syrian goods going the other way
were taxed or restricted. The UAR regime saw Syria as an agricultural region whose
economic activities should serve the interests of the Egyptian metropole, much
the way Britain had regarded colonial India. Syrian merchants and business people were forced to import from Egypt, not from other suppliers. Cairo introduced
exchange controls in 1961, precipitating a flight of Syrian capital abroad.

In addition to subjecting Syrians to the modern police state and economic servitude, the UAR also brought Syria's first land reform law (1958) and Nasser's nationalization decrees in July 1961. The former was modeled on one in Egypt, and it did not reflect Syrian conditions where much agriculture was extensive and rain fed. Nonetheless, it established the principle of limits to individual landholding and the distribution of title to qualified cultivators. Where land was redistributed, cultivators would establish state-supported agricultural cooperatives to provide the credit, seeds, and so on, that landlords previously had supplied. Actual implementation of the land reform law during the UAR period was patchy, but it did create pockets of pro-Nasser political sympathy among agriculturalists of the Houran and the Jazira. Land reform also had the effect of reducing the political power of landlords. Once their control over villages and village life was curtailed, landlords lost some of the political clout that they had enjoyed under various government systems, from the Ottomans through the French, through the first decade of independence. As it happened, the land reform law and the period of union with Egypt coincided with a severe drought in the Syrian countryside, a hardship that became associated with the law in the minds of many.

Nasser's July 1961 nationalization decrees affected banks, insurance companies and selected industrial firms in Syria. The Syrians harmed were 'national' capitalists, not absentee foreign owners. The rationale of the nationalization decrees (in both the Egyptian and Syrian regions of the UAR) was to supplant profit-driven private capitalists with a 'socialist' system that could be counted on to meet the patriotic goals of national economic development. Nationalizations aimed to deprive private capital of its political power, to transfer economic decision making authority to state officials, and to extend state authority to include workers' unions in nationalized enterprises, since now all of them were public employees. There was little time to implement these decrees in Syria before the secessionist coup of September 1961, but they set a precedent for government intervention in the economy that would be renewed shortly thereafter.

SECESSION

Nasser was impatient to hasten Syria's restructuring, and remained suspicious of Sarraj's lingering power base in the Syrian region even after he had transferred him to Egypt. Therefore Nasser abolished the Syrian regional administration in August 1961 and broke up the country into a number of discrete governorates that answered directly to Cairo. (In this the celebrated Arab nationalist was following in the footsteps of the French colonial authority, who also had worked to fragment Syria administratively and politically.) Capitalizing on the unhappiness that UAR policies had produced, a group of rebellious Syrian army officers confronted Nasser's plenipotentiary Amer in his Damascus headquarters in September 1961. They demanded a renegotiation of the union. Amer seemed willing to engage but he did not have the final word; Nasser did.

Initially Nasser wished to crush the rebellious officers, but when he issued orders he discovered that he had no loyal forces in Syria willing to obey him and march on Damascus to quash the coup. Nasser grudgingly accepted the secession as a *fait accompli* but he unleashed a fierce propaganda campaign against the officers and politicians who assumed power in Damascus, now once again the capital of a sovereign state. Though many Syrians had supported Syria's withdrawal from the UAR, Nasser was particularly angry with the Baath, erstwhile supporters of union whom he now accused of 'betrayal.' It was a rocky beginning to Syria's final episode of pluralistic parliamentary life, and it did not end well.

The architects of the September 1961 military coup made a show of withdrawing from public political life, but they remained active in the background in the run-up to the December 1961 elections. Cairo called on Syrians to boycott the elections, but turnout was relatively high. Parties were officially banned, but factions and groupings were identifiable nonetheless. The Baath were shut out, whereas Hourani (who had distanced himself from the Baath) and his candidates did well. So too did the political independent and industrialist Khalid al-Azm, whose reputation was enhanced by his unyielding opposition to the UAR project. Candidates affiliated with the old-line People's Party and National Party also won seats, and People's Party candidates were selected for the presidency and premiership.

The 'secessionist' government undid many of the UAR nationalizations. Nasser's government supported two coup attempts in 1962, which failed to overturn the government but added to the sense of political fragility and insecurity in post-UAR Syria. The Syrian officer corps once more became embroiled in factional partisan politics. The Baath fragmented as the historic civilian leadership of Aflaq and Salah al-Din al-Bitar (d. 1980, like Aflaq a Damascene schoolteacher) expelled Hourani from the party's ranks. The Baath Military Committee, operating separately from the civilian leadership, extended its networks of influence in the officer corps. Azm and Hourani spearheaded public campaigns to bring an end to emergency laws and to fully restore free constitutional and associational life in the trades unions. In September 1962 Azm became prime minister, pre-Baathist Syria's last, since he was the candidate who was most acceptable to the spectrum of elected representatives.

The Baathist military coup in March 1963 brought down the curtain on this phase of Syria's political life. At the time it seemed to be just one more military intervention in a country that had experienced many since 1949. Khalid al-Azm became a kind of symbolic bookend for the collapse of multiparty constitutional life in Syria. He had been ousted as prime minister by Husni al-Zaim's first military coup in 1949, and the Baathist coup of 1963 ousted him again. Post-independence Syria's most respected and durable statesman died in exile in Beirut two years later.

THE BAATH TAKES POWER

The new Baath regime was insecure. It enjoyed no political legitimacy, arising as it had from a conspiratorial coup d'état. Nasser and his propaganda apparatus kept up a relentless campaign against the Baath, questioning their Arab nationalist credentials and inciting Syrians to reject them. Pro-Nasser officers in the Syrian army vainly attempted a counter-coup. The Baath itself was divided between a civilian apparatus that dominated public offices and positions, and a secretive military apparatus rooted in the Military Committee and their supporters. In terms of the structure of the party, allies of the civilian leadership, including cofounders Aflaq and Bitar, dominated the party's 'National' (= pan-Arab) Command, while the 'Regional' (= Syrian) Command was controlled by the Military Committee. Mirroring the makeup of the Military Committee, men of rural and non-Sunni background dominated the Regional Command. Alawites were especially prominent but they were not the only ones.

The principal figure in the Regional Command was Salah Jadid (d. 1993). He was an Alawite officer who had been stationed in Cairo during the UAR period. Because the Baath had come to power by conspiracy, and military factions were critical to the power struggles that unfolded afterward, politically powerful military officers like Jadid built up their personal clienteles and recruited supporters into the armed forces. This had the effect of making region, clan, tribe and sect key elements of political organizing in the post-1963 Baath.

The new Baath regime was widely disliked in the major inland cities. Historically these were the centers of Syrian commerce, and in the independence period old-line nationalists had dominated them politically. In May 1963 the new regime renationalized the banks, sparking capital flight and bankruptcies. Facing a revenue crisis, the government reduced expenditures, adding to public unhappiness. By 1964 the economic malaise was widespread, and anti-government protests were spreading. Protests were organized and supported by an unstable coalition of Nasserists and

Muslim Brothers. Meanwhile, in some countryside regions peasants complained of government inaction on the declared goals of land reform.

More and more, opponents of the Baath regime (Nasserists and Muslim Brothers alike) portrayed it as a 'regime of minorities', and Radio Cairo (reviving an argument it had used against the Druzes in 1954) suggested that the Baathists were not even Arabs. Sectarian rhetoric in and around Hama was particularly sharp. In April 1964 Muslim leaders in the town invoked symbols of jihad in their struggle, and raised the slogan 'Islam or the Baath'.[7] Armed clashes erupted in the old city between pro- and anti-government forces. The government's use of artillery against a venerable mosque in old Hama became a key symbol in raising religious opposition against the Baath government in other parts of the country. Baathist Druze officers were said to have been especially eager to repay Hama for the suffering that Shishakli and his Hama-dominated inner circle had inflicted on the Jabal Druze ten years before.

The new regime's insecurity promoted clannish and sectarian behavior in efforts to bolster its position. Although the party's rhetoric avoided overt sectarian or tribal references – preferring to frame conflicts in the language of progressive or revolutionary Baath nationalists versus traitorous and reactionary enemies – the fact that power came from the barrels of guns, and that the party and military were factionalized, meant that political actors recruited support from where they thought it to be most reliable. For the Alawite and Druze officers who had major voices in the Military Committee, recruitment occurred among kith, kin and reliable elements bound by personal and communal ties. The ruralization of the armed forces proceeded apace. In a country that was developing a culture of coups, different factions within the armed forces jostled for the upper hand. Rhetorical or ideological abstractions were less important in these kinds of calculations than primordialist and clientelist ties of loyalty.

In March 1964 a major purge of the armed forces occurred as members of the Baath Military Committee weeded out politically unreliable officers. Those affected – either discharged or transferred to marginal posts – were predominantly Sunnis, a development that added fuel to opposition accusations about the minoritarian (anti-Muslim, even anti-Arab) nature of the regime. Such arguments conflated Arab identity with Sunni identity, a persistent undercurrent in the development of twentieth-century Arab nationalism comparable to Irish nationalists' conflation of Gaelic ethnic and Catholic religious identities. Against anti-government violence, a 'Labor Militia' led by an Ismaili Baathist fought back against the Hama protesters.

The urban bourgeoisie and big landowners were against the regime. Feeling they had little to gain by temporizing, the Baath moved in a more radical direction.

The party's rural-dominated Regional Command set the tone. In fall 1964 the government resumed implementation of land reform. On new year's day 1965 it announced a wave of nationalizations of virtually all modern industries. Other nationalizations followed including utilities and foreign trade. More army purges ensued, with Alawites and Druzes replacing Sunnis who were suspected of wavering or of being sympathetic to disparate forces of the opposition. The nationalizations offered new patronage opportunities, as managerial and administrative positions could now be thrown open to clients of the Regional Command.

These policy initiatives deepened the split within the Baath between the old guard of Aflaq and Bitar, who were taken aback by the rapid dispossession of the country's old commercial classes, and the radicals of the Regional Command whose principal representative was Salah Jadid. The President of Syria, General Amin al-Hafez (d. 2009, a Sunni from Aleppo), was aligned with the National Command and he sought to promote his protégés and allies. Internal tensions in the Baath reached a breaking point when Jadid and the Regional Command launched a coup against Amin al-Hafez, party cofounders Aflaq and Bitar, and the National Command in February 1966.

The old guard of the Baath were gone, forced into exile. A Sunni ally of the Regional Command, Nureddin al-Atassi (d. 1992, a radical member of the prominent Homs family), became president. The Regional Command of Salah Jadid and his allies, including air force commander Hafez al-Assad, took the reins. They declared the old National Command to be illegitimate and replaced it with a new National Command molded in the Regional Command's image. (Henceforth the Syrian Baath's National Command had no independent institutional power. It followed the Regional Command's dictates and operated pro-Syrian Baath parties in other Arab countries.) The 1966 coup opened a phase of Syria's political history, lasting until November 1970, usually referred to as the ascendancy of the Neo-Baath.

THE NEO-BAATH

The Neo-Baath decisively took power away from urban people and set out to remake Syrian society. Many of its governing measures were typical of those where administrations seek to overcome the heritage of underdevelopment *and* to develop new constituencies of support. The Neo-Baath promoted the expansion of education and the development of economic infrastructure, including railways and major dam projects whose promise was to produce electricity and allow reclamation of farmland. Principal beneficiaries of these policies would be people from rural and small-town backgrounds, who now would have better access to formal education and whose rural communities were promised electrification. To mobilize support the Neo-Baath encouraged and organized 'general unions' (of peasants, workers, students, women) both to act as instruments of government and party influence, and to strengthen the presence of the party among various elements of the population. In this way, urban bourgeois and landlord opposition (including the Muslim Brotherhood) could be sidelined.

Under the Neo-Baath new elements of the population were brought into the 'political nation,' no longer synonymous solely with urban merchants and land-lords who had set the tone since the later Ottoman period. Ambitious young people of rural and small-town origins saw opportunities that their parents could only have dreamed of. Also, in keeping with the liberationist spirit of the times, the Neo-Baath argued that the emancipation of women was an important revolutionary value, and the party's women's organization advocated for their greater participation in public life. Sometimes these aspirations collided with populations whose values (especially in rural and small-town settings) were deeply patriarchal. But the argument that the 'strength of the nation' depended on improvement in women's status seemed no less useful in the 1960s than it had been in the 1920s, but now with reference to deeper swathes of the population beyond prosperous urban elites.

Although Baathist rhetoric denounced 'tribalism,' realities of life in the Jazira and elsewhere meant that alliances with key tribal or clan figures were needed to get things done locally, and this affected recruitment to the party and its organizations. Moreover, the core leadership of the Neo-Baath depended on clan and tribal patterns of recruitment and loyalty. To give the Neo-Baath its due, the party's principals and advocates did have a vision of a transformed society, more progressive and egalitarian than any Syria had known. But the top-down structures that they constructed did not challenge deeply rooted social conservatism. The Baathists' conspiratorial reflexes prevented the development of democratic traditions useful for discussing and treating persistent problems and challenges – to the contrary. Therefore, difficult or contentious issues were sidelined or suppressed rather than honestly confronted. Moreover, the party's reliance on patronage and connections meant that the kinds of 'corruption' that had characterized the old merchant–landlord establishment regimes were no less characteristic of the Neo-Baath setup. The beneficiaries of neo-Baathist policies tended mostly to be people of some stature in the small towns and rural areas, who grasped the opportunities offered to become important parts of the developing bureaucratic apparatus and patronage system. They were people much like the leaders of the Neo-Baath themselves, in terms of their socioeconomic backgrounds. Although the personnel and circumstances would change over time, patronage, clientage and primordial ties (kinship and confession) would remain leitmotifs of Baathist authoritarian rule from that point onward.

Jadid remained the power behind the scenes, in charge of the party apparatus of the Regional Command, while front men like President Atassi performed the public functions of government. Now people from modest (but not poor or landless) rural and small-town backgrounds were in charge. The rhetoric of the Neo-Baath was socialist and couched in the language of Global South solidarity, in keeping with the tenor of the times. They sought – and got – political credit for actions such as cutting off the (foreign-owned) Iraqi oil company pipeline across Syria until Syria received a higher royalty rate. The Neo-Baath spoke the rhetoric of radical Arab nationalism. With respect to Palestine – the Arab nationalist cause par excellence – they were second to none (including Nasser's Egypt) in their rhetorical support for the Palestinian cause and their material support for the recently emerged Palestinian armed resistance (guerrilla) movement led by Yasser Arafat (d. 2004) and the Fatah organization.

Jadid and the Regional Command faced factional opposition from those who had assisted the February 1966 coup but felt that they had not been duly rewarded. One of these was Salim Hatum, a Druze major who had played important roles in both the March 1963 and February 1966 coups. In September he attempted a coup of his own, but it failed. Hatum fled into exile and his army followers (mostly from the Druze community) were arrested and purged. After this, the only real powers to speak of in the Neo-Baath Regional Command and regime structure were Alawites.

Anyone seeking to gain or hold power in Syria needed to have military allies onside. Eventually, as we have seen, the military actors marginalized civilians in terms of who wielded actual power. Given the factional fragmentation inherent in this conspiratorial atmosphere, political–military actors built up loyal followings who would secure their positions and defend them in ensuing political struggles. This meant recruiting clients, who were most reliably cultivated among kith, kin, clan, tribe or sect – or combinations of all of these. When the Neo-Baath exercised power it did so in the name of Arab nationalism, and the public functions of administration were carried out by Syrians from a broad range of regional and confessional backgrounds. But the core elements of power – commanders of key military units, officers in charge of police and security services – were drawn from a narrower range of the population. After 1966 these were almost exclusively Alawites.

THE JUNE 1967 WAR

Despite growing homogeneity (i.e., Alawite and rural backgrounds) at the heart of the Neo-Baath regime, its experience of coups and intrigues were not yet finished. The outcome and consequences of the June 1967 Arab–Israeli war set the stage for a showdown between Salah Jadid, who wielded authority through the Regional Command with his control of the party apparatus, and Hafez al-Assad, defense minister during the Neo-Baath period. The outcome of their internecine power struggle set the template for Syria's political regime for the rest of the twentieth century.

Leading up to the June 1967 war were continued tensions between Israel and Syria in the 1949 demilitarized zones, and Syrian-supported Palestinian guerrilla attacks against Israel. The demilitarized zones were three small areas of former Palestine that had been left under Syrian army control in 1949. According to the armistice agreements, they were to be demilitarized and not incorporated into Israel. But the Israeli leadership saw these territories as 'unredeemed' portions of the homeland, and from time to time they would send armored bulldozers into them to clear land and to claim it for Jewish farmers, drawing Syrian military fire and endemic small-scale armed clashes along the front.

Partly as a response, and partly to demonstrate the regime's nationalist credentials (at a time when it faced significant internal opposition), Damascus supported Palestinian Fatah. Since 1965 Fatah had waged 'armed struggle' against Israel, typically from Jordanian-controlled territory in the West Bank. These attacks complicated Jordanian King Hussein's sensitive position and exposed his army to Israeli counterstrikes. Jordan's embarrassment was a bonus, from the Syrian government's point of view, since Damascus regarded him and his Hashemite Kingdom as reactionary vestiges of the old British colonial order, ripe for replacement by Baath-like 'revolutionaries.'

The Baath's support for Fatah was also a way for Damascus to show up Nasser. As the putative 'leader of the Arabs,' Nasser wanted to control the Palestine issue in a way that maximized the political benefit to Egypt and minimized the risk of a new war with Israel. His solution to this dilemma had been creation of the Palestine Liberation Organization under Arab League auspices in 1964. The PLO was intended mainly to be a political instrument, and Nasser supported it with generous doses of grandiloquent speechifying. Syria's support for Fatah guerrillas (who operated outside of the PLO framework) risked upstaging Nasser in the wider contest for Arab public opinion.

In November 1966 Nasser and the Neo-Baath signed an alliance, a surprising development in light of the mutual hostility between Nasser and the Baath since the 1961 Syrian secession. However, both parties expected benefits from the sudden reconciliation. Damascus believed that it was bringing Egypt closer to Syria's preferred strategy of escalating tensions with Israel in support of a 'people's war' that would produce Arab unity. Nasser believed that he was gaining authority over Syrian actions, and he would be able to stop Syria from behaving in ways that jeopardized Egyptian interests.

One reason for Nasser's reluctance to consider an outright military engagement against Israel was that some of the best units of the Egyptian army were nowhere near the Egyptian–Israeli border and armistice lines. Since 1962 Egypt had been bogged down in a difficult war in Yemen, in the Arabian Peninsula, supporting a pro-Nasser republican regime against its royalist enemies who were supported by Jordan, Saudi Arabia and Israel.

But events developed their own dynamic. Israel held Syria responsible for Palestinian attacks. Syrian–Israeli tensions and clashes escalated. Rhetoric from Israeli leaders, and a warning from Nasser's Soviet allies, convinced the Egyptian president that Israel was preparing to deal a major blow against Syria. Determined to assert Egypt's regional leadership (and sensitive to taunts from his Arab enemies, including Jordan, that Egypt was all talk and no action), Nasser closed the Straits of Tiran to Israeli shipping (an act of war, reversing an arrangement that had been made at the end of the 1956 Suez War). He ordered the UN force present in the Sinai Peninsula since 1956 to withdraw. War fever gripped the Arab countries, and Jordan's King Hussein felt compelled to sign onto the Egyptian–Syrian alliance against Israel at the end of May 1967.

The main question now was, would the crisis be de-escalated by diplomacy, or would it explode into open war? After receiving assurances from back channels in Washington that Israel would not be diplomatically isolated if it took the first military move, the Israeli air force and army launched a 'preemptive' war against the Arab states on 5 June 1967. With their air forces destroyed in the first wave of attacks, there was little that the Arabs could do militarily. The Egyptian and Jordanian armies were consecutively defeated, and in the final days Israel's forces scaled the Syrian Golan Heights. In addition to their loss of air cover, the Syrian forces were hobbled by politicization of the officer corps and the endemic purges of preceding years. Damascus radio wrongly reported that Israel had captured the regional administrative center of Quneitra before it fell, sowing panic in the ranks of Syrian front-line forces who feared they had been cut off. Nothing stood between the Israeli army and Damascus when the ceasefire came into effect on 10 June 1967.

In the Gaza Strip, East Jerusalem and the West Bank, Israel took over thickly settled Palestinian populations – both original residents and refugee populations from the 1948–9 war. Occupation of Egypt's Sinai Peninsula gave Israel control of the Straits of Tiran waterway (whose closure by Egypt had been a precipitating factor in the war) and control of the eastern bank of the Suez Canal. Eleven years after Nasser's celebrated nationalization of it, the Suez Canal was now closed. (It did not reopen until 1974, in the wake of yet another Arab–Israeli war.) Israeli occupation of the Gaza Strip, East Jerusalem and the West Bank meant that all the lands of the erstwhile Palestine mandate were administered once again from Jerusalem. Israel became, *de facto*, the sole successor state of the old Palestine mandate. Israel's capture of the Syrian Golan Heights secured the Jewish state's northeastern flank and placed the Israeli army within striking range of Damascus. In the Golan Heights most of the Syrian population fled or were expelled, though the populations of four Druze villages were permitted to remain under Israeli rule.

The outcome of the war was a grievous blow to the Neo-Baath. Recriminations flew back and forth. The defeat provoked a sharp internal debate about future policies. Arguments around policy became polarized between the military and the party leadership, personified respectively by Defense Minister Hafez al-Assad and Regional Command Secretary-General Salah Jadid. Both men had been stalwarts of the Neo-Baath against the old, historic Baath leadership. Both were Alawites who had risen to power in the military, although Jadid had retired from the military in 1965 and now wielded power through the party apparatus.

Jadid and the civilian party leadership argued for a radicalization of policy. The proper response to the defeat, they believed, was to deepen the popular and revolutionary aspects of society at home, and to prepare for a 'people's war' against Israel that would sound the death-knell of 'Arab reaction.' Quaint as all this may sound from the perspective of today, the world of 50 years ago was different. Popular revolutions against colonialism and imperialism were leitmotifs of struggles in Algeria, Vietnam and elsewhere. Activists and thinkers attracted to varieties of Global South solidarity, Castroism and/or Maoism believed these to be the wave of the future, and to be the only sure way for 'the masses' to defeat their imperialist and colonialist enemies.

In contrast, Assad and his supporters argued for policies of (in their estimation) pragmatism and realpolitik. The sobered military did not wish to be dragged into further misadventures. The idea of waging a popular war against Israel and against 'Arab reaction' was an illusion that would likely result in further catastrophic misfortunes, given the balance of forces regionally and internationally. Instead, Assad argued for strengthening the capability of the Syrian state and its armed forces, for bridging the urban and rural divide by seeking conciliation with at least some of the country's commercial interests, and for working with other Arab states (regardless of their ideological coloring) and with international powers and institutions (the superpowers and the UN) to undo the consequences of the 1967 defeat.

Coordinated Arab state action to undo the consequences of 1967 was programmatically and philosophically quite different from the idea of inspiring a people's war to liberate Palestine and bring down Arab reaction. The tension between Assad and Jadid and their respective viewpoints played out with increasing urgency from October 1968 onward. Assad effectively took the armed forces out of the supervision of the Regional Command, declaring, 'I do not recognize this political leadership!'[8] In February 1969 he sacked Jadid's allies from the major party and government newspapers. Jadid still controlled the party apparatus and a powerful armored brigade near the capital, but Assad controlled the bulk of the military. He also began quietly to cultivate mercantile circles, especially in Damascus, who had been wrong-footed and alienated by Baath nationalizations. The duality of power between the party and army created a situation where government and party posts were in the hands of Jadid and his allies, including President Nureddin al-Atassi, but most of the military answered to Assad.

In February 1969 forces loyal to Assad arrested members of the Latakia branch of the party, and Assad tried to sever connections between the Regional Command and local party organizations in other provinces. The party's auxiliary organizations rallied to the civilian leadership's side, resulting in a prolongation of the political standoff for most of the remainder of the year. Jadid and the party leadership tried to strengthen their position by organizing a client Palestinian militia that would answer to the Regional Command, but Assad's army closed all branches of the militia (called al-Saiqa) in August 1970. (Subsequently, when Assad consolidated power, he revived Saiqa as an instrument of Syria's Palestinian policy.)

In September 1970, the Regional Command ordered Palestinian regular units of the Syrian army (the 'Palestine Liberation Army') to intervene in northern Jordan where Palestinian guerrillas were fighting pitched battles against the Jordanian army, a clash that became known as 'Black September.' But when Israeli or American aerial intervention threatened, Assad ordered the withdrawal of the Syrian-commanded forces. He argued that withdrawal was a realistic course; his opponents accused him of running away from the battlefield and from defense of the Palestinian cause (just as, they whispered, his defense ministry had abandoned the Quneitra battlefield in 1967).

The party–army contest came to a head in November 1970, when an emergency National Congress of the (pro-Syrian Baath) party ordered Assad to stop transferring officers deemed sympathetic to the party apparatus, excoriated him and his associates for flouting party discipline, and accused him of advocating a 'defeatist reactionary line.'[9] The Congress ordered the removal of Assad and his allies from their posts. In response, Assad launched a coup d'état on 16 November that disestablished the hostile party apparatus. The month before, Assad finally had gained control of a key powerful armored brigade near Damascus, so Jadid and the Regional Command had no effective military allies on which to rely. Jadid and Atassi were arrested, and their followers were purged. Assad and his allies became arbiters of what the Baath's policies and personnel would be. Jadid died in prison in 1993, and Atassi died shortly after being released from prison in 1994.

For the duration of Assad's rule, and continuing up to the present day under his son Bashar, the 16 November coup was called the 'Corrective Movement,' one in which the allegedly proper path of Baathist rule was restored. Party–army dualism ended; Assad and his allies now were in charge of everything. Hafez al-Assad stayed at the top of the heap for the rest of the twentieth century until his death in 2000.

CULTURAL LIFE IN A TIME OF TROUBLES

The political story of Syria in the 1950s and 1960s is therefore marked by repeated traumas and setbacks – coups, internal political violence, annexation by Egypt, defeat and territorial losses in war. Paradoxically, Syria's cultural presence loomed larger than it had in the preceding period. While it is true that, after World War II, Arabic mass media and cultural production continued to be centered in Egypt (because of its size and its head start in Arabic mass media) and in Lebanon (because of Beirut's liberal cultural and intellectual atmosphere), new Arabic literature from Syria found its footing in the 1950s and 1960s. The achievement of Syria's independence coincided with an upsurge in writers who reflected on the tumult and transformations that they and their country experienced. Many Syrians published in Beirut, given its proximity and well-developed literary infrastructure.

Two poets who gained audiences in Syria and beyond in this era were the Damascene Nizar Qabbani (d. 1998) and Ali Ahmad Said (b. 1930) from Latakia province, who publishes under the pen name Adonis. Qabbani's early poetry was in the romantic vein. He came to be regarded as Syria's unofficial 'national' poet, and his wide readership made him one of the most popular poets in the entire Arab world.[10] Though romantic poetry, almost by definition, dealt with personal feelings and relationships, social and political concerns were never absent from Qabbani's writing and became salient after the June 1967 defeat. Then and later his verse included caustic commentaries on the failings that had led Syria and other Arab societies to disasters and dead ends.[11]

Adonis is a central figure in the Arabic modernist movement. He was politically committed from a young age, identified as a supporter of the SSNP in the 1950s. Through his writings, editorial work and collaborations he has demonstrated a commitment to rethinking Arabic poetry and its relationship to society. Arabs required a revolution in consciousness, and language was the expression of consciousness. Though it can be overly simplistic to correlate cultural change directly with political events, the defeat of 1967 was a profound shock, and it amplified the critical consciousness of Adonis (and many other Arab intellectuals) regarding the pressing need for cultural and social transformations. His pen name hearkens back to the ancient Near Eastern resurrection myth of Tammuz or Adonis, signaling a quest for resurrection that incorporates and transcends both the recent and more distant pasts. In his work Adonis consciously invokes ancient myths and Sufi mysticism, and his oeuvre is central to any understanding of Arab literary and cultural modernism.

Qabbani lived the later years of his life in Beirut and London, while Adonis moved to Beirut in the 1950s and to Paris (where he has since remained) in 1975. Neither got on particularly well with Assad's state, but their international prominence meant that the government did not seek openly to stifle or repress them.

Notable Syrian-born novelists emerged in the 1950s and 1960s as well. Novels became vehicles for political and social commentary in tumultuous times. Hanna Mina (b. 1924) was born in Latakia and raised in humble circumstances, the son of itinerant sharecroppers who eked out livings on owners' estates. He began publishing short stories and novels in the 1940s. His most celebrated novel, translated into English as *Fragments of Memory*, came out in 1975. It is a novelized autobiography that depicts the hard lives of peasant families in the 1930s, one of the rare records of such lives written by someone who grew up living the experience. Mina has lived in Syria throughout his long career. Halim Barakat (b. 1936) was born in the Ansariyeh mountains above Tartous, and raised in Beirut. His most widely acclaimed novel appeared in Arabic in 1969, and was translated into English as *Days of Dust* a few years later. Literary critic Roger Allen called it 'one of the most effective commentaries on the 1967 debacle and its implications [...]. A monument of Arabic fiction written during [the twentieth] century.'[12] A third novelist of note whose publications became known in the 1950s and 1960s is Colette Khoury (b. 1931), granddaughter of National Bloc politician Faris al-Khoury. Her social commentary approached issues from a feminist vantage point. Her first novel, *The Days with Him* (1961), caused a stir because it was widely assumed to be an only slightly fictionalized account of an affair she had had with married poet Nizar al-Qabbani. Her bold promotion of individual female subjectivity that avoided pious moralizing represented a fresh (and to some, a shocking) literary departure. Khoury published regularly and prolifically in the years after that, giving voice to a woman's perspectives, thoughts and feelings in a patriarchal culture and society.

Syrian drama (theater) came of age in the 1960s, principally identified with the playwright Saadallah Wannous (d. 1997). Like novelist Halim Barakat, he was born in the Ansariyeh mountains near Tartous. Unlike Barakat, he spent most of his life and career in Syria after receiving theater training in Paris. His first major play was a critical social and political commentary born of the 1967 defeat, titled *An Evening's Entertainment for the 5th of June* (the starting date of the 1967 war). He went on to have a long career in Syria. He filled prominent positions in public cultural life, while maintaining theater as a source of critical commentary through the years of Hafez al-Assad's dictatorship.

Syrian cinema established a modest artistic foothold during the first two decades of independence. The first Syrian talkie was produced in 1947, and the popular burlesque comedies of actor–comedian Durayd Lahham were a staple of the 1960s. The new Baath regime established the National Film Organization in 1963, and six years later the NFO was given a monopoly on film production in Syria. Private ventures disappeared. The NFO's initial impact was felt in documentaries such as a 1970 paean to the Tabqa Dam project on the Euphrates river directed by Omar Amiralay (d. 2011). Amiralay went on to do many more documentaries, and his attitude toward conditions in Syria became increasingly critical. Documentaries made their way to television, and were a way of consciousness-raising or promoting the kinds of revolutionary or developmentalist changes befitting the ideological outlook of the Baath (socialist, revolutionary, etc.). The first NFO feature films to have a critical impact, and that would in time earn Syria a respected place in the world of Arab and international cinema, began to appear in the 1970s.

The work of Syrian writers and cultural producers in the first quarter century of independence offers another angle for exploring the work of nation-building. A nation is an idea held in common by a community of people who are bound together by a shared institutional life and who develop a sense of shared history and a common destiny. The Syrian state and the political life of Syria were unstable and unsettled, and the country even disappeared for three years under the rubric of the United Arab Republic. Yet amidst the tumult, Syrian writers and cultural workers built the foundations for expressions of a national culture, at least among a reading and listening public who through prose, poetry, radio and television could begin to imagine the arbitrary territorial legacy of the French Mandate as a nation state within a wider Arab environment.

Even so, the existence and salience of political fault-lines and of ethnic and inter-communal tensions pointed to acute vulnerabilities in the Syrian national project. These tensions and fault-lines included the uprooting of most of Syria's Jews, demonization of non-Sunnis in some renderings of Arab nationalism, interventions of outside powers in the country's politics, and reliance on primordial ties of clan and confession in the conspiratorial politics of the era. All of these phenomena underscore the continuing unsettled nature of Syria as a fragile national project. Assad's coup in 1970 began a new era, after which the Syrian state would appear stronger than ever before. Nevertheless, doubts about national identity and national cohesion continued to characterize Syria, along with sharp differences in Syrians' efforts to develop and to articulate a national culture.

7

THIRTY YEARS OF HAFEZ AL-ASSAD

UPRISING IN HAMA

Early in the morning of 3 February 1982, government forces 'combing' the old city of Hama for Muslim Brotherhood militants and their weapons fell into an ambush. They had come across the hideout of a significant local commander. Government reinforcements rushed in, and the Muslim Brotherhood commander called for a general insurrection in the city. As calls from the city's minarets rang out, hundreds of armed men arose, attacked symbols of government authority and besieged the local governor's headquarters. Facing a large-scale urban insurrection, the Damascus authorities treated Hama as a hostile city. Handpicked loyalist forces, drawn mostly from ranks of Syria's Alawites, fought to recapture the town using artillery and air power. As the militants took refuge in densely built-up parts of the old city, entire neighborhoods were destroyed in the indiscriminate fire. For two weeks after retaking the city, state forces moved through pulverized neighborhoods, looking for militants and taking revenge with summary executions of entire families. Thousands died. A news blackout kept these events from being known at the time, and only gradually did the word of them leak out. The Hama violence of 1982 marked the nadir of Hafez al-Assad's 30-year rule of Syria. After crushing the revolt, the government erected a large statue of the president at a major intersection on the outskirts of Hama, so that everyone approaching it by road from Damascus would understand who had won, and would internalize knowledge of the high cost of defiance. Independent Syria finally possessed a powerful state, only to see its weapons turned against Hama, which had been one of the nationalist bastions of the colonial era.

HAFEZ AL-ASSAD COMES TO POWER

From 1970 to his death in 2000, Hafez al-Assad constructed a durable authoritarian regime. He built it around him, his family, his Alawite community and his allies from a wider spectrum of Syrian society. During these years Assad's personal authority, and the patronage networks that he enabled, ensured the consolidation of a cohesive ruling group in Syria for the first time in the modern state's history. Unlike the 1950s and 1960s, when Syria was a coup-ridden pawn in regional and international power struggles, Assad's Syria projected power outside its frontiers (especially in Lebanon) and for a time became a key actor in Arab regional and Arab–Israeli politics. As part of his stabilization of rule and projection of power, Assad also consolidated and extended a police state model of governance that Syrians had first met during the 1958–61 union with Egypt. Assad's political opponents, Syrians who ran afoul of the regime and its control networks, or members of the regime elite who fell out of favor, bore the full impact of arbitrary and unaccountable police-state authority. Political opponents were subject to torture, extrajudicial killings and massacre.

Assad's bloodless coup in November 1970, followed by his March 1971 elevation to the presidency after a referendum, ushered in an initial five-year period when most Syrians actively supported him. His alliance with the private sector, and in particular with the (Sunni) merchants of Damascus, signaled that the era of nationalizations and Baathist campaigns against bastions of private property were over. Support of the merchant community, though not represented in a formal institutional way until many years later, gave the Assad presidency some ballast in the capital city. Likewise, Assad's coup allowed him to take over the Baath party apparatus and turn it into his personal instrument. Remaining Jadid loyalists, many of them Alawites, were purged from the officer corps and from party membership rolls.

Assad's monopolization of power brought an end to debilitating political factionalism in the officer corps, which helped to produce a new level of professionalism in the military that bore fruit during the October 1973 war with Israel. The Syrian and Egyptian armies caught Israel by surprise and held the upper hand in the early days of fighting, though by the time ceasefires were agreed Israel had taken the military initiative and captured more territory. But the October 1973 war was packaged as a political victory that added luster to Assad's reputation as a competent and responsible leader in time of war, in sharp contrast to the experience of 1967 (where Assad, as defense minister, bore a major share of responsibility for the loss of the Golan Heights and its administrative center of Quneitra). In US-brokered disengagement negotiations following the 1973 war, Israel evacuated Quneitra and Assad personally raised the Syrian flag there. It flew over a destroyed and demilitarized town in the shadow of Israeli hilltop observation posts in the occupied Golan Heights. Still, the October War was victory enough for the time being, and the government went on a spree of naming various buildings, institutions and places 'October' to capitalize on the achievement.

The 1973 war also marked the accumulation of fabulous wealth in the hands of Arab oil-exporting countries. Oil-producing countries in the developing world inside and outside of the Middle East, Arab and non-Arab alike, took control of production and pricing from the Western oil companies that had dominated the international industry until then. Though not yet a significant oil exporter, Syria benefited from oil producers' windfalls by seeing a dramatic increase in Arab aid and investment, and in remittances from Syrians working in oil-rich Arab countries.

Syria's role as a 'front-line state' (against Israel in 1973) gave it a political claim on Arab largesse. Assad's pragmatic approach to relations with other Arab countries meant that Syria now formed partnerships with Arab states based on interests not ideologies. The old Baathist (and Nasserite) rhetoric about 'progressive' versus 'reactionary' Arab states was shelved. Instead, Assad promoted Syria as being in the vanguard of the 'Arab cause', and Syria's relations with other Arab states were assessed solely through that prism. So in the first part of the 1970s, 'socialist' and republican Syria developed a workmanlike relationship with 'conservative' and monarchical Saudi Arabia, based on mutual self-interest enveloped in the rhetoric of Arab solidarity. The resulting flow of Arab private and state capital into Syria made more resources available for the public sector economy. The relative success of the 1973 war, in combination with rising incomes from relatives' remittances and from new business opportunities, redounded to Assad's benefit.

On the political scene, the early years of Assad's rule promised a degree of relaxation compared to what had come immediately before. Because Assad was relatively popular, it was mainly his avowed (and defeated) political opponents like Salah Jadid who suffered. Organized opposition (principally the Muslim Brotherhood) was weak and fragmented, not yet seen as a real threat. Indeed the regime's qualified pro-business stance undercut some of the traditional urban support for the Brotherhood. The organization broke into three. One group remained loyal to the older and more quietist leadership of Damascus, who favored efforts to Islamize society without directly confronting the regime. Another faction was loyal to an Aleppo-based leadership that presented itself as more assertive and willing to challenge the regime than the Damascus group. A third faction followed a militant leadership, based principally in Hama and called the Fighting Vanguard.

The ascent to the presidency of an Alawite naturally upset Sunni traditionalists, and Assad needed to tread carefully regarding this matter in view of the symbolism involved. So when a draft constitution failed to designate Islam as the official religion of Syria (in contrast to earlier constitutions and charters), protests in major urban centers (especially in Hama) drove home to Assad the necessity of a symbolic compromise. The final version of the 1973 constitution designated that the president of Syria must *always* be a Muslim. In 1972 Assad obtained a statement from a prominent Shiite Lebanese religious and political figure that Alawites were in fact Shiites, and therefore they were indeed Muslims. Assad was thereafter careful to perform the public role of a Muslim head of state: he attended mosque on major feast days and expressed support for the country's clerical establishment headed by the quietist Syrian–Kurdish Naqshbandi Sufi Sheikh Ahmed Kuftaro, Mufti of the Republic from 1964 until his death in 2004. Assad also forged an enduring alliance with prominent scholar Mohamed Said Ramadan al-Bouti, dean of the School of Islamic Sharia at Damascus University and preacher at the Umayyad Mosque. (Bouti would eventually die in a bomb attack in 2013.)

In addition to trying to defuse the symbolic religious issue, Assad also sought to neutralize political movements that had been competitors with the Baath for nationalist and progressive support in the 1960s. He orchestrated the creation of the Progressive National Front in 1972, which grouped together legal communist and Nasserite organizations into a political body that was formally represented in parliament and in government. According to the 1973 constitution, though, the Baath would always be the leader of state and society. Communists still enjoyed some support in Syrian society, but the Nasserites by this time were shell parties. The National Progressive Front was a convenient piece of window dressing and communists who could not abide working in subordination to Assad's Baath broke away from the official party and founded separate, illegal organizations.

In the regime's 'good years' of 1970–5 formation of the Front and the legalization of the smaller parties within it signaled that Assad was open to partnerships (as with the private sector) so long as there was no doubt regarding who the dominant partner was. Later, in response to criticism of Syria as a one-party dictatorship, Assad's defenders would cite the National Patriotic Front to argue that under his presidency Syria had institutionalized political 'pluralism.'

At the core of the regime were loyalists from Assad's family, clan and confessional community, plus a handful of trusted non-Alawite associates from the military and the Baath. Keenly aware of Syria's history of military coups, and the author or a major participant in three of them (1966, 1969, 1970), Assad was determined to 'coup-proof' his regime. He did so by ensuring that key striking units in and near Damascus were under the command of people related to him by tribal or clan affiliation, including by marriage. (These were the Makhloufs, the family of his wife Anisa.) Even in cases where the nominal commander of a key unit or military branch was not a kinsman or an Alawite, such units would typically have Alawite deputies whose authorization would be needed for non-routine deployments and operations. Headships of the country's multiple security and secret police services were similarly structured. Commanders of all key military units and of all intelligence and security services were bound to Assad personally. Moreover, the security services had overlapping responsibilities and they spied on each other as well as on society at large.

If the predominantly Alawite commanders of key units and of the security, intelligence and secret police agencies were the inner core of Assad's regime, a secondary (and more public) layer were his trusted associates from the military and the Baath. They were army men and civilians who had come up with Assad through party or military ranks. Reflecting the Baath's appeal to people of rural-notable and provincial background, they included a number of small-town Sunnis.

A third layer of regime loyalists who filled out government rosters were the senior members of the Baath party Regional Command. They controlled patronage, guided public policymaking and staffed high-ranking public offices. The Regional Command and the Baath in general were broadly representative of Syria's regions and its various Arab communities, but above all they were instruments for regime power. The Baath mustered loyalty to Assad and acted as a sounding board for those aspects of policy that Assad did not tend to personally. Representatives of this group were long-serving Regional Command member Zuhair Masharqa (d. 2007, also a vice president from 1984 to 2006) and the prime ministers of Syria (invariably Sunnis and longtime Baathists).

CHALLENGE OF THE MUSLIM BROTHERHOOD, 1976–82

The 'troubles' began around 1976 through a confluence of pressures and events when the general sense of wellbeing and optimism that had allowed Assad and his version of the Baath to enjoy a degree of popular acceptance came to an abrupt end. A cocktail of price inflation, a dropping off of Arab investment, flagrant corruption and profiteering by those at the heart of the regime, an unpopular intervention in Lebanon, and a violent anti-government insurgency expressed in Islamic terms all contributed to the disquiet.

Because the stability of the regime depended on its patronage networks, those at the center of power looked out for their clients in order to keep their loyalty. Although from time to time Assad or the state media would rail against such informal relationships or 'corruption,' in reality these commissions, payoffs and favors were what kept the system going. This state of affairs especially irked those in the cities who found that people with connections froze them out of lucrative opportunities. In the northern cities (Homs, Hama and Aleppo) unhappiness with the regime's 'injustice' and 'corruption' encouraged the growth of a militant faction of the Muslim Brotherhood, the Fighting Vanguard, who were impatient with the older, politically oriented Brotherhood leadership. Emphasizing that key people in the regime's power structure were Alawites, and claiming that the regime's Sunni faces (ministers, members of parliament) were mere window dressing, the Sunni militants characterized the Assad government as unjust and non-Islamic (referencing the widespread conviction that Islam stands for justice). Muslim Brothers therefore chastised Assad as the sectarian leader of a corrupt sectarian regime, representing a non-Muslim minority who were lording it over the majority. To Sunni militants, the Alawites were not Muslims at all, but (in the words of their clandestine newsletter) 'infidel Nusayris'[1] (in the modern context, as we have seen, a pejorative term for Alawites).

The Muslim Brotherhood articulated and drew upon deeper grievances than corruption. Merchant-landowners of the northern cities had played pivotal roles in the emergence of Syria during the mandate and in the early post-colonial years and, in the late 1940s and 1950s, the Aleppo-based People's Party had usually been the largest bloc in elected parliaments, while their key ally the Homs patrician Hashim al-Atassi had served as Syria's president periodically between 1936 and 1955. Populist, socially conservative Muslim movements had been a feature of Syria's old market towns since the demise of the Ottoman Empire decades before. These movements evolved into the Muslim Brotherhood, and the Islamists' increased militancy of the 1970s was symptomatic of the marginalization that northern urban interests had suffered since the 1960s.

In the first 15 years of independence, Aleppo and its hinterland had been among the most prosperous and lucrative regions of the country. Aleppo entrepreneurs had invested in the expansion of wheat and cotton cultivation in the Jazira. But these gains were jeopardized in the era of Baathist land reform. Aleppo was also a center of light industry, particularly textiles. The Baath nationalizations of the 1960s had hurt the northern merchants and industrialists. Beneficiaries of these changes were small-town and/or religious minority Baathists who had ridden the party and army to preeminence. These parvenus and 'upstarts' displaced the older, Sunni urban figures who had been a leading political class in Syria since late Ottoman times.

Assad's olive branches to the Syrian private sector, and especially to merchants, mainly focused on Damascus where the regime formed its strongest mercantile political alliances. As opposition to the Baath and Assad mounted from 1976 onward, the strongholds of opposition tended to be in the northern cities rather than in the capital.

Fueling consternation about the regime, and the assertion that it was 'non-Islamic' (for those who were open to such claims), was Assad's policy in Lebanon. The Lebanese state disintegrated as civil war broke out in 1975 between mostly Christian loyalist militias and predominantly Muslim opposition militias supported by Yasser Arafat's Palestine Liberation Organization. In this conflict, Baathist ideology and Syria's self-proclaimed role as 'champion of the Arab and Palestinian cause' should have placed it on the side of Lebanon's 'progressive' and 'Arab nationalist' forces and their Palestinian allies. Yet when Assad intervened militarily in 1976, it was to prevent the opposition militias and their Palestinian allies from scoring a military success against the Christian militias. Syrians inclined to view politics through sectarian lenses saw Assad's alliance with Lebanon's Christian loyalists as further evidence of his regime's non-Muslim character, and its 'betrayal' of the sacred Muslim and Arab nationalist Palestinian cause. The Muslim Brotherhood made political hay out of the sectarian interpretation of Assad's Lebanon intervention.

Most likely, though, Assad's intervention in Lebanon was designed to ensure that Syria, not Israel, would be the arbiter of events there. In the course of the next 15 years, Syria's struggle with Israel for regional influence, especially in Lebanon, formed the overarching strategic impetus of Assad's regional policies.

In the late 1970s the Fighting Vanguard of the Muslim Brotherhood escalated their armed campaign against what they called the 'Alawite regime.' They assassinated prominent Alawites in professional and public life, seeking to highlight the new status and powers enjoyed by members of the minority community. The use of violence was meant not only to draw attention to their viewpoint, but also to provoke a response that would further polarize society – in this case, between the regime's Alawite core and the broader Sunni population, especially the urban population. Predictably, as if following a script, the regime's security services fought violence with violence, terror with terror. The northern cities in particular turned into virtual battlegrounds, with gunfights, protest strikes, demolition of buildings, heavy-handed checkpoints and military raids becoming features of daily life. Syria's secret police forces and their prisons developed reputations for being among the world's worst and most brutal.

President Anwar Sadat of Egypt (d. 1981) endorsed and supported the sectarian, anti-Alawite rhetoric of Syria's militant opposition. Sadat had been stung by Syria's fierce criticism of his 'treasonous' separate peace treaty negotiated with Israel in

1978 and signed in 1979. Sadat publicly dismissed Syria's Baath regime as nothing more than a vehicle for Alawite interests:

> I was prepared [in the negotiations with Israel] to speak on behalf of the [Israeli-occupied Syrian] Golan. But no. Let these dirty Alawis speak for it. These are people who have lost all life's meaning. By God, let them face their people in Syria and let them solve it. We shall see what they will achieve. I could have brought them the Golan, but I am not responsible for it while the Alawis are in power […]. We all know what the Alawis are in the eyes of the Syrian people. The Syrian people will deal with them. Afterwards things will be different […]. [King] Faysal [of Saudi Arabia] told me that Hafiz al-Asad is Alawi and Baathist, and the one is more evil than the other.[2]

Sadat's denunciation of Alawites, which calls to mind Cairo's anti-Druze rhetoric in the Shishakli era, showed official Egypt working once again to fan the flames of sectarian difference in Syria.

In his pushback against these kinds of statements and claims, Assad declared that he was a Muslim, that true Islam respected all religions, and that he exercised authority not because of his confessional background, but because of his headship of the (secular) Baath party. Assad and his supporters denounced the sectarianism of their opponents, and denied that sectarian considerations played a part in the regime's exercise of power.

The campaign of tit-for-tat brutality between the regime and militants escalated in June 1979, when the Fighting Vanguard of the Muslim Brotherhood killed scores of unarmed military cadets in their barracks in Aleppo. A captain who was in league with the Brotherhood, Ibrahim Yusuf (d. 1980), summoned the cadets for an assembly, and then ordered specific cadets to leave the room. Fighting Vanguard accomplices in purloined military uniforms opened fire on those who remained, most if not all of whom were Alawites. The militant opposition lionized Captain Yusuf as a hero. Many years later, during the civil war in post-2011 Syria, Islamist fighters in northern Syria named one of their anti-government offensives after him.

From the perspective of the government, its supporters, and unknown numbers of the non-committed who were not aligned with the Muslim Brotherhood, the massacre of cadets in Aleppo was not a heroic deed. The victims were young, unarmed officer trainees wearing the uniform of Syria's state armed forces. Given that the Baath regime drew on the support of rural and small-town communities and notables, and that these (including many Sunnis among them) were a majority of the country's population, the militants' 'Islamic struggle' drew little support or sympathy outside of core urban constituencies. Among the major cities they had the least success in Damascus, where Assad's cultivation of the city's (historically pious and conservative) Sunni merchant classes paid off. The Brotherhood failed to establish a significant foothold in the capital where their less-militant predecessors had once enjoyed a substantial following.

In spite of this, the Fighting Vanguard believed they needed to jolt awake the slumbering Sunni majority who, when awakened, would surely see matters their way. Assisting the militants' efforts was encouragement and support from Iraq, Jordan and Saudi Arabia, other Arab countries with which Syria was on the outs due to Assad's pro-Iranian regional policies in the wake of Iran's 1979 revolution, as Iraq and Iran headed toward war in 1980.

Muslim Brotherhood gunmen attempted to assassinate Assad in June 1980 but they failed. After that, membership in the Muslim Brotherhood became a capital offense, punishable by death. In retaliation for the assassination attempt, elite regime forces commanded by Assad's younger brother Rifaat massacred 550 Muslim Brotherhood political prisoners who were being held in the notorious desert prison at Tadmur (Palmyra). The Alawite soldiers of the praetorian units (Rifaat's 'Defense Companies') were exhorted:

> The Muslim Brothers have killed officers, they have killed religious shaykhs, they have killed doctors, and finally they have tried to kill President Hafiz al-Asad. Therefore we now entrust you with your first combat mission.[3]

The soldiers did not have to be told that the victimized officers, sheikhs and doctors were (like President Assad) Alawites. The Tadmur prison killings were carried out in retaliation for injuries inflicted on the Alawite community.

At the end of 1980 various Islamist groups (i.e., those advocating one kind or another of 'Islamic government') formed the Islamic Salvation Front, dominated by the Muslim Brotherhood, whose stated goal was to overthrow the regime. In the months that followed, Fighting Vanguard militants began to prepare for an armed uprising, focusing on the northern cities where they were strongest. The regime responded with 'combing' operations, where urban neighborhoods were searched house by house for activists and weapons, accompanied by arrests, torture and gunfights. In Hama in February 1982, security forces' discovery of the arms cache forced the hand of the local Armed Vanguard leadership who launched an immediate uprising in the city. They seized Hama's historic center, killed Baath administrators and government employees, and called on sympathizers in other parts of the country to follow suit. But Hama remained isolated, a sign that the militants had overplayed their hand. Cutting off all of Hama's communication with the outside world (something that was possible to do in the pre-internet, pre-satellite telephone age), mostly Alawite security forces (spearheaded once again by Rifaat al-Assad's Defense Companies) surrounded Hama, besieged it, and pounded the city with artillery and air strikes. Moving street by street, house by house, Rifaat's forces killed the Brotherhood fighters, their supporters and anyone else unlucky enough to be in the way of determined and vengeful praetorian troops. Lots of people lived in the densely populated, densely built neighborhoods of the old city. There has never been a formal accounting of the government's violence, and estimates of the number of dead range from 15,000 to 30,000. Whole sections of the old city were devastated and flattened, a fate that, chillingly, proved to be a harbinger what would befall built-up parts of Homs and Aleppo three decades later when Syria collapsed into full-scale civil war.

For many, not just supporters or partisans of the Muslim Brotherhood, the death and destruction in Hama represented a 'tragedy of the age' (the title of a Brotherhood-published accounting of the events). The Assad regime showed no mercy, hesitation or doubt. They wielded an iron fist that effectively destroyed the Muslim Brotherhood as a political–military force inside of Syria for many decades. Syrians appalled by this turn of events had no way to express themselves. People could discuss Hama's fate only in whispers. The inescapable lesson was that politics in Syria was a deadly business. The legacy of Hama was a depoliticized population, cowed and/or apathetic, who kept their heads down and tried to ensure a modicum of safety and predictability in their lives by eschewing politics and obediently performing the public rituals demanded of them.

While the tragedy of Hama 1982 was deeply felt (and, as events of 2011–12 would demonstrate, well remembered), this did not necessarily translate into sympathy or support for the Muslim Brotherhood. They too had not conducted themselves wisely or well. The Brotherhood's divisive sectarian rhetoric and behavior convinced many that, in an existential conflict between the difficult reality that they knew (the Assad regime) and the apocalyptic rhetoric and vision of the Muslim Brotherhood, Syrians preferred the devil they knew.

The events of 1982 conclusively demonstrated that a determined, militant and armed opposition could not overthrow the regime. But a different kind of test lay ahead, namely, an intra-elite power struggle in 1983–4 sparked by Assad's temporary incapacity as he recovered from a heart attack.

ASSAD'S ILLNESS AND THE PERSONALITY CULT

At first, Assad's recovery was uncertain. In the immediate aftermath, his brother
Rifaat al-Assad used his command of the Defense Companies to make a bid for
power, although officers close to the president blocked his way. Devoted to the
regime and the maintenance of their own personal authority, they maneuvered to
limit Rifaat's ambitions, resulting in a tense Damascene armed standoff in the streets
between rival units of the security forces in February 1984. The standoff pointed to
a key weakness in the personalized system that Hafez al-Assad had constructed:
without him to hold the state together, it might well come apart.

When the president recovered his strength and it was clear that he would continue in his position, Hafez personally intervened to curb his brother's ambitions.
He drove to Rifaat's residence, dressed him down in front of their visiting mother
and demanded Rifaat's obedience. In a face-saving gesture Rifaat was named one
of three vice presidents as part of a government reorganization, although Rifaat's
Defense Companies were dissolved and he was stripped of all substantive power
and influence. He spent many years afterward living in luxurious exile in Europe.
After the events of 1983–4, Rifaat was more or less the forgotten man of Syrian politics, though he held on to the empty title of vice president until 1998.

Hafez al-Assad's reassertion of authority after his recovery reaffirmed that he was
the major, if not the only, political asset remaining for the regime. By 1984–5, all
of the key officeholders in the state and armed forces were completely beholden to
him. The Baath party had been molded in his image and packed with loyalists, an
instrument of patronage and control dominated by careerists rather than (as it once
had been) a party of radical nationalists and revolutionaries. Public sector institutions were in the hands of Baath apparatchiks, not only at the managerial level but
also at the level of trade union leaders, who represented the regime to the workers not the reverse. Centers of independent liberal thought had been crushed and
brought to heel in 1980, in the midst of the struggle with the Muslim Brotherhood,
when associations of lawyers, engineers and physicians who called for respect for
personal and legal freedoms were dissolved and their leadership arrested, replaced
by party appointees.

In this environment, Assad's personality cult, in place since the 1970s, reached
its zenith. Upon his recovery the Baath declared him to be Syria's 'eternal leader.'
Monuments and statues funded by the state and by sycophantic private donors dot-
ted the landscape. Public buildings and monuments were named after him, including the new national library building at Umayyad Circle in Damascus. Expensive
reconstructions of the Damascus citadel and the enclosure wall of the venerable

Umayyad Mosque made sure to inscribe his name on their stones. Visitors to the country were even met by signs welcoming them to 'Assad's Syria.' Every seven years the parliament would nominate him for another presidential term, and the public referendum campaign urging Syrians to vote 'yes' (in a public ballot) were occasions for the Assad cult to reach new heights of hyperbolic affirmation. It is unlikely that most who mouthed these slogans actually believed them. Acting 'as if' they did sufficed.[4] Public employees (a large proportion of the workforce in 1980s–1990s Syria), soldiers, schoolchildren and university students had little choice. These affirmations were rituals of belonging, which projected a patrimonial and patriarchal image of Hafez al-Assad as the 'founder of modern Syria,' comparable to the way former Ottoman general Mustafa Kemal became idolized as Ataturk, the founder of modern Turkey earlier in the twentieth century.

The rituals of obedience embedded in the Assad personality cult were an attempted shortcut to nation-building. Demanding that everyone in Syria demonstrate public fealty to Hafez al-Assad was a way for the regime to differentiate Syria from its neighbors. Turkey had the Ataturk cult; in Iraq the figure of Saddam Hussein served a function comparable to the Assad cult; in Jordan the image of King Hussein dominated the public and political landscape. In countries where national identity is fragile or contested, the ability of the state to impose one archetypal 'father figure' on people's consciousness is a fast way to demonstrate its domestic political hegemony and to assert a common national belonging in the face of rival or alternative claims to loyalty.

In Turkey the Ataturk cult served the interests ultimately of the army, which for at least half a century was the main political force in the country notwithstanding Turkey's façade of multiparty parliamentary government. Iraq's Saddam cult was similar to Syria's Assad cult, inasmuch as both men built authoritarian regimes that depended on them, their relatives and their regional or tribal allies as core groups at the heart of the state, with key institutions and political actors linked to them by ties of patronage and dependency. Formal institutions were secondary, serving administrative and patronage functions rather than having any kind of autonomous institutional or political weight. In the event of the displacement of the core group (in Syria, Assad and his close allies) or their mutual falling out (as almost happened in 1983–4), institutions' resilience would be tested and their fundamental weaknesses exposed. So even if Hafez al-Assad was 'the founder of modern Syria,' this was a personal accomplishment not guaranteed to survive him. For all that the Assad cult attempted to portray the regime's strength, it was mainly a way of papering over unresolved issues of Syrian nationhood, and concealing a hollowness at the heart of the country's institutions.

POLITICAL STASIS AND ECONOMIC LIBERALIZATION

The last 15 years of Assad's rule were in many ways politically quiet since most elements of potential opposition had been killed, jailed, exiled, cowed or co-opted. Regionally, too, Assad had good reason to feel secure. He had bested Israel in the struggle for Lebanon, rallying Syria's Lebanese allies in a way that assured continued Syrian hegemony in most of the country. Among Syria's most effective Lebanese allies were the predominantly Shiite parties and militias of Amal and Hezbollah, the latter closely tied to Iran with which Syria had a burgeoning alliance. New political arrangements for Lebanon agreed at Taif in Saudi Arabia in 1989 enabled Syria to assert full control over Lebanon's governing institutions, assisted by mysterious (and convenient) assassinations of public figures thought to be less amenable to Syrian guidance (the Sunni mufti; a newly elected Lebanese president who served for barely one month).

In 1990 and 1991 Syria's strained relations with the US and oil-rich Gulf Arab states warmed up. When Syria's Baathist rival Iraq invaded and occupied Kuwait in 1990, Assad joined most Arab states plus the US in supporting a military campaign to drive Iraq out of Kuwait. Subsequently Syria took part in the 1991 Madrid Peace Conference organized by the US administration of George H. W. Bush. With the collapse of the USSR that same year, Assad recognized that he could no longer count on Syria's alliance with Moscow as a counterweight to Washington, and that Syria would need to find a place for itself in the emerging era of US political hegemony and military dominance. As a reward for Syria's helping to provide broader Arab political cover for the US military campaign against Iraq in Kuwait, the George H. W. Bush administration allowed Syria forcibly to assert its dominance in all of Lebanon except for the southern border strip still occupied by Israel. At this time, Assad lifted restrictions on Syrian Jewish emigration. All but a handful of the country's remaining Jews departed Damascus, mostly for the US and Israel.

The Gulf Arab states, who had been angry at Assad's support for Iran during the Iran–Iraq war of 1980–8, reopened the funding spigots to Syria when Assad sided with them and Kuwait against Iraq. In the meantime, occasioned by the Iraqi invasion of Kuwait, Syria reconciled with Egypt too. Now Assad could rely on Egyptian political support for Syria's role in Lebanon and in Syria's 1990s negotiations with Israel. Without abandoning Syria's connection to Iran, and retaining ties to Syria's weakened Russian partner, Assad worked to ensure that Washington would want to work with Syria. In the years that followed the short-lived 1991 Madrid conference, serious Syrian–Israeli negotiations took place, for the most part clandestinely, that came close to agreement on a peace treaty. Assad met in Geneva with Presidents Bush (1990) and Clinton (1994 and 2000) in connection with this goal.

By weathering the challenges of the 1980s, ensuring Syrian hegemony in Lebanon and establishing Syria as a key player in the political affairs of the region, Assad earned international plaudits as a skilled political operator. Syria, a country that two decades before had been an object of regional and international intrigues, now projected power beyond its frontiers and forced consideration from those who wished to shape regional politics.

With Assad's regional and international status secured, structural shifts were afoot within Syria during his final 15 years. A rare Regional Congress of the Baath party convened in 1985 to ratify Assad's political decisions of the previous period, including the establishment of three vice presidencies that amplified Assad's power and underscored others' dependence on him. In addition to his weakened brother Rifaat, the other two vice presidents were Sunni allies and functionaries. Abdul Halim Khaddam, former foreign minister, was an old Baathist from the Mediterranean port town of Banias in the Tartus governorate. He had long served as Assad's point man in Lebanon. As vice president Khaddam continued in this role, while the Syrian intelligence chief in Lebanon oversaw matters in the country from day to day. The third was party functionary Zuhair Masharqa, a lawyer from Aleppo who oversaw the party and its bureaucratic apparatus.

Structural changes at home, plus Syria's post-1991 reconciliation with the Gulf Arab states allowed Assad to address immediate economic crises. During the 1980s Syria suffered a severe foreign exchange shortage. Assad had embarked on an expensive military build-up (said to be for the sake of achieving 'strategic parity' with Israel). But beginning in 1986 markets saw a dramatic drop in the international price of oil, reducing remittances from Syrians working abroad. Bailouts and grants from oil-rich Arab states had dried up years before, due to Syria's alignment with Iran in the 1980s Iran–Iraq war. (However, Iran partially compensated with subsidized oil shipments to Syria.) During the 1980s Syria's per capita income fell, agricultural production stagnated and the country had to import food. The economic crisis caused chronic shortages of electricity, fresh foods and basic consumer products in the cities. Nationalized industries worked at reduced capacity, especially where manufacturing inputs had to be imported. Private merchants had trouble obtaining foreign exchange legally through the state-owned commercial bank, driving them to the black market. Paid-off authorities turned a blind eye to endemic smuggling, or patronized smuggling networks themselves.

The formal, 'socialist' system of employment and commodity distribution was failing. Assad and his allies looked to mobilize sources of private capital to make up for the shortages and inefficiencies of the state-run economy. The early policies of import-substituting industrialization were in crisis and could no longer sustain employment. Moreover, because they were protected industries, they were uncompetitive in regional markets and they were expensive to maintain. A course change was unavoidable.

To this end the rubber-stamp national parliament brought in new laws to encourage private investment in commercial agriculture (1989) and in industry (1991). These changes were meant to appeal to expatriate Syrians, so that they would bring some of their capital back to their home country, and to individual and institutional investors in the Arab world, especially the Gulf countries. Legal exchange rates were adjusted to make them closer to the actual 'black market' rate, now recognized as the 'neighboring country' rate (i.e., what Syrian pounds would garner in Jordan and Lebanon).

The passage of the investment laws marked a formal abandonment of the Baath's earlier focus on state-led economic development. Such ideas had been born in the heady period of post-colonial independence, when new social forces (in Syria's case, small-town and rural notables allied with the military) took power away from the urban merchants and absentee landlords who had dominated local politics in colonial times. These older private interests had been represented by the National Bloc, then the National and People's Parties, and also by prominent independents such as Khalid al-Azm.

The post-1985 opening to private capital was not entirely new, but it did mark a formal ideological shift. Now the public sector was defined as something that needed to be protected or managed (for the sake of people's subsistence and regime stability), but hopes for economic growth were vested in the private sector. The weight of the state, and the importance of the public sector to social and regime stability, is reflected in the estimate that one-third of the working population was employed by the state in the early 1990s, including military and security personnel. With the freeing up of foreign exchange controls and the green light given to new privately owned industrial and service companies and agricultural enterprises, Syria's gross domestic product (GDP) did grow, helped along by the coincidence that Syria began to produce modest quantities of petroleum for export in the late 1980s. (The oilfields were in Syria's northeast, the Jazira, giving this relatively remote region a new, outsized importance in Syria's balance of payments.)

Opening up to private capital brought immediate benefits to those in a position to exploit these changes. The quality and quantity of consumer goods and foodstuffs increased, new investments refurbished dilapidated cityscapes in the two principal cities of Damascus and Aleppo, and expatriate Syrians felt more relaxed about investing and spending their hard currency in the home country. People who prospered were less hesitant than before to show off their prosperity and poorly lit major thoroughfares turned into bustling commercial hubs. For the regular visitor to Syria's cities, the transformation within the course of a few years was remarkable. Domestic unrest had been almost entirely suppressed or marginalized, and the heavy pall of fear that accompanied the deprivations of the 1980s also lifted to a certain degree, as people adapted to and learned what was permitted and what was not.

Dire economic conditions pushed the government toward economic liberalization, but these policies were not literally imposed on Syria. Syria had no significant foreign debt to Western banking institutions, because its major debts were to the USSR and the USSR's principal successor state, Russia. Such debts could be politically managed (i.e., reduced) and paid back in kind rather than in cash. Syria's relationship to international (Western) financial institutions was limited, so the latter had no direct leverage in terms of imposing international monetary fund (IMF)-style 'restructuring' on the country. Syria's piecemeal adoption of neoliberal policies was therefore a local response to changing international and regional conditions. This is a subtle distinction but it is worth making, in contrast for example to Egypt's experience. There, under IMF pressure, the Mubarak government in the 1990s began to sell off public assets to private investors, keeping mostly the unprofitable and money-losing ones in public hands.

To a degree economic liberalization succeeded, giving Syrians with money more confidence to spend, invest and repatriate it. GDP growth (assisted by oil revenues) in the 1990s was modest but steady. This included, after a certain time lag, a growth in light industries around Aleppo, whose products (especially textiles) were exported to regional markets.

Syria's political institutions now also opened up to representatives of the private sector. This opening, the regime asserted, was an expansion of the 'pluralism' that it claimed had long been a part of the country's political system. The official understanding of pluralism was a narrow one, and it was not the equivalent of most people's understanding of democratization. Since 1972, official reasoning went, the Baath-led Progressive National Front had represented 'political pluralism,' and Syria's mixed public–private economy was another example of 'pluralism.' Assad himself used this concept to explain, post-1989, why Syria would not be vulnerable to the types of changes that had brought down Syrian-allied communist regimes in Europe, including the family-led regime of Nicolas Ceausescu in Romania. (Punning graffiti in Damascus in 1989 referred to Assad as Shamsescu, 'Sham' being a reference to Damascus and Syria.)[5]

As a way of co-opting some of the private sector whose businesses were increasingly important to the economy, a number of seats in parliament were allotted to non-party people. Elections for these seats could be genuinely competitive. In the 1990s one-third of elected parliamentarians were independents, including businessmen, tribal leaders and urban professionals. The businessmen in particular were expected to act as advocates for the private sector in deliberations around economic policy and drafting laws. But parliament as an institution remained a weak body. Major areas of concern remained off limits to public discussion – including foreign policy, high-level corruption, the prerogatives of the president and his close associates, issues of sectarianism, and extraordinary powers granted to security services through the emergency laws in place since 1963. In 1995 an anonymous 'Damascene notable' told one foreign researcher, 'The party and the government are like Qasiun [the mountain overlooking Damascus]. You may like it or not like it; it's still there.'[6] Nonetheless, compared to the grim nadir of the early 1980s, it seemed that new winds were blowing through Syria.

Whereas previously the dour and dowdy face of 'socialist' Syria had concealed inequalities, or at least discouraged those with wealth from flaunting it too much, these restraints were lifted by the 1990s. More and more, Syria's major urban centers were sharply distinguished geographically between neighborhoods of privilege and neighborhoods of poverty, with the well-to-do living the high life and not feeling shy or embarrassed about it. The public sector that had been the regime's bulwark in its socialist days was increasingly residual, and was becoming the poor cousin of the national economy.

Whereas at one time workers in the public sector and the bureaucracy might have comforted themselves by thinking that they were at the center of a national project, now they were increasingly forgotten, unappreciated and underpaid employees who were not well-connected enough to prosper in an increasingly privatized market economy. Workers in public factories, in agricultural co-ops, and public employees generally had previously enjoyed subsidized benefits – consumer goods, publicly supported health care and recreation activities. Now, though, not only did their salaries not keep pace with inflation, but the benefits that once came along with public employment deteriorated as the government's commitment to benefits fell behind also.

Peasants in the countryside had generally benefited from the Baath's improvement in rural conditions (linked to policies that were crafted by ranking Baathists of rural and small-town backgrounds, who rose to power from the 1960s onward). But the more egalitarian aspects of the early Baathist program were abandoned in the name of economic efficiency. Increasing differentiation in the countryside between rich and poor accelerated rural migration to the cities. Even where the government did not 'cut' support for public services in nominal terms, maintenance of the same salaries or same supports as in previous budgets were in fact felt as budget cuts since they did not acknowledge the general rise in prices. This meant that, except for those in managerial positions who were able to profit from their positions by deal-making ('corruption'), most public employees struggled to make ends meet and usually had to moonlight or rely on petty bribery (for providing their routine services) in order to support themselves and their families. Patronage remained baked into the system. If people needed to obtain a service or get a job, or gain access to resources, they needed a patron or an intermediary to provide these. This situation strengthened personal ties, including 'primordial' ties based on region or sect, and pointed to the continued entropy of institutions that might have put Syria's modern state formation on a sounder and more regularized footing. Corruption, in the sense of exchanging money or favors for help from those in administration, was built in and further detracted from any sense of respect people might have had for 'the state' in the abstract.

In Assad's last decade a rot set into the public institutions that formerly had been bulwarks of regime stability, in terms of their ability to purchase public acquiescence at least. The socially disintegrative effects of privatization and the abandonment of egalitarian goals was reflected in remarks made by Syrian playwright Saadallah Wannous addressing UNESCO in 1996, by which time he was recognized as one of Syria's most important artists, Wannous lamented:

Unfortunately, the globalization that is taking place at the end of this century [...] seems to be widening [...] the gap between the obscenely rich and the destitute poor, [...] mercilessly destroying all forms of cohesion within societies, and breaking them up into individual lonely and depressed souls.[7]

As someone who had come the fore during the revolutionary 1960s, and who had written socially committed and critical literature aimed at contributing to a collective project of progressive change, Wannous was keenly aware of how these sentiments had dissipated by the mid-1990s.

RELIGIOSITY, HISTORY AND CULTURE IN HAFEZ AL-ASSAD'S TWILIGHT YEARS

With opportunities for open discussion of Syria's issues closed off, people looked to various means, movements or forums for self-expression in this period.

Expressions of quietist piety offered one recourse. Among the Assad regime's insurance policies during the Muslim Brotherhood challenge, was a broad understanding that Assad reached with the Sunni and socially conservative merchants and traders of Damascus, who were represented by the Damascus Chamber of Commerce. In a symbolic gesture that underscored this bond, during the 1991 referendum to affirm his fourth seven-year term, Assad made a point of voting in the company of the head of the Chamber, Badr al-Din Shallah (d. 1996). The government looked for ways to be supportive of (quietist and pietist) Islam, as a way of reinforcing this message and of channeling religiosity into politically unthreatening channels.

The late 1980s and the 1990s saw a steady growth of modern Islamic associations in Syria's cities. Adherents of these associations included well-to-do, educated men and women, often with professional training and backgrounds. They specifically eschewed the kind of polarizing militancy that had characterized the defeated Brotherhood activists, working instead to advance religious education, raise consciousness and to carve out a distinctively Islamic space in their personal and associational lives. Quietist piety marked a kind of psychological disengagement from mandatory public displays of cultish devotion to Assad.

However, 'disengagement' was not 'opposition,' and the regime was prepared to live and let live, apparently relieved that the development of a demonstrably pious urban Sunni outlook did not need to take the form of political opposition to the state. Quietist piety represented a kind of dropping out or away (as much as one could) from the ideological foundations of Baathism.

In its promotion of quietist piety, the regime had a valuable ally in Sheikh Ahmed Kuftaro, a Naqshbandi Sufi who had been Mufti of the Republic since 1964. Kuftaro and the religious establishment were onside, and in the 1980s and 1990s they gained access to state media for religious programming in ways that had not been possible in earlier periods of more outspoken Baathist secularism. The sterility of official discourse, the suppression of viable political ideas in Syria, and the co-optation of the communists and Nasserites whose official organizations in the 1990s were inconsequential and mere shadows of their former (1960s) selves, meant that when a renewed public political discourse did emerge in the decade of the 2010s, it was more heavily inflected with Islamic imagery and symbols than had been the case in an earlier period (1950s) of political openness and greater freedom of expression.

Another sign of the times during Assad's final decade was a persistent debate about old Damascus, its heritage, and who might lay claim to it. During the colonial period and in the early independence era, much public discourse in Syria was future-oriented. Syrian and Arab nationalists argued that France was preventing the modern Syrian nation from being born. Later, Syria's and the Arabs' defeat in

Palestine in 1948–9 required a range of new and modernizing forces to confront and displace the old 'corrupt' elites inherited from the Ottoman and colonial days. Under the flag of Arab nationalism (whether of the Baathist or Nasserite variety), the Syrian Arab people would construct a heroic future and assume their rightful role in the modern world. In Egypt, the Aswan High Dam came to symbolize this optimistic, technocratic and heroic vision of the future. In Syria its counterpart was the Tabqa Dam on the Euphrates, begun in 1968 and opened in 1973.

By the 1990s, this idea of a modern nation with a bright future ceased to inspire. To be sure, late-period Assad invoked the dam as a symbol of the 'modern Syria' for which he claimed credit. But by the mid-1980s the slogans of a vibrant, modern Arab renewal no longer had the same cachet. Israel's decisive defeat of the Arab armies in 1967 was one nail in the coffin of this particular dream. The brief respite of the Arabs' relative success in the 1973 war, and the beginning of the 1970s oil boom, was quickly followed by the outbreak of the Lebanese civil war. This was a kind of Arab civil war in which different Arab countries including Syria supported different parties. The putative Arab 'front' against Israel was broken in 1979 with Egypt's signature of a separate peace with Israel. Also in 1979, Iranian revolutionaries overthrew the Shah's US-allied government and replaced it with an avowedly Islamic one led by clerics. This achievement raised the prestige of Islamic movements at the expense of the erstwhile (and failing) future-oriented ideologies of communism and Arab nationalism. Syria's support for Iran against Iraq was one more demonstration (if any more were needed) that 'Arab solidarity' as a slogan counted for very little and was not a basis for any attainable future-oriented project. The Syrian regime's destruction of Hama and the adoption of a hyperbolic cult of personality around Hafez al-Assad drove the last nails into the coffin of the older future-oriented ideologies of the 1950s and 1960s.

As in politics, so too in culture: authoritarianism marked Syria public life, and Assad's state tried to use intellectuals and artists to project a positive image for the regime. Playwright Wannous wrote of Arab regimes,

> They have worked to turn them [intellectuals] into official mouthpieces. Their methods include oppression and pursuit, confiscation and prison [...]. There is agreement that the writer is a witness whose witness must be silenced [...] so that tyranny can relax and spread.[8]

Although the Assad government could not stifle the creativity of determined artists, it could restrict or limit the public reach of critical arts. Some Syrian writers, such as the poet Adonis, worked mostly outside the country.

In the 1990s former prisoners in Syria began to produce literature rooted in their experiences of incarceration. The Syrian Ministry of Culture published one such work, the book *Banana Fingers* (1994) by Ghassan al-Jaba'i (b. 1956), though it was not distributed to any significant degree.[9] After his release from prison Jaba'i taught theater in Damascus. His story, and that of other critical artists, illustrates the paradoxical use of what one scholar calls 'commissioned criticism'.[10] The state authorized, published or permitted critical work to appear, but then ensured that such work was little read or seen.

A similar dynamic was at work in the Syrian film industry. The National Film Organization had a monopoly on feature film production, and produced only one or two films per year. These were serious, 'auteur' films by Soviet-trained directors who brought personal visions and critical sensibilities to their work. Their stories were of individual lives set against the background of important national events, told in ways that pushed against heroic national narratives and instead recounted tales of discontent, disillusion and dashed dreams.[11]

Two directors who made their reputations the 1980s and 1990s were Mohammad Malas (b. 1945) and Ossama Mohammed (b. 1954). Malas's feature *The Night* (1989) was set in his hometown of Quneitra in the Golan Heights. The protagonist was a resident of Quneitra with roots in Hama. The story was set at a time when Quneitra was near the front lines with Israel. When the story reaches the point of Quneitra's capture by Israel in 1967, and it is emptied and destroyed by the occupiers, the protagonist thinks back to his home town of Hama. The character evokes his life in Hama, juxtaposed with scenes of destruction in Quneitra. This juxtaposition was a daring reminder of Hama's fate, a subject that could not be openly aired or discussed in Hafez al-Assad's Syria. In 1988 Ossama Mohammed made *Stars in Broad Daylight*, about an authoritarian patriarch from a village in the coastal region whose abuse of dictatorial power brings sorrow to his family. The actor who played the patriarch bore an unmistakable physical resemblance to Assad. The National Film Organization funded both of these films, but neither got a theatrical run in Syria.

So what was the logic of 'commissioned criticism'? Because of restrictions in distribution, the impact of critical books and movies on the Syrian public was small. These products could, however, be used for international consumption (book fairs and film festivals) where they projected an image of a more open cultural life than actually existed. Artists who wished to work in Syria had little choice but to maneuver within these constraints, to encourage each other and to cultivate a homegrown critical sensibility. The alternatives were to go silent or to go into exile. Filmmaker Mohammad Malas remarked to an American researcher in the mid-1990s, 'Prison narratives reflect our daily life'.[12]

Live theater had the greatest license for criticism. Perhaps this was because, unlike books or films, live theater could not circulate among a wide audience but would only affect the relatively small numbers of people who attended performances. (Camcorders were not a common consumer item in 1990s Syria.) The preeminent playwrights of the decade were the veteran Saadallah Wannous and his contemporary Mamdouh Adwan (d. 2004), who was born in a mountain town west of Hama called Masyaf (famous for its medieval fortress). Both playwrights used thinly disguised historical allegories to explore the subject of tyranny.

In Wannous's *Historical Miniatures*, published in 1993, he reimagines the fifteenth-century encounter between the bloodthirsty conqueror Tamerlane and the celebrated medieval Arab intellectual Ibn Khaldun as Tamerlane approached Damascus. Ibn Khaldun was sent out of Damascus to negotiate with Tamerlane. Wannous uses this encounter to stage a debate between the conqueror and the intellectual, exploring the nature of tyranny and intellectuals' role or responsibility in the face of it. Ibn Khaldun accommodated himself to Tamerlane, which lends a tragic dimension to Wannous's work.[13] In 1995 playwright Mamdouh Adwan staged *The Ghoul*, whose central character is Jemal Pasha, the tyrannical Turkish governor of Syria during World War I. The play imagines a hypothetical trial of Jemal for the atrocities and miseries that he inflicted on the population: conscription, famine and mass death. Historical figures, such as the journalist and intellectual Muhammad Kurd Ali, and the mufti of Acre who extended religious legitimacy to Jemal Pasha, feature in the play.[14] The contemporary relevance of the script's investigation of tyranny and its enablers was lost on no one who saw it.

These forays into history and memory, heritage and cultural appropriation, and the experiences of individualism and self-expression versus prison and tyranny, were responses from Syrian artists, activists and cultural producers to the difficult circumstances that they faced. Syria was no longer being problematized. The state had unequivocally established itself. But what kind of state and nation would it become, once the strongman was gone? Hafez al-Assad claimed to be the builder of modern Syria. Yet much of the state's efficacy depended on one man and the patronage networks that he oversaw or enabled, with the result that personal ties were paramount and institutions were weak. The regime's propaganda emphasized loyalty to and unity around the symbols of Assad and of Arab and Syrian identities. This did little to resolve or honestly confront the tensions, disparities and differences in Syrian society. Hafez al-Assad died in June 2000, and his son Bashar took the reins of government. No one quite knew what this change at the top would produce. They would soon find out.

8

A FALSE 'SPRING' AND GATHERING STORMS

BASHAR'S SUCCESSION

When Bashar al-Assad succeeded his father as Syria's president in July 2000, many hoped that the young man's ascent would mark a new and reformist turn in Syria's public life. Like most of the sons and daughters of the Baath elite, and unlike their parents, the younger Assad was a person of the city. He had lived most of his life in Damascus, and he also had lived and worked for nearly two years in London, England where he received training as an ophthalmologist. He seemed open to new ideas and new ways of doing things. Initially he had not been meant for a political role at all. Hafez al-Assad had been preparing his oldest son, Basil, for a likely succession. However, after Basil was killed in an automobile accident in January 1994, his father recalled Bashar from London. The 28 year old began an intense period of training and networking intended to smooth the way for him to succeed his father.

Like his brother Basil, Bashar received officers' training. He served in the Republican Guards, an elite regime-protection unit that had supplanted his uncle Rifaat's disbanded Defense Companies. Bashar's promotion through the ranks was swift. Beginning as a lieutenant early in 1994, he became a full colonel by 1999. In 1998 his father also began to entrust him with political duties. Bashar supplanted Vice President Abdul Halim Khaddam in responsibility for the Lebanon political file, and he began to cultivate ties to Lebanese political elites acting as his father's emissary. (Day-to-day management of Syria's interests in Lebanon – including managing most of its politicians – remained in the hands of Syria's intelligence chief.) Because Hafez al-Assad ordered this change, Khaddam bowed to his patron's wishes.

In addition to his rapid ascent in the officer corps, Bashar also succeeded his late brother as head of the Syria Computer Society. This appointment burnished his reputation as a forward-looking modernizer, and he became publicly identified with the spread of computer technology and the internet in Syria. Bashar's boosters identified him as an innovator, as someone in tune with the rising generation and the demands of the rapidly approaching new century. In contrast to the atmosphere of stasis that hung over Syria in his father's declining years, Bashar appeared to be someone who was aware of Syria's need for change. In early 2000, shortly before Hafez al-Assad's death, Bashar commented: 'Bill Gates [of Microsoft] functions in a cultural and technological environment that helps explain his achievements and therefore, if Syrians wish to advance themselves in these areas, they must create a similar environment in Syria itself.'[1]

The elder Assad died suddenly on 10 June 2000 while talking on the phone with his handpicked president of Lebanon. After 30 years of presidential rule in Syria, Assad's death was a shock, though not a total surprise. His health had been failing for some time, and awareness of approaching mortality explained the urgency with which he promoted Bashar to succeed him. Assad's last major international meeting had been in Geneva in March 2000 with US President Bill Clinton, marking the final futile effort to advance peace talks between Syria and Israel during Assad's lifetime. In photographs of the encounter the 69-year-old Syrian president looked at least a decade older.

Hafez may have been hoping to hang on long enough so that Bashar (aged 34 in 2000) could reach the constitutionally mandated age of 40 required to become Syria's president. At the time of Hafez's death, a rare Regional Congress of the Baath party was due to convene, at which it was expected Bashar would join the ranks of the party leadership, a distinction that he had not yet attained.

Bashar's smooth ascent to Syria's presidency one month after his father died demonstrates that Syria's elite were prepared for the event. The success of the transition depended on the key power centers of the regime – the intelligence services and prominent public personalities like Khaddam – subordinating their ambitions to the requirements of regime survival. They saw a quick transition to Bashar as a way to preserve the regime's essential features and power structures. The scheduled meeting of the Baath party Regional Congress went ahead. Bashar was elected to the leadership of the Baath party, he became commander in chief of the armed forces with the rank of marshal, parliament changed the constitution to lower the age of presidential eligibility to 34, and the parliament nominated him to be the sole presidential candidate. A referendum on 10 July sealed the deal and Bashar al-Assad delivered his inaugural address in parliament on 17 July.

Given the repressive political atmosphere, few Syrians expressed public qualms about the *de facto* establishment of a republican hereditary presidency. Perhaps most were relieved that the transition did not open or reopen fractious political divisions, with unpredictable consequences.

A FALSE PROMISE OF SPRING

Though he came into office as the candidate of the regime status quo, Bashar's inaugural address emphasized themes of reform and renewal:

> We must rid ourselves of those old ideas that have become obstacles. In order to succeed we need modern thinking [...]. Some people may believe that creative minds are linked to age and that they can frequently be found with the old, but this is not quite accurate. Some young people have strong minds that are still lively and creative.[2]

At first it seemed that a fresh breeze was blowing through the corridors of power and political activists, business interests, cultural figures and intellectuals fast began to test the limits of what could now publicly be said and done. An independent parliamentarian and businessman who controlled the Adidas franchise in Syria, Riad Seif (b. 1946), established a 'forum' in his Damascus home at the end of August 2000 to debate political and social matters and to strengthen civil society. Though technically illegal (because convened without a permit), Seif's forum drew no immediate rebuke from the authorities. This encouraged others in Damascus and elsewhere to do the same. Alongside questions of human rights and civil society, the issue of Syria's largest ethnic minority, the Kurds, made its appearance. In the northeastern city of Qamishli, established as an administrative center during the French Mandate and home to large numbers of Kurds and Assyrian Christians as well as Arabs, activists established a pro-Kurdish forum. Its participants demanded that 'the authorities recognize about two million Kurds living in Syria as a national minority and take steps to end the ongoing violations of their human rights.'[3]

These efforts to carve out spaces for national dialogue were complemented by a public petition from 99 Syrian artists and intellectuals. Published in Beirut in September 2000, the signatories called on the state to restore people's freedoms and the rule of law. Among the signatories were internationally known philosopher Sadiq Jalal al-Azm (d. 2016), poet Adonis, parliamentarian and businessman Riad Seif, playwright Mamdouh Adwan, and filmmakers Mohammad Malas, Ossama Mohammed and Omar Amiralay. They demanded:

> the release of all the political prisoners and prisoners of conscience, the return of all exiles, the establishment of a law-abiding state, the granting of freedoms and the recognition of political and ideological pluralism, the right

to organize, freedom of the press, speech and expression and the release of public life from supervision.[4]

This call was followed a few months later by a similar petition signed by one thousand intellectuals. In January, the signatories announced the formation in Damascus of a coordination committee to strengthen civil society. Important sectors of Syria's intelligentsia and parts of its business community were eager to test the limits of the new president's stated commitment to reform and renewal. Print media, too, became more pluralistic in the early months of Bashar's administration. Internationally recognized cartoonist Ali Farzat (b. 1951) obtained a license to publish the first independent publication of the Baath era, a satirical periodical titled *The Lamplighter*. According to Farzat, the president was a fan of his work, including his sendups of pompous officials and sinister security men. Abroad, Syrians' new opportunity for freer public discussion and criticism was christened the 'Damascus spring.'

By 2001's actual, calendar spring, key figures in the regime feared that liberalization of political life was getting out of hand. Modernizing Syria's authoritarian structures was one thing, but the intensifying public debate threatened to undermine them altogether. Bashar al-Assad was a product of the system that his father had built, and in March 2001 he warned that public criticism of the system's fundamentals would not be allowed. Areas off limits to public discussion included national unity (that is, questions of regionalism and sectarianism), the leading role of the Baath party, the role of the armed forces, and the 'path of the late leader Hafez al-Assad.'[5] Mustafa Tlas, the long-serving defense minister whom Bashar had inherited, was blunt: 'We will not accept that anybody take the power from us, because it comes from the barrel of the gun, and we are its masters.'[6] The discussion forums were closed down, some high-profile signatories of the two public petitions were arrested, and preliminary moves by independent parliamentarians to form a non-Baathist voting bloc were stopped. Cartoonist Farzat remarked, 'We are like someone in the bathroom who finds the water is hot one minute and cold the next [...]. Change is there, but it has been overshadowed by what remains the same.'[7]

SYRIA AND THE 'GLOBAL WAR ON TERRORISM'

The harsh official reaction to the 'Damascus spring' was inevitable. Assad's regime was built for survival, based on the security services and on permanent emergency laws that obviated claims to human rights. Prolonged public questioning of these pillars would call the whole system into question. The government's renewed hard line was made easier, in political terms, by the increasingly perilous political environment of the Middle East. At a time when Syria faced threats and challenges, the government argument went, it would be irresponsible to allow the enemy within to sow doubt and discord.

Syria–Israel negotiations had collapsed after the elder Assad's March 2000 meeting with Bill Clinton in Geneva. Bashar took office in July, and that autumn the second Palestinian uprising against Israeli occupation broke out. This second intifada was a much bloodier affair than the first of the late 1980s, which had paved the way for the 1993 Oslo agreement that established Palestinian self-rule in parts of the occupied West Bank and Gaza Strip. By the year 2000 the political hopes and political capital that the 1993 Oslo agreement had represented were spent. In the meantime Israeli settlements in the West Bank and East Jerusalem had expanded, and the existence of the Fatah-dominated Palestinian Authority did not stop more radical Palestinian groups like Hamas from organizing attacks against 'soft' Israeli–Jewish targets like cafes and buses. The second intifada of 2000–5 was marked by Palestinian suicide bombings and harsh Israeli countermeasures.

Damascus housed offices for two of the militant Palestinian organizations, Hamas and Islamic Jihad, rivals or adversaries of the mainstream Fatah movement. The Assads, father and son, saw Syria's ties to Hamas and Islamic Jihad as cards to play in regional politics. Moreover, for propaganda purposes Syrian support for Hamas and Islamic Jihad allowed the Assads to claim that they were onside with the 'resistance' to Israel. Similar considerations lay behind Syria's close association with Lebanon's powerful Hezbollah militia, an alliance that gave Syria a potential pressure point against Israel and that strengthened Syria's alliance with Hezbollah's ultimate patron, Iran.

Following al Qaeda's 9/11 attacks and Washington's declaration of a 'global war on terrorism' and because Syria was an ally of Hamas, Islamic Jihad and Hezbollah, the Assad regime found itself in the crosshairs of Washington's global war on terrorism – even though al Qaeda had nothing to do with the Syrian state. Pressure on Syria ramped up when the US invaded Iraq and destroyed Saddam Hussein's rival Baath regime in April 2003. Syria and Saddam's Iraq had reestablished a regular relationship in 1997, and Bashar's government opposed the developing American plans to invade Iraq on the pretext of finding and destroying 'weapons of mass destruction.' Syria's warming relationship with Saddam's Iraq had helped Syria's balance of payments. Because of international sanctions against Iraq limiting the country's oil exports, Syria profited by buying surplus Iraqi oil at a discount, and then exporting equivalent amounts of Syria's own oil at world market rates. But after the US invasion of April 2003, Saddam was gone and the US was Syria's new eastern (occupying) neighbor. Official Damascus cited regional circumstances of emergency, war and invasion to push back against any loosening or liberalization of political life in Syria.

GOODBYE SOCIALISM: THE OPEN EMBRACE OF A MARKET ECONOMY

Following the 'Damascus spring' and its suppression, Assad shifted his rhetorical approach regarding the domestic front. Rather than reiterate slogans of reform and renewal, which had led to public questioning of the country's fundamental political and security structures, the president instead emphasized economic and administrative modernization. Among measures taken were the establishment of private banks (including Lebanese-connected commercial banks and Islamic banking linked to Arab Gulf money), establishment of private universities (including one with a European Union connection), the retirement of many members of his father's old guard, and the promotion of technocrats to key ministries. In June 2005, a rare Baath party congress formalized the country's retreat from 'socialism' toward greater economic liberalization, by proclaiming the party's support for a 'social market economy.' Market principles now would apply to wider and wider sectors of Syria's economic life, but legacy state enterprises would not be sold off or privatized.

A key business ally in the government's move to wider market relations was Rateb Shallah (b. 1932), a Damascene banker and businessman who had succeeded his father (and Hafez al-Assad's ally) Badr al-Din Shallah as the head of the Damascus Chamber of Commerce. Rateb subsequently became president of the federation of Syrian chambers of commerce, making him the principal spokesman for the country's private sector. Syrian advocates of the 'social market economy' compared it to China's experience of economic modernization, which was not accompanied by any diminution of the Chinese Communist Party's monopoly of political power. More skeptical observers described the developing Syrian system as a 'market-oriented autocracy.'

Syria certainly was in need of economic and structural modernization in the early 2000s. The final years of Hafez al-Assad's presidency had been marred by stagnant growth and high unemployment, alongside rapid population increase. By the early 2000s, 40 percent of the country's population was under 15 years of age.[8] Government schools did not keep up with the need for education and training, and job creation was desultory. Adding to people's woes was a severe drought at the end of the 1990s, in what was still a heavily agricultural country where the well being of people in many regions depended on precarious rainfall. The collapse of a newly constructed dam in the Ghab region north of Hama in 2002 left 80,000 people homeless and highlighted the poor condition of Syria's infrastructure.[9] Although Syria experienced economic growth between 2000–2, this was due mainly to its sanctions-busting economic opening with Saddam's Iraq. (This opening ended for a while after the US invasion of Iraq in 2003.) Looking for new sources of investment, and to expand Syria's access to regional markets, in 2004 the Assad government signed an association agreement with the European Union (though it was never ratified), and the Syrian president paid a friendly visit to Ankara, the capital of Turkey.

Implementation of the 'social market economy' accelerated transformations to the central business and commercial areas of major cities (Damascus and Aleppo, plus the port of Latakia). They took on a prosperous air, as Syrians with access to hard currency opened new businesses and upgraded their private properties. In Damascus official buildings more and more stood out as grey and dowdy in contrast to the shining new or renovated structures that went up around them. Café culture spread, rundown historical buildings were repurposed as restaurants and boutique hotels, shopkeepers had more goods to sell, and they found more customers willing and able to buy. Beneficiaries of the social market economy felt that, with the drabness and austerity of the former socialist era now a memory, their lives in Syria were more and more approaching a transnational globalized standard.

The business community, by and large, were willing to work with the regime and they appreciated the pro-business orientation of the social market economy, but entrepreneurs' opportunities were conditioned by connections and patronage rather than regulated or guaranteed by an arm's length or third-party legal and judicial structure. Such a pattern was not new, because favored businessmen close to Hafez al-Assad's regime had become prominent and wealthy in the 1980s and 1990s. But in the unabashedly liberal, openly market-oriented economy of the 2000s, the advantages of those with regime ties became more glaring as they built their fortunes and lived lives of opulence. The principal corrupt symbol of this 'crony capitalist' dynamic was Bashar al-Assad's maternal cousin Rami Makhlouf, who leveraged his relationship to the ruling clan to build a fortune on the wireless telecommunications industry (cell phones). At one point Makhlouf had a junior partner, the Egypt-based Orascom telecom company, but in a commercial dispute in 2002 Makhlouf seized Orascom's Syrian assets. Makhlouf's influence ensured that Syrian courts would not protect Orascom. The fleeced Egyptians were forced to negotiate a settlement, and such experiences discouraged more wide-ranging foreign (Arab) investment. Money that did come in mostly focused on real estate including new luxury hotels.

Ultimately the market-oriented policies of Bashar al-Assad and the Baath proved unable to meet the needs of Syria's population and to address crises of subsistence. With money flowing into the cities, and with agriculture increasingly privatized, impoverished rural folk migrated to cities, especially Damascus and Aleppo. They settled in neighborhoods that once had been outlying villages, but that now became underserviced slums and shantytowns. The glittering lights and swanky shops of the central city were a world away from the informally built housing, rutted roads and patchy services (water and electricity) of the shantytowns/suburbs. Adding to the pressures was a severe, multi-year drought in Syria from 2006–10. Widespread and massive crop failures were a consequence, driving rural people away from their native regions to the cities. Once there, they jostled with the nearly one million Iraqi refugees who had taken refuge in Syria following the US invasion in 2003 and the intensifying civil war in Iraq (with strong sectarian overtones) since 2005.

The social market economy was of course not responsible for the drought, and Syria deserved more credit than it got for accommodating Iraqis whose lives had been overturned by events whose triggers lay in Washington, Riyadh and Tehran and not in Damascus. But even before the double blow of drought and the Iraqi influx, residents of poor urban neighborhoods lived in deprived conditions, with population densities of 70,000 per square kilometer, and families of 10–12 people living in a single dwelling with three to four persons per room.[10] The confluence of these remarkable pressures in the late 2000s, at a time when the state no longer had the resources, interest or intention to maintain the 'socialist' welfare and support systems of its predecessors, created a perfect storm of misery. A migrant from Qamishli on the Syrian–Turkish border was living in an informal (illegally constructed) suburb of Damascus, Jebel Aruz, in 2009. He said to a visiting journalist, 'It's not easy here. We try to work, we try to make lives for ourselves and our families, but it's hard. There were no jobs at home and there aren't really any here. There's no money, there's no future.' A veteran actor, Khalid Taja, who was starring in a socially conscious television serial set in Jebel Aruz, added:

> They have problems in their villages and then come here and have more problems. Some of them are forced into being criminals, not necessarily serious things, just petty thieves as a way of surviving [...]. There can be drug abuse and [domestic] violence.[11]

Disenfranchisement of urban newcomers in a system that depended on informal patronage networks for distribution of resources, combined with absence of legal avenues for protest or redress, sowed the seeds for a sociopolitical protest movement.

SYRIA'S RELIGIOUS COMMUNITIES AND THE SOCIAL MARKET ECONOMY

The retreat of the state from a universal social welfare model created a space, and growing need, for private charities. In a country where NGOs were strictly limited, the principal domestic charitable bodies were organized around religious identities. Both Muslim and Christian charities had long histories, but traditionally the Muslim charities were more closely regulated because institutional Islam could potentially form a counterweight or a challenge to the Baath party and the security regime built around the Assad family. Christian charities were less burdened. But as early as the 1980s, with Hafez al-Assad's cultivation of a quietist, practical, non-political Islam, Muslim charities in the regime's good graces found wider scope to operate. Patronized by the Mufti of the Republic, Sheikh Kuftaro, and other clergy and scholars, Muslim charities channeled the resources of Syria's Muslim bourgeoisie into schools and welfare associations. The neoliberalism of the 1990s, and the formal adoption of the social market economy in the 2000s, allowed the Sunni *ulama* to expound on and to promote middle-class values of thrift, sobriety and hard work. Clergy often were, themselves, investors in or partners in small and medium-sized businesses associated with the Sunni bourgeoisie. With the Baath's adoption of the social market economy in 2005, private donations to the clergy-run Islamic associations and schools rose. Among other things, this ascendancy of the clergy at a time when the older imaginaries of Arab nationalism and socialism were discredited or in retreat, meant that when political space for populist mobilizing ideologies opened up a few years later, Islamic discourse would be powerfully positioned.

As for the country's Arabic-speaking Christians, these were mostly Orthodox rite, whether Greek Orthodox (linked to the Patriarch of Antioch, long resident in Damascus) or Greek Catholic (linked to the papacy in Rome). Institutionally, Syria's Christians mostly expressed loyalty to the Baath regime, appreciative that the Baath were formally committed to a secular political identity that did not favor the Muslim majority except with respect to the religion of the head of state. Christians as individuals played roles in the ruling Baath party and in the army. For instance, in 2009 a Christian general became the army's chief of staff. However, Christians were never a sectarian 'power bloc' in ways that Sunnis, Alawites and Druzes were or had been at one time or another. Apparently this absence of a communal political profile suited most Christians just fine, as it kept them and their communities out of the often-brutal intra-Syrian political crossfire.

Christian charities, like their Muslim counterparts, grew in importance during the years of neo-liberalization. Their importance expanded with the confluence of the government's social market economy policies and the influx of Iraqi refugees.

By the later 2000s, institutional Christianity in Syria was becoming more and more pro-regime in a proactive or affirmative way. The victimization of Iraq's Christians by sectarian militias in the Iraqi civil war underscored to Syrian Christians the importance of keeping militant Muslim political forces at bay. Bashar al-Assad's government presented itself as a guarantor of Syrian Christians' communal security. Moreover, the liberal cultural policies that Bashar al-Assad pursued throughout the decade of the 2000s (on which, see more below) encouraged Christians to affirm and demonstrate their membership in the Syrian national community. Assad and his British-born wife Asma (née Akhras, a Sunni family with roots in Homs) endorsed and encouraged Christian expressions of belonging to the Syrian national community. The first couple made a point of patronizing Christian events, especially Christmas concerts organized by Fr. Elias Zahlawi's Choir of Joy, who performed in the presidential palace. Pope John Paul II's visit to Damascus in 2001, early in Bashar's presidency, likewise boosted the visibility of Syria's Christian dimension.

Among Ismaili Muslims, minority-community assertiveness and integration had its own particular path. Like other non-Sunni Muslims in Syria, Ismailis were historically rooted in small town and rural regions away from the major cities. Their principal centers were Salamiyya southeast of Homs and a handful of historic villages in the Ansariyeh mountains, whence many had emigrated to Salamiyya in the nineteenth century after tribal clashes with more numerous Alawites. This small community was usually on the margins of Syrian politics, but at one point during the intra-Baath power struggles of the 1960s some Ismaili officers played significant roles. But after the triumph of the Neo-Baath in 1966 and then Hafez al-Assad in 1970, Ismailis ceased to count politically as a community. As with the Christians, this low political profile probably helped to keep them out of the crossfire of political battles, particularly when Muslim Brotherhood militant began their campaign against Alawites as 'unbeliever Nusayris' in the later 1970s.

Like Christians, Ismailis were not seen as a community that could or would challenge the Baath monopoly of power, so they were allowed to cultivate ties to their international fellow believers (whose Imam is the Aga Khan) without heavy-handed government interference. And like Christians, Ismailis as a community were well positioned to take advantage of new openings and opportunities in the 1990s and 2000s. Beginning in 1999 the Aga Khan Development Network, in cooperation with UNESCO and the Syrian government, undertook a major project of renewal and restoration in the old city of Aleppo. This renewal became part and parcel of the gentrification process that took root in Syria's major urban centers in the 1990s and 2000s. The association of the Aga Khan Development Network (and therefore the Ismaili community) with the restoration of Syria's historic merchant metropolis helped Syrian Ismailis to feel that they were being mainstreamed as part of the wider Syrian national community, similar to the sense of belonging expressed by Syrian Christians in the same years. (Most of the Aga Khan Development Network's undertakings in Aleppo would be destroyed in the city's post-2012 warfare.)

Establishment-oriented Muslim and Christian clerics alike had reason to express support for Bashar al-Assad's government and offer their cooperation. Muslim clerics welcomed the government's embrace of markets and the sanctity of private property that dovetailed with the *ulama's* interests and the interests of their principal constituencies and backers, namely the Sunni urban bourgeoisie. Recall that the nationalizations of 1964 had led to the initial wave of popular religious-inspired mobilizations against the new Baath regime in the major cities. Hafez al-Assad had halted the further extension of those policies, and now it seemed the Muslim clergy and their constituencies had won the ideological battle clearly and unequivocally. They might still, in a philosophical sense, be 'opposed to the regime.' However, there were many practical advantages to working with and through the state to achieve concrete institutional and social outcomes.

Christian clergy and community leaders, for their part, appreciated the wider scope they now had for institution-building and social action (through their charities), and they welcomed high-profile symbolic inclusion of Christians and Christian symbols into the government's presentation of Syria and Syrian society. In this sense they regarded the Assad regime as a guarantor of their collective safety, particularly in light of Christians' horrific experiences of persecution and killings in Iraq at the hands of sectarian Muslim militias.

Given their happiness with the government's retreat from 1960s 'socialism,' most prominent Muslim clerics did not dwell on the costs of the new policies. An exception that proves the rule was Mahmud Ghul Aghasi, popularly known as Abu al-Qa'qa (d. 2007). He preached in a working-class neighborhood of Aleppo in strongly worded (or rabble-rousing) sermons directed against enemies external to Syria, namely the US and Israel. He seemed to have good relations with the Assad regime, and in the mid-2000s he became director of Aleppo's sharia high school. In September 2007 he delivered an address that sharply criticized what he called 'mafias' within the regime, and lamented the displays of wealth and disregard for the poor that marked the new era:

> There are poor people, modest people who sell some parsley, tomatoes and fruits on their handcart for their livelihood. Then patrols of the municipal police swoop down on them, as if we were in Tel Aviv. They beat [them] and

they break [their handcart] on their head. But this is only for the poor, O Leader of this Homeland! As for the rich who are involved in drug trafficking, who protects them? And the organized mafias that steal billions, who protects them? [...] O Leader of this Homeland! State officials build houses, estates and palaces, and nobody asks them why, and the law that provides for the destruction [of illegal buildings] is not implemented against them. But when a poor man builds a bedroom for his children, he has it broken on his head![12]

Abu al-Qa'qa's sharp criticism of the costs associated with the social market economy, and of the vulgarity and heedlessness of some who had done well under the regime, made him enemies. Unknown persons assassinated him two weeks after he delivered this sermon. Another Muslim cleric who sounded a warning note was Moaz al-Khatib (b. 1960), at one time the preacher (Ar. *khatib*, his family name) at Damascus's historic Umayyad Mosque, marking him as a prominent and mainstream figure. In the 2000s Khatib expressed sympathy for the poor and evoked Qur'anic and sharia concepts of justice and equity to criticize the status quo. (In the following decade he became a prominent figure in the exiled opposition to Bashar al-Assad's government.)

NEW KURDISH ASSERTIVENESS IN SYRIA'S NORTHEAST

One straw in the wind indicating trouble ahead was a sharpening of ethnic tensions in the Jazira. The American promotion of Kurdish self-government in Iraq after the US invasion of that country spilled over into Syria's northeast, where Kurds were a substantial part of the population along with Assyrian Christians and Arab Muslims. The Syrian Baath refused minority rights to Kurds. The only formally acknowledged minorities with their own institutional structures were non-Muslim religious communities, that is, Jews and Christians. Because most Syrian Kurds were Sunni Muslims they did not have any specific 'Kurdish' institutions, though Arabized Kurds had long been a part of urban life in Ottoman and post-Ottoman Syria. (In the Assads' time, the most prominent of these was the long-serving Mufti of the Republic, the Naqshbandi Sheikh Ahmed Kuftaro.)

When the French first drew Syria's boundaries in the 1920s, Kurds constituted about ten percent of the country's population. Kurds had long been part of the Syrian lands' ethnic mix, and Kurdish neighborhoods, communities and families were found in various parts of the country including the cities of Damascus and Aleppo.

In independent Syria, Kurdish nationalists campaigned for recognition as a national and ethnic minority, with rights to Kurdish education, language instruction and representation in parliament. However, due to Kurds' thick demographic presence along parts of the Turkish and Iraqi frontiers, fragile Syrian governments feared Turkey or Iraq might use the Kurdish issue to slice off Syria's borderlands, and so Damascus refused to recognize Kurdish distinctiveness. In the early 1960s a Kurdish insurgency in Iraq carved out an autonomous zone in Iraq, so the apprehensive government in Damascus moved to strip of Syrian citizenship large numbers of Kurds who lived in the adjoining Syrian Jazira. The 1962 Jazira census deprived about 20 percent of Syria's Kurdish population of their citizenship, on the grounds that they were 'recent immigrants' to Syria from Turkey. Irregularities in the administration of the census (arrival of census officials with no notice; no effort to identify people whom they had overlooked) were signs of Damascus's bad faith. As a result thousands of Syrian Kurds were deprived of basic civic and legal rights that other Syrian citizens enjoyed. (The denationalized Kurds were, however, subject to military conscription.) An Arabization policy, carried out for a decade from 1966 to 1976, added insult to injury as Baathist governments settled Arabs (including those displaced by the Tabqa Dam project) onto Kurdish lands in the Jazira border region, as part of a project to create an 'Arab belt' that displaced thousands of Kurds. All of this formed a background to the emergence, during the brief 2000–1 'Damascus spring', of a public forum in the Jazira town of Qamishli dedicated to promoting institutional recognition of Kurdish identity in Syria.

Three years later, Iraqi Kurds' achievement of formal self-government after the US invasion raised Syrian Kurds' expectations. In Qamishli in March 2004, police suppression of a fight between fans of rival Kurdish and Arab soccer clubs spilled over into widespread Kurdish protests against police brutality. Reverberations of these protests were felt as far away as Damascus, in Kurdish neighborhoods and among Kurdish university students. The regime's response in this instance was conciliatory. Feeling vulnerable, uncertain of US intentions but worried about American hostility, Damascus sought to quell the unrest by releasing prisoners and issuing identity cards (i.e., citizenship) to tens of thousands of stateless Kurds who resided in the northeastern region. Within a decade, the Kurdish issue would emerge again as one of the defining issues in Syria as a consequence of the Syrian civil war.

CULTURAL LIBERALISM AND REGIME LEGITIMIZATION

The cultural field in Bashar al-Assad's first decade enjoyed freer rein than before, despite the government's political clampdown after the 'Damascus spring.'

This greater freedom to discuss contentious issues in print and on film was evidenced by novels that took up the subject of the security state versus Islamists, and that treated one-party authoritarian rule in a satirical way. Syrian writers of the 2000s were of course not the first to use literature to advance social and political critiques, but now their language was less circumspect and their critical references more open and transparent.

The relatively liberal cultural atmosphere of the 2000s reached the widest audiences in the field of television drama. Television serials made for broadcast during Ramadan had long been a staple of Arab television, and Syria had secured a notable place for its productions, second only to Egypt. Changes in investment laws starting in the 1990s meant that private investors, often from the Arab Gulf countries where the Ramadan television serials found an appreciative market, could coproduce Syrian dramas. Television attracted top-drawer talent, because it had become a burgeoning industry where creative people could earn a living from their art, rather than (as was often the case with writers) needing to moonlight or to supplement their income with other activities.

Aware of television's influence, Bashar al-Assad was personally interested in encouraging these productions as a way to develop Syria's 'soft power' in the cultural domain. Moreover the president wished to be seen as a patron by and for Syria's creative class. Producers of the serials had good contacts with the regime and its agencies, and if they encountered obstacles from the government's censorship department they knew they could appeal to Assad who from time to time overruled censorship panels. People associated with the television industry, including producers, directors, and actors, met the president at public functions, which demonstrated that he supported their industry and wished to be seen as their patron.

The storylines of the serials – whether set in contemporary times or in more distant eras – included cultural and political criticism. Scripts critiqued conservative social mores (presented as 'backward'), repression of women, public corruption and political arbitrariness (whether Ottoman Turkish, French or police-state depending on the era). Cultural producers might be philosophically opposed to the 'regime' (defined at its core by secret police and security services and by crony capitalism), but they were able to negotiate with the government (from the president on down) regarding the expression of critical perspectives. In this way, Bashar al-Assad was able to maintain some kind of reputation as a 'reformer,' or at least as an open-minded patron of creative folk.

The president as a patron of the arts, and of artists, also found expression in the lavishly supported official campaign that made Damascus in 2008 the Arab League's 'capital of Arab culture,' complete with numerous national, Arab and international shows and exhibitions. Some of these took place in the city's newly renovated Ottoman citadel, formerly used as a prison, and in Asaad Pasha al-Azm's eighteenth-century caravanserai, renovated into an exhibition space. The first couple's patronage of the city's new opera house and of Syria's premier modern dance troupe reinforced their culturally 'progressive' image. The Assads' patronage of the arts helps to explain and to contextualize the admiring article that *Vogue* magazine published about Asma al-Assad, awkwardly timed to appear (in March 2011) just when widespread anti-government protests were breaking out.

The Assads' association with the country's cultural scene fit an image-making political agenda, but also was part of the more liberal and cosmopolitan cultural atmosphere that privileged residents of Damascus and Aleppo were coming to enjoy. Much of Syria's creative community was willing to give Bashar al-Assad the benefit of the doubt during the 2000s. (There were prominent exceptions, of course. Veteran documentary filmmaker Omar Amiralay's low-key, yet devastating, critique of Baathist rural social engineering, *A Flood in Baath Country*, appeared in 2003.) However, many among Syria's cultural producers sensed opportunities to build a new and more satisfactory relationship with the state during Bashar al-Assad's first decade of rule.

WEATHERING AND SURVIVING REGIONAL STORMS

The years 2003–5 had been Bashar al-Assad's most perilous up to that point, when his government found itself on the wrong side of major regional developments. George W. Bush's 'war on terrorism' after the 11 September 2001 attacks placed Syria in the US rogues' gallery. The Assad regime's support for Palestinian and Lebanese 'resistance' organizations (Hamas and Hezbollah, respectively) risked making the country an honorary (though unnamed) member of Bush's 'axis of evil.' Since 1997 Syria had been improving relations with Saddam's Iraq. Helping Iraq to bust international oil sanctions had given a boost to Syria's balance of payments. But the US invasion of Iraq in 2003 put an end to the Damascus–Baghdad relationship, at least for a while.

Adapting to the new situation, the Syrian security services offered the US a degree of help and cooperation in identifying, arresting and torturing individuals identified as al Qaeda suspects; this cooperation became publicly known when Arab suspects, some with European or North American citizenship, were outsourced to Syria for brutal interrogations. (The case of the Canadian–Syrian engineer Maher Arar is one notorious example.) Despite this gesture of cooperation with the US,

Syria was strategically opposed to the ongoing US occupation of Iraq and sought to make it more difficult.

To that end, the Assad government facilitated the passage from Syria into Iraq of al Qaeda recruits who, in combination with deposed Iraqi Baathists, organized a guerrilla war against the US occupying forces. Damascus's logic for allowing Islamists to transit Syria was that if the US became bogged down in Iraq, Washington was less likely to try overthrowing the other remaining Baathist regime in Damascus. Also, by enabling al Qaeda recruits to go to Iraq, Syria could channel the energies of Islamist militants away from its own territory.

Officially Syria did not acknowledge assisting the anti-US guerrilla forces in this manner, and the Syrian government would occasionally make a public show of strengthening its monitoring of the porous Iraqi–Syrian border. But fears of a US military campaign against Syria hung over Damascus for some time after the US conquest of Iraq. Because one long-standing autocratic Baathist regime had been brought down by means of a lightning military campaign (President Bush's 'mission accomplished' moment), generating little immediate international or regional pushback, there seemed little to stop the US from trying an encore in Syria.

Syria's beleaguered international position was also reflected in Lebanon. Faced with mounting Lebanese criticism of Syria's presence in the country, the Syrian government exerted heavy-handed pressure on the Lebanese parliament in September 2004 to approve a three-year extension to the presidential term of Emile Lahoud, seen as Syria's man in the Lebanese presidency. This maneuver – decried as 'unconstitutional' – alienated many in the Lebanese political elite who had previously been willing to accommodate themselves to Damascus's agenda, most significantly the prime minister, Rafiq al-Hariri (d. 2005). Shortly before, the US and France, although at odds over Iraq, had come together to push through the UN Security Council a resolution calling on 'all foreign forces' to be withdrawn from Lebanon and for all militias to be disbanded. Because Israel had withdrawn from all Lebanese territory (as certified by the United Nations) in 2000, the reference to 'all foreign forces' clearly meant Syria. The only significant armed militia left in the country was Hezbollah, supported by Syria and Iran. Damascus was loath to surrender its military role in Lebanon, citing the friendship agreement that Syria and a dependent Lebanese government had signed in 1991. Moreover, Hezbollah's strength among Lebanon's Shiite community (the country's largest) gave Syria a direct entrée into Lebanon's politics, and a potential card to play in relations with Israel.

Hariri resigned the Lebanese premiership and cast his lot with the opposition. He was Lebanon's preeminent Sunni Muslim political figure, who in the 1990s had used his political and business connections in Saudi Arabia, France and Syria to carve out a political space for himself and his domestic economic policies. But in late 2004 and early 2005, annoyed by the imposed extension of President Lahoud's term, wary of Bashar's agenda in Lebanon now that Hariri's friend Abdul Halim Khaddam was no longer influential in Damascus, and encouraged by France, the US and Saudi Arabia, Hariri began planning an electoral alliance with like-minded anti-Syrian politicians for upcoming Lebanese parliamentary elections.

On Valentine's Day 2005 a truck bomb killed Hariri (and many of his companions) when it exploded alongside his fast-moving motorcade in Beirut. The Syrian government professed its innocence, but large numbers of Lebanese – especially Lebanese Christians, Druzes and Sunni Muslims, who altogether formed a majority of the country's population – blamed Damascus for the assassination. A series of huge protest demonstrations took place, which dwarfed efforts by Hezbollah to rally countervailing pro-Syria crowds. The United Nations formed an extraordinary court to investigate the assassination. (The UN investigation initially focused on Syria, before moving on to Syria's Lebanese ally Hezbollah.) In April 2005, bowing to the political pressures that these events had set in train, Assad withdrew the last uniformed Syrian soldiers from Lebanon after a presence of 29 years. This was the low point of Bashar's young presidency, and many wondered if he would survive the political humiliation that it represented.

But survive he did. In June 2005 Assad ousted Hariri's former patron Khaddam from the position of first vice president. Assad accused Syrian oppositionists of being in league with the US, an accusation designed to weaken them but one that also happened to be true, inasmuch as Washington encouraged the formation of pro-Western Syrian opposition groups and funneled resources to them in the name of 'promoting democracy' (a rhetorical leitmotif of George W. Bush's Middle East policy). Seeking to reinforce his nationalist legitimacy, Assad reiterated Syria's alignment with the 'resistance bloc' of Hamas and Hezbollah, a policy that garnered clear political dividends for him when Hezbollah fought Israel to a standstill in Lebanon in the summer of 2006. The Hezbollah leader, Sayyid Hasan Nasrallah (b. 1960), momentarily acquired a pan-Arab reputation as a popular resistance hero, and Assad basked in reflected glory of being Nasrallah's strongest and most consistent Arab backer.

In the meantime, Syria and the new US-backed government in Iraq reestablished relations in November 2006. That year al Qaeda in Iraq launched a sectarian, anti-Shiite war that hastened the US's political climb-down in that country. The US handed over authority in Iraq to the pro-Iranian (and historically anti-Baath) Daawa party, led after 2007 by Nouri al-Maliki (b. 1950) who became Iraq's prime minister. Like Maliki and his Daawa party, Syria was also an Iranian ally and Syria was the Arab patron of Iran's Lebanese ally Hezbollah. So Damascus had gained a degree of strategic depth in Iraq, now once again a friendly country. In the short term, al Qaeda's unleashing of open sectarian warfare in Iraq worked to Assad's advantage, because the large-scale fighting and ethnic cleansing that resulted forced the Americans to scale back their ambitions.

The upshot of all these developments was the creation of a durable political bond among Damascus, Baghdad, Tehran and Lebanon's Hezbollah rooted in common interests and lent moral force by assertions of Shiite identity. Syria was officially a secular state with national institutions that encompassed multiple religious communities. But the key levers of power in Syria had been in the hands of Alawites for more than a generation, and in the twentieth century Alawites had chosen to define their creed as a variant of Shiism.

By the end of 2007 Syria and the US were supporting the same side in Iraq, that is, the pro-Iranian Maliki government in Baghdad. Damascus and Bashar al-Assad were breaking out of their diplomatic isolation. In May 2008 Assad visited Paris as part of discussions on European–Mediterranean relations. Syria's ties with Turkey had been developing for many years, as both parties sought greater economic cooperation and had a shared interest in the development of the Kurdish question in Iraq. Both Turkey and Syria have significant Kurdish populations in regions that border Iraqi Kurdistan. In 2004 Assad visited Ankara, and the Turkish president returned the visit in 2008. Turkey also agreed to be a mediator in secret peace talks between Syria and Israel, which however broke down after the Israeli military campaign against Hamas-ruled Gaza in December 2008–January 2009.

Bouncing back from the nadir of 2003–5, Assad in the final years of the decade looked secure. In an unopposed referendum he was re-elected to the presidency in 2007. This was hardly a gauge of authentic popularity, but some of the support he received seemed genuine. His boosters could claim that he had kept the country independent and intact, in sharp contrast to foreign invasion and civil war in neighboring Iraq. Syria's opposition to the US invasion of Iraq and Damascus's support for Hezbollah against Israel allowed Assad to play the 'anti-imperialism' card, and to claim that under his leadership Syria remained a nodal point of resistance to American and Israeli regional designs. Syria's business-like relations with Saudi Arabia, Turkey and the European Union demonstrated the leadership's pragmatic maintenance of diplomatic equilibrium in the midst of the world's post-9/11 turmoil.

In 2008 Damascus's Lebanese allies were party to a Qatari-brokered agreement that allowed the election of a consensus figure to succeed Emile Lahoud as Lebanon's president, and led to Syria's allies sharing power in Lebanon with the

Saudis' principal allies, a bloc led by the son of the assassinated Rafiq al-Hariri. The younger Hariri, appointed Lebanese prime minister in 2009, subsequently paid a cordial visit to Damascus. This marked a *de facto* end to his party's effort to have Syria held internationally accountable through the United Nations for his father's death. The inauguration of a new American president, Barack Obama, in January 2009 allowed Damascus to put the hostile George W. Bush administration in the rear-view mirror, and to hope for a modest improvement in US–Syrian relations.

With political opponents sidelined, jailed or in exile, with improving international and regional ties, with a veneer of prosperity in the major cities, with positive international attention on Syria for its state-patronized cultural productions and its tourism potential, Bashar al-Assad and those around him might well have been tempted to take a victory lap at the end of the first decade of the twenty-first century. But events, and important segments of the Syrian population, had a different tale to tell.

9

UPRISING, CIVIL WAR AND FRAGMENTATION

SPRING 2011: THE SYRIAN UPRISING

Major anti-government protests broke out in Syria in mid-March 2011, catching the government by surprise. Perhaps they should not have been surprised. A wave of popular protests was already sweeping across different parts of the Arab world in the early months of 2011. In January, unable to count on the loyalty of his army as unrest moved from the provinces to the capital, the longtime authoritarian dictator of Tunisia, Zine El Abidine Ben Ali (b. 1936), fled into exile with his family and his fortune. Mass demonstrations in Egypt, unopposed by the Egyptian army who stood aside, forced the longtime president of the country, Hosni Mubarak (b. 1928), to resign on 11 February 2011. A few days later, large crowds gathered in Benghazi in eastern Libya, rallying against years of neglect and tyranny at the hands of Muammar Gaddafi (d. 2011), the self-proclaimed Leader who had seized power in a military coup in 1969. (Armed rebels would eventually kill him in August.) Meanwhile, sit-ins and demonstrations against Yemen's long-ensconced president, Ali Abdullah Saleh (d. 2017), broke out in January leading eventually to his negotiated departure from office.

All of these men were widely disliked or despised authoritarian figures who had burned through whatever political capital they may once have had. Over the decades they had built regimes that enriched them, their families and their cronies while denying meaningful participation to the vast majority of their countrymen who were outside of the charmed circle of patronage. Each country had its particular features, but the parallels with Syria were obvious.

The rapid downfall of Ben Ali and Mubarak led to some initial self-congratulatory gloating among pro-government circles in Damascus. The Tunisian and Egyptian presidents had fallen, Assad's boosters claimed, because they were pro-American tools of the West who had lost touch with the anti-imperialist sentiments of their peoples. In contrast, Assad had placed Syria at the center of the Arab resistance bloc, acting with its allies Hezbollah and the militant Palestinian group Hamas to frustrate Israeli and American designs for the Arab region. This difference was critical, so the reasoning went.

Even those (like the present author) who were not convinced by the ideological argument nevertheless thought it unlikely that the wave of unrest (called the 'Arab spring' by the international media) would spread to Syria. These doubts were rooted in an understanding of the depth and effectiveness of the regime's patronage networks (an understanding that had become outdated by 2010, especially for rural and outlying areas), and the efficacy of fear in discouraging mass political action. The shadow of Hama's 1982 experience had hung over the country for a generation, and who (the thinking went) would want to expose themselves and their communities to a repetition of such violence? Turnout was small for two opposition-organized demonstrations in Damascus in February 2011 that were called to express solidarity with Egyptians and Libyans. Also in February, a demonstration in the old city of Damascus against police mistreatment of a merchant drew a crowd, but it was quickly dispersed. The fact that these demonstrations happened at all was significant in retrospect, but at the time there was still little sign that they might be harbingers of a wider movement.

But the uprisings in Tunisia, Egypt, Libya and Yemen had a demonstration effect, and showed Syrians what could be done (and what people were doing) in other Arab countries. Slogans that arose in one country – 'the people want the fall of the regime' – were easily transferrable. Video images of these dramatic events were widely disseminated, both through satellite television and through newer social media. The wall of fear in Syria had already started to crack. Though the 'Damascus spring' of one decade earlier had been stymied, it did open up a period of freer and more assertive criticism of the status quo. Prison literature and dissident novels of the 2000s may not have been widely circulated, but their existence was significant, and social criticism had become a feature of Syrian television serials. Transnational satellite television, especially Qatar-based al-Jazeera, likewise weakened the wall of fear inasmuch as al-Jazeera and its competitors accustomed Syrians to hearing critical commentary on live television, albeit little that impugned Syria or the Assad regime directly. But public culture had come to life, and the way was being prepared for dramatic developments.

The regime's ability to control and co-opt populations in smaller towns and the countryside had eroded. Whereas in the first decades of its rule the Baath's base had been in the small towns and countryside, including among lesser rural notables, these political tools were rusted by 2010. With its adoption of the social market economy policy and its alliance with state-linked businessmen, the ruling system had allowed crises in the countryside to go untreated. Their symptoms were growing poverty and large-scale rural to urban migration. When the Syrian uprisings did occur, they represented a revolt of the peripheries against the center, using vocabulary of protest developed in Syria as well as borrowed from other Arab uprisings.

The benefits of Bashar al-Assad's first decade in power had flowed to the regime's core supporters: the security apparatus, recipients of protection and patronage, business figures tied to the state, and (more generally) the better-off populations of central Damascus and central Aleppo. The costs were widely borne elsewhere, in poor neighborhoods, district towns and rural areas.

The Syrian uprising broke out when schoolboys wrote anti-regime graffiti on walls in the southern district town of Deraa, close to Houran and the Jordanian border, in early March. The children were arrested, tortured (one of them was killed), and detained for two weeks. On 15 March, crowds of people in Deraa began demonstrating demanding the release of the children and the dismissal of the local governor, a cousin of Assad's. The protesters were met with a brutal response from security men who fired live ammunition into unarmed crowds. News and images of the events spread on social media, and comparable demonstrations – demanding an end to brutality and demanding the recognition of people's rights – broke out in smaller towns in other parts of the country.

During the first two weeks as the protests spread, Assad was nowhere to be seen. When he finally did make a public statement about the unrest, in a speech to parliament on 30 March, he mostly reiterated stale themes that had been heard in Syria before: that the opposition were subversives in the pay of foreign powers, and they threatened the integrity of Syria. He acknowledged the need for 'reform,' but conceded nothing to the protesters' demands for accountability, due process and political freedom. Subsequent public speeches before handpicked audiences were similar.

In the early weeks and months protesters were locally organized, unarmed, and called for reform and accountability, not revolution. Many within and without Syria still hoped that Assad's tattered reputation as a 'reformer' – viable enough still to be cited by US Secretary of State Hillary Clinton in the summer of 2011 – would open the space for a dialogue between the government and protesters. But the authorities responded to the spreading unrest with rising violence of their own, firing into crowds, unleashing paramilitary hit men (*shabiha* – criminal gangs who acted as plainclothes enforcers) to intimidate and murder, and torturing prisoners to death. Mutilated corpses served as warnings to others not to defy the government.

These were the reflexes of a regime built to survive by defeating and intimidating opposition that it could not co-opt or sideline. Any concessions that the government might make would be cosmetic.

There is no gainsaying the exhilaration that Syrians felt in the early months as they overcame the wall of fear, and began to speak, sing and write openly to each other about their dreams and aspirations. The anti-government movement was punctuated by a creative outpouring of expression. Crowds performed the *dabka*, a style of chain dance rooted in village life, which reinforced their bonds of solidarity that countered the 'official' versions of the dance that had been a staple of government-sponsored cultural heritage festivals. Satire and humor, using social media, mocked the president and the police state that he and his father controlled. Songs and chants, often with the repeated refrain 'go away' (*irhal*) directed at the president, animated crowds. Celebrated cartoonist Ali Farzat, who briefly had edited a licensed, independent journal during 2002–3, explicitly lampooned the country's torturers. Syrians who had been hesitant to share their thoughts with people they did not know well (for fear of police informants) now found solidarity and community in large crowds and rallies. People's creativity – long in evidence, often suppressed, frequently fully expressed only in lands of exile or emigration – burst out in a myriad of ways. These expressions of solidarity and creativity were accompanied by critiques of the status quo that drew on Syria's battered yet resilient traditions of liberal and progressive thought to imagine the birth of a new society.

FROM UPRISING TO CIVIL WAR

But the exhilaration did not last. By its quick recourse to lethal force, the government gave protesters few choices between surrender or self-defense and counter-militarization. This was not a mistake or a 'bug' in the government's approach, but a feature. If intimidation worked, the protests would end and the state would re-establish the wall of fear that had been one part of the father-and-son Assad regime's formula for political stability. If intimidation did not work and government opponents took up arms, this would reinforce the official discourse that the government faced insurgents or 'terrorists' whom it was duty-bound to combat and to destroy.

Based on what had happened in neighboring Iraq, a prolonged insurgency would likely take on an Islamist flavor. This would allow Damascus to assert that its battle was against armed religious fanatics. Domestically, an armed confrontation would heighten minority anxieties and ensure their adhesion to the Assad government – better the mediocre status quo than an unknown (and likely hazardous) future under the rule of Islamist militants. Early in the uprising, Assad released a number of known militants from prison under the pretext of an amnesty. The release of these prisoners seeded the opposition with figures whose subsequent behavior would reinforce the government's narrative of events. One of those released was Zahran Alloush (d. 2015), discussed further below.

A massacre of 108 people at Houla near Homs in May 2011 at the hands of pro-government *shabiha* and regular military forces showed where the uprising – soon to be a conflict – was headed. The last, faint hopes that Syria could avoid full-scale civil war died during the month of Ramadan, which coincided with August in 2011. Large nightly demonstrations in many parts of the country (though still not so much in central Damascus or central Aleppo, or in the Alawite-dominated Latakia region) demonstrated the breadth and depth of Syrians' unhappiness with the regime. Invariably the government used deadly force in response. Armed men began to make a significant appearance in the ranks of the opposition. Initially these were lower-ranking army defectors, later to be joined by local militiamen identifying with themes of Islamic struggle, and (from January 2012 onward) a contingent who answered to al Qaeda in Iraq.

At this point it is worth considering why the Syrian opposition, an uneasy coalition of urban intellectuals and professionals, Muslim Brotherhood sympathizers, and local militias, opted to carry on the struggle despite the toll that it was certain to exact. No one in August 2011 knew how high the ultimate cost would be. Apart from the subjective reasons that individuals or communities might have for sustaining armed resistance against a ruthless state – a wish for revenge, a sense of local solidarity and defense, and so forth – there were two overarching factors at work that encouraged (or compelled) the opposition to take up arms and persist. The Libyan opposition had just triumphed in the face of Muammar Gaddafi's military forces, a victory made possible because NATO air forces intervened on their behalf in the name of preventing a massacre of civilians in Benghazi. NATO aircraft destroyed Gaddafi's air power and served as the tactical air arm for Libyan rebels, who captured Libya's capital Tripoli and killed Gaddafi in August. Syrian oppositionists hoped that a comparable Western intervention might be provoked in Syria. Therefore it would be not only the rebels and their local militias against the Syrian army and air force, but the opposition would enjoy a robust Western military intervention on their behalf.

Signals from the US administration of Barack Obama encouraged the opposition to believe that strong American support was forthcoming. In July the US ambassador to Syria, accompanied by his French counterpart, visited opposition protesters in Hama ostensibly to ensure that human rights were being protected, but in fact to give the protesters political encouragement and support. In August, as the daily accounts of Ramadan violence dominated international news headlines, Obama dispensed with Washington's earlier ambiguity and stated categorically, 'For the sake of the Syrian people, the time has come for President Assad to step aside.'[1]

To better ensure that they would follow in their Libyan counterparts' footsteps, oppositionists formed an umbrella body, the Syrian National Council, in August 2011. Headquartered in Istanbul, the SNC hoped to become the recipient of NATO largesse. Military defectors who had formed the 'Free Syrian Army' announced the creation of a military coalition allied with and nominally subject to the SNC. These expectations of significant external military support, badly mistaken as it turned out, were reinforced by oppositionists' conviction that they had come too far by August 2011 to turn back. If the Assad regime survived, those who had defected or taken part in opposition activities would have no future in the country. The Syrian security services and secret police had a long reach, and 'amnesties,' even if promised, could not be relied upon.

Opposition activists had already crossed the Rubicon. Their choices were victory, or permanent exile, or imprisonment and torture in Syria, or death. They would fight on. One activist ruefully commented, 'If we had known it would reach this point, we probably wouldn't have dared oppose the regime. But we did it, and now we can't stop, because if we do, they will kill us all.'[2]

The emergence of Istanbul (and Turkey more generally) as a haven for the Syrian opposition is significant. Official relations between Turkey and Assad's government had been friendly, even warm, during the first decade of the twenty-first century, especially after the electoral victory of the Justice and Development Party in Turkey in 2003. This was a center-right party with Islamist roots, whose dominant figure was the then prime minister (and today President) Recep Tayyip Erdoğan (b. 1954). He sought to expand Turkey's profile in the Arab world. With their shared Ottoman history Turkey and Syria had much to offer each other. Turkish firms invested in Syria and marketed their products there; Syrian businessmen in Aleppo, especially, expanded their markets in Turkey and rediscovered the old regional trading emporia that Aleppo once had dominated prior to the breakup of the Ottoman Empire. The lifting of visa requirements between Turkey and Syria turned the border into a bustling market area, where Turks and Syrians began to think of the neighboring country as a place to visit and to shop (cf. the US–Canada border). In Syria, newly friendly discourse on Turkey offered paeans to the shared Ottoman legacy of cuisine, music and spiritual culture (Sufism), briefly replacing the zero-sum nationalist demagoguery and finger pointing of the post-colonial era. The Syrian government de-emphasized the issue of the lost district of Iskanderun (Turkish Hatay), instead seeing opportunities to renew or expand cultural and economic ties with Arabic-speaking Turkish citizens in the district. (Large numbers of them, incidentally, were Alawites well disposed to deepening Turkish–Syrian ties.)

When the anti-government protests broke out in Syria, the Erdoğan government pressed Assad to introduce substantive reforms to resolve the political crisis. Elsewhere, in Tunisia, Egypt and Libya, Turkey had been in the forefront of regional states that supported Arab protesters' demands. Turkey's alignment with Arab peoples' popular mood would (Ankara hoped) serve the country's interests in the long run. Assad had been a close ally, but his reluctance to offer anything substantive on the political front while the government's security forces used live ammunition to suppress demonstrations prompted Erdoğan to break with him decisively. An attack by the Syrian army on the opposition center of Jisr al-Shaghur in June 2011 seems to have been a tipping point. This small town near the Turkish border, on the road between Latakia and Aleppo, was emptied of most of its people, many of whom took refuge in Turkey. With the breakdown in official relations between Ankara and Damascus, Turkey became a principal refuge for opposition organizers. The long, meandering Syrian–Turkish border became a prime staging ground for manpower and supplies destined for opposition-held areas in northern Syria.

Nearly one year after the outbreak of the protests, in February 2012, the Assad government brought in a new constitution that a few years earlier, and in more peaceful times, might have been greeted as a step toward political liberalization. The new constitution formally abolished the leading role of the Baath party and, under restrictive conditions, allowed for the legalization of new political parties and for contested presidential elections. In these respects it resembled the kind of authoritarian pluralism that had prevailed in Egypt under former President Mubarak. But in the context of the Syrian civil war, in which the state exercised unchecked authority in government-controlled areas while shooting at or bombing opposition-controlled areas, the new constitution was too little, too late. It did not curb the arbitrary authority of the security services or subject the government or its agents to any kind of judicial review.

Once the Syrian uprising turned into a civil war and became a drawn-out fight to the death (or to exhaustion), Islamic language was bound to become the vocabulary of sustained mass mobilization. Most of the population in disadvantaged areas, the geographic heart of the opposition, were Sunnis. Rural areas and district towns dominated the anti-government rebellion, and in the main these populations were socially and religiously conservative. Sunni Arabs were the principal victims of government violence. The use of Islam as an expression of communal solidarity and a symbol of resistance has deep roots: recall populist/communal resistance to the Ottoman Tanzimat in Damascus in 1860, to the colonizing French in the 1920s, and to the 'socialist' Baath in the 1960s and 1970s. Meanwhile, the radical secularist ideologies of the mid-twentieth century (Arab nationalism, socialism, communism) now were associated with the regime, its slogans and its institutions. (While the Baath was doctrinally anti-communist, Syria's established communist party had been formally aligned with the Baath since the early 1970s.)

In the 1980s and after, the increasing prominence of Islamic discourse and public display (clothing, public mosque attendance) helped prepare the way for the hegemony of Islam – or invocations of Islam – as a mobilizing discourse. Alternatives were few. In the Assad dictatorship, other forms of social solidarity or action (professional associations, political parties) were banned or tightly controlled. So as the Syrian uprising transformed from one of demonstrators demanding rights, to a sustained and bitter civil war dividing opposition areas from pro-government populations, variations of Islamic identity and ideology came to the fore. Liberals and progressives, who had penned the declarations of the 'Damascus spring,' who relied on a vocabulary of universal rights and who worked to create and promote an inclusive 'culture of resistance' through art, literature, music and drama, were pushed to the margins.

Because of Syria's central geographic position, the conflict quickly drew in a variety of regional and international powers. Russia and Iran supported their ally, Bashar al-Assad. For Russia, Syria was a valuable regional client state and host to Russia's only overseas naval base at Tartous. A weakened Russia had previously stood by helplessly as US-led forces destroyed two other former Russian and Soviet allies, namely Saddam Hussein in Iraq (2003) and Muammar Gaddafi in Libya (2011). Although NATO had intervened in Libya with UN authorization to protect civilian lives, the Russian leadership believed that NATO had opportunistically turned a humanitarian mission into a military campaign to force regime change there. Assad's Syrian government was to be Russia's 'red line.' As for Iran, its leaders supported the Assad government because Syria had been Iran's most consistent Arab ally for 30 years. Syria was a conduit through which Iran could support its client movement Hezbollah in Lebanon. Hezbollah controlled a powerful militia on Lebanon's border with Israel, and was the preeminent representative of Lebanon's large Shiite community in the Lebanese government. Preserving Tehran's tie to Syria was crucial for Iran's regional position.

The opposition drew support from a variety of regional governments, plus the US. Regional backers of opposition forces included Qatar, Saudi Arabia, Turkey and Jordan, as well as wealthy private donors in the Arab Gulf states.

They responded to opposition appeals for arms and money. Saudi misgivings about the expansion of Iranian influence in the Fertile Crescent motivated Saudi intervention in Syria. Riyadh had been taken aback at Iraq's transformation into an Iranian client state, a fast-developing consequence of the US invasion of 2003. At Saudi urging, Syria's membership in the Arab League was suspended in November 2011. The Saudi leadership worked to bring down the Iranian-allied Assad regime in favor of another that would emphasize Sunni identity and pursue anti-Iranian and pro-Saudi policies. Qatar was sympathetic to the Muslim Brotherhood and was keen to bolster the opposition parties and groups that derived from the Muslim Brotherhood movement. This was a way of extending Qatar's reach and influence in the Arab world (the al-Jazeera television network was another), despite Qatar's small size.

Turkey wished to ensure that Syria (or at least the Syrian–Turkish border regions) would be in the hands of forces friendly to Turkey, and in particular Ankara wished to limit the ambitions of Syria's Kurds. As the civil war in Syria polarized between the Assad government and Sunni/Islamic militias, and the Syrian government was forced to retrench, Kurdish local authorities took over in northern regions where Kurds were a majority of the population. As for the Obama administration in the US, it engaged in a quixotic and ultimately futile quest to sponsor opposition militias that were not connected to armed Islamically oriented militants and radicals. In the end, the groups the Americans funded came up short. They were outfought and outmaneuvered by rival groups that had greater élan and more street-fighting credibility, and that enjoyed generous funding from their various backers. In some cases US-funded groups found themselves acting as junior partners to more radical opposition militias, who helped themselves to a share of the US-supplied weaponry. The opposition as a whole was too divided to win.

SECTARIANISM

Islamically oriented groups' domination of armed opposition reinforced the regime's message that it was on the front lines of a war against 'religious extremism.' Faced with what appeared to be a binary choice, the country's various minorities either supported the regime or gave it resigned assent. Moreover, the rural roots of opposition militias gave pause to city dwellers. Urbanites might originally have sympathized with the pro-democracy demands of the 2011 uprising, but now many feared the consequences of a rebel victory that would see the cities taken over by armed people from the countryside.

Rhetoric from some of the principal militia leaders reinforced the government's propaganda campaign. A case in point is offered by Zahran Alloush, the powerful commander of the 'Army of Islam' in the Ghouta east of Damascus, and one of those whom Assad released from prison in 2011. As a militia leader Alloush received support from Turkey and Saudi Arabia. The last US ambassador to Syria (an advocate of US assistance to the rebels) once described Alloush as a 'moderate' in the spectrum of militant Syrian opposition leaders. Alloush became famous (or notorious) for a barn-burning speech he delivered in 2013, when he called on Syria to be cleansed of Alawites and Shiites. He referred to Alawites by the old name of Nusayris, implicitly denying that they were Muslims at all. He called Shiites *Rafida* ('Rejectionists' of the Sunni tradition) and *Majous* ('magi,' or crypto-Persians and therefore not Arabs). He glorified the memory of the Umayyads (the Banu Umayya), who had established the first Muslim dynasty in the seventh century and whose leaders had killed the prophet's grandson Hussein, a pretender to Muslim leadership, at Karbala in Iraq. (Shiite sacred history mourns Hussein's death at Karbala, and castigates the Umayyads who murdered him.) Alloush pressed various sectarian buttons in his 2013 speech:

The mujahidin of Sham [Damascus and Syria] will wash the filth of the Rafida and [their doctrine] from Sham, they will wash it forever, if God wills it, until they cleanse the lands of Sham from the filth of the Majous who have fought the religion of God [...]. You people of Sham are carrying the banner of Islam today [...]. Majous, including Rafida and Nusayris, besieged al-Ghouta, they claimed, to prevent the creation of a state, such as that of the Banu Umayya. And I bid you, O unclean Rafida, that as the Banu Umayya destroyed your skulls in the past, the people of Ghouta and the people of Sham will destroy your skulls in the future. We are proud of the Banu Umayya state, the capital of which was Damascus [...]. We welcome the mujahidin from all over the world to be an aid and support for us, to fight in our ranks [...] until the humiliation and destruction is on the Majous, the enemies of God. Until we cleanse Sham from their filth and uncleanliness, so go and support your brethren O believers.[3]

Two years afterward, when visiting Istanbul to solicit international assistance for his militia, Alloush claimed that he had not really meant what he said in 2013, and that he merely was attempting to boost his followers' morale. Regardless, the political damage was done. Anti-Shiite and anti-Alawite rhetoric of this kind from a powerful militant opposition figure played into the government's hands. Non-Sunnis, as well as the many thousands of urban Syrians of whatever sect who depended directly on the government for employment and services, feared the consequences of a regime defeat and so lent Assad their acquiescence if not active support. (Alloush died in a government airstrike at the end of 2015.)

SCORCHED-EARTH TACTICS AND CHEMICAL WEAPONS

In the meantime, the regime instilled fear of its own through scorched-earth tactics against neighborhoods and districts that came under rebel control. The military and political logic behind these tactics appeared twofold: to make ordinary life difficult if not impossible in rebel-held areas, and to pound selected rebel-held areas into submission using artillery, rockets and air power as a way to force the evacuation of fighters, their families and most residents. Hafez al-Assad's destruction of Hama in 1982 had been a test run, not a one-off. An early example of these tactics post-2011 was the punishment meted out to the Baba Amr neighborhood in Homs, taken over by rebels in October 2011, and reduced to a ruined ghost town by the time the last rebels withdrew in March 2012. The government used these tactics again and again in its bids to recapture lost towns and villages, most spectacularly in eastern Aleppo where an intensive 17-month siege ended with its recapture by the government in December 2016. Evacuations of civilians from recaptured rebel-held districts to other government-held areas or to rebel-controlled regions elsewhere created depopulated areas, such as the corridor linking Damascus via mountain valleys to the Beqaa valley in Lebanon. Population shifts produced by war had the potential to change permanently the demographic and confessional character of strategic regions, mimicking what happened in Palestine (1948–9), in Lebanon (1975–90) and in Iraq after 2006. Collectively, uprooted Sunni Arab populations were the biggest losers.

Among the weapons that government forces used were 'barrel bombs,' shrapnel-filled containers dropped from the air into places where people lived, worked and shopped. Use of these weapons was a violation of international law. From experience, people in the Middle East know that regional states can violate international law with impunity so long as offenders have protection from a great power patron that provides political cover. In this case Russia played the principal patron role, usually supported by China. (China was reluctant to endorse international criticism of the Assad government, for fear of legitimizing international strictures against Beijing on issues like Tibet and Xinjiang.)

But the Syrian government's use of chemical weapons against rebel-held areas of the Ghouta in August 2013 did precipitate an international crisis. Earlier Obama had warned that the Assad government's use of chemical weapons would constitute a 'red line' and provoke direct US intervention in the war. The August 2013 attacks tested Obama's threat, and exposed its failure as a verbal deterrent. Obama found it difficult, however, to muster support for direct US intervention from a Congress and public wary of new (mis-)adventures in the Middle East. He was given an out when Russia proposed that the US and Russia work jointly to account for and remove Syria's chemical weapons, in collaboration with the Assad government. Obama climbed down from a politically untenable position (intervention in the Syrian war), and Russia was able to ensure its client (the Assad government) participated in an international arrangement to dispose of chemical weapons. After that the Syrian government's use of chemical weapons decreased but did not completely end. A chlorine gas attack at Khan Shaykhun near Aleppo in April 2017 precipitated a US retaliatory strike against a Syrian airbase, but by then a one-off US military intervention of this nature was not going to change the parameters of the war. (One year later, the US bombed government targets again after another gas attack against a rebel-held enclave in Douma near Damascus. Nonetheless, the US government and public showed little appetite for a sustained US military campaign against the Syrian government.)

When Obama failed to follow through with the threat of US military intervention in 2013, Syrian oppositionists felt betrayed. Obama's political adversaries were quick to seize on his decision as an example of the American president's alleged fecklessness and to describe it as an opportunity lost. However, US military intervention in 2013 is unlikely to have ended the Syrian war. More likely it merely would have escalated the war by drawing in additional combatants more rapidly.

Very quickly, given the centrality of Syria to the Middle East region, external parties took an interest. The dynamic of external intervention reinforced the singleness of purpose of the pro-government forces, and further divided an already fractionalized opposition. The core of the Assad regime – the security services, top officials, predominantly Alawite praetorian guard units, and the civilian militias – knew they had to hang together or they would hang separately (as the saying goes). Russian and Iranian support strengthened the determination of the regime and its allied irregulars to hang on and to win against the opposition, at any price. The opposition, on the other hand, were geographically divided and politically at odds: pro-Turkish, pro-Saudi, pro-Qatari and pro-US elements contended with each other for influence. Moreover, the opposition was internationally compromised when two radical movements emerged on the anti-government scene, namely, al Qaeda and the self-styled Islamic State.

AL QAEDA AND ISIS

In January 2012 al Qaeda in Iraq sent fighters across the border into Syria, including Syrians whom Assad had earlier released from jail to fight the US in Iraq. In Syria they established what became the Nusra Front. (Nusra subsequently changed names, and after 2016 it was called the Syrian Conquest Front.) Nusra established itself in the leading ranks of the Islam-oriented militias fighting against the government. Nusra were well trained and experienced, and in time they became a dominant force among anti-government militants on the front lines. A Nusra-led group seized Raqqa in 2013, the first provincial capital to fall under rebel control.

In the meantime, al Qaeda in Iraq declared itself to be the 'Islamic State of Iraq and Syria' (ISIS) in 2013. It was based in parts of the Syrian Jazira and in territories and towns in the northwest of Iraq that the organization had taken following the US military withdrawal from Iraq in 2011. The Baghdad government failed effectively to integrate US-armed northern Sunni tribal militias into Iraqi government forces. Rising Sunni disenchantment with the Shiite sectarian regime of Iraqi Prime Minister Nouri al-Maliki opened the way for ISIS to seize most of Iraq's Arab Sunni areas with ease. When ISIS was declared, Nusra split from it and the international al Qaeda leadership disavowed ISIS as well, criticizing its hypersectarian and anti-Shiite program. After the 2013 split Nusra represented al Qaeda in Syria, and ISIS no longer recognized the international al Qaeda leadership.

In June 2014 ISIS achieved its greatest success, capturing Iraq's second city of Mosul, and gaining control of the bulk of Iraq's Sunni Arab heartland north of Baghdad. ISIS already controlled much of the Syrian Jazira and Raqqa. In June 2014 the ISIS leadership announced the creation of a new 'caliphate,' with its capital at Raqqa. ISIS built up an administration in the now-extensive territories it controlled. With a flourish the Islamic State made a point of removing Iraq–Syria border markers, declaring that it had put an end to Britain and France's post-World War I partition of the region.

ISIS used exemplary violence against populations who were deemed unsuited to share in their version of a righteous caliphate. Christians, Yazidi Kurds, Shiites and homosexuals were fiercely excoriated, brutalized and murdered. ISIS's unapologetic embrace of rape, sex slavery (concubinage), gruesome public executions and wanton destruction of historical artifacts underscored to its global audience the movement's rejection of supposed international standards, imposed as they had been by the victorious Western powers after the two world wars. (Never mind that the last widely recognized caliphate state, the Ottoman Empire, had subscribed to the developing international law of the modern era.)

As a norms-shattering movement ISIS attracted militants, dreamers, the angry and the alienated from around the globe who wished to dedicate their lives to the construction of (what they saw as) a model Islamic state. Added to this was an opportunity to participate in a world-changing apocalypse. ISIS made much of its control of Dabiq, the place near Aleppo that gave its name to Marj Dabiq, 'the plain of Dabiq,' where Selim the Ottoman Sultan had defeated his Mamluk counterpart Qansuh al-Ghawri in the sixteenth century. Medieval Muslim apocalyptic literature prophesied that Dabiq would be the site of the 'final battle' between Muslims and their enemies from *Rum* – that is, Rome. *Dabiq* became the name of ISIS's online newsletter.

For a time ISIS enjoyed considerable income from their seizure of assets in conquered areas (especially the bank vaults of Mosul), and from the sale of oil through intermediaries. At its peak, ISIS controlled some 60 percent of Syria's oil wells. The organization fielded an effective military force. Because ISIS's most immediate military adversaries were Syria's Kurds, the Turkish government did not staunch or stifle the flow of arms, recruits and material across the Turkish border into ISIS-controlled regions of northern Syria.

The advent of ISIS was a propaganda boon for Assad's government, as the organization's extremist ideology and behavior were perfect foils for official Damascus's claim to be standing up against religious fanaticism and 'terror.' For some time, however, clashes between government forces and ISIS were relatively few, because the government's war priorities lay mostly elsewhere against assorted other opposition groups in provinces of Aleppo, Hama, Idlib and Deraa and around Damascus.

THE KURDISH DIMENSION

The Assad regime developed a tacit understanding with Syrian Kurds, whose enemies (Islamists supported by Turkey, Qatar and Saudi Arabia) were also the government's foes. As the 2011 protests in Syria gathered steam, and as Damascus concentrated its forces to suppress demonstrations and uprisings elsewhere in the country, Kurdish activists took over public spaces in the north as government forces withdrew. In October 2011 a coalition of previously underground (but semi-tolerated) political parties formed the Kurdish National Council to speak for Syria's Kurdish regions.

However, what soon would emerge as the most important Kurdish organization was not a part of this grouping. The Democratic Union Party, known by its Kurdish initials PYD, was formed in 2003. The PYD was allied with the (Turkish) Kurdistan Workers' Party (PKK), and it acknowledged the overall leadership of PKK leader Abdullah Ocalan (b. 1948), imprisoned in Turkey since 1998. Hafez al-Assad's Syrian government had supported the PKK as a pressure card against Turkey until 1998. Because of the PYD's connection to the PKK, and the PKK's historical connection to the Assad regime, older established Syrian Kurdish parties looked askance at the PYD. But alone among Syria's Kurdish parties, the PYD had an effective military organization called the Syrian Democratic Forces (building on the long guerrilla war that the PKK had waged in Turkey). Therefore the PYD gradually asserted control over Syrian Kurdish areas beginning in November 2011.

Kurdish parties as a whole kept their distance from the post-2011 Syrian opposition. Kurdish representatives' focus on Kurdish issues, including rights to citizenship, language, and cultural expression and education, were distinct from the agendas of demonstrators and rebels elsewhere in Syria. The domination of opposition groupings (such as the Syrian National Council) by Islamists and Arab nationalists caused Kurds to worry about what an opposition-led Syria might look like. Leading figures in the Arab opposition made negative reference to Kurds. Prominent among these was an early head of the Syrian National Council, academician Burhan Ghalioun (b. 1945), who declared in an October 2011 interview:

> Of course, Syria is an Arab state [...] there is no discussion about this [...] there is no debate that Syria is an Arab country because the majority of the population are Arabs [...]. The discussion is not about the identity for Syria. Kurds [...] you cannot tell the Syrian Arabs that you are not Arabs [...] is that OK? Here is the wall.[4]

De facto collaboration with Kurds paid off for the Assad regime in Aleppo, where a PYD enclave formed part of the siege perimeter of rebel-held eastern Aleppo prior to its recapture by government forces in late 2016. Where the longer-term strategic relations between Damascus and Syria's Kurds will go is an open question. In 2012 Assad acceded to a long-standing Kurdish demand that the Syrian government recognize the Kurdish new year – Nawruz – as a public holiday. The PYD's proclamation of the 'Democratic Federation of Rojava' in March 2016 signaled a long-term political objective of establishing a self-governing region in northern Syria aka Rojava (western Kurdistan), a vision at odds with Damascus's insistence on preserving Syria as a unitary Arab state. But for the time being the Damascus government and the PYD continued to have some interests and some enemies in common.

When Turkey, bowing to US pressure, agreed to join the military campaign against ISIS in mid-2015, it did so mainly to ensure that Syria's Kurds would not be the main beneficiaries of ISIS retreats. Complicating matters, the PYD leadership welcomed American patronage and allowed US forces to operate in Syrian territory that the Kurds controlled. The US military sent an expeditionary force to Kurdish-administered Syria in October 2015. There, US forces provided tactical assistance (artillery and air support, reconnaissance, and special forces operations) to the PYD's ethnically mixed militia units (including, in addition to Kurds, Arab tribal and Assyrian Christian formations). Washington saw these forces as the only effective pro-Western proxy in the country capable of seizing and holding territory. In May 2017 Kurdish-led forces took the Tabqa Dam on the Euphrates from ISIS, and subsequently fought their way into the ISIS capital of Raqqa. The Turkish government of Tayyip Erdoğan viewed these developments warily, fearing the consolidation of a Kurdish self-governing territory along Turkey's Syrian border.

The irruption of ISIS into Syria and the ongoing presence of al Qaeda (i.e., Nusra) there introduced new complications into international alignments. Western powers, including the US now saw the Islamic State presence in Syria and Iraq as the foremost problem. Opposition militias that formerly were recipients of US aid became tainted by their association with Syria's al Qaeda franchise. For the US and its European allies, combating the Assad regime moved down the list of priorities. Militants inspired by or trained by ISIS unleashed a series of bombings in European capitals, driving home the danger of Syrian developments to Europeans' well being. Compared to these new threats and challenges, the continued survival of Assad's government appeared to be a lesser problem. Moreover, wave upon wave of refugees from Syria, seeing no quick end to their exile in Turkey, contributed to a flood of a million migrants who made their way to the European Union in 2015. Syrian refugees complemented an already significant migration of people across the Mediterranean that accelerated with the downfall of Gaddafi's authoritarian state in Libya and the opening up of the Libyan coast to people smugglers.

THE GOVERNMENT'S SECOND WIND

In spring 2015 Syrian government forces suffered a number of battlefield setbacks. Most international attention focused on the government's loss to ISIS of Palmyra (Tadmur), a UNESCO world heritage site where ISIS executed the director of the Palmyra museum and melodramatically destroyed ancient artifacts and monuments as they had done in Iraq. (ISIS also made a point of destroying Tadmur prison, site of Rifaat al-Assad's notorious massacre of Muslim Brotherhood prisoners in 1980.) ISIS's capture of Palmyra put the jihadist group within striking distance of the government's remaining natural gas fields. Possibly even more worrying from Damascus's point of view was the government's loss of most of the province of Idlib (including the provincial capital) to opposition rebels. This was the Zawiya mountain region, which had been such a thorn in the side of the French in 1920–1. The way was now open for rebels to press southward, toward Hama, and westward toward the Alawite heartland.

These defeats were symptoms of growing exhaustion in government ranks: manpower shortages, a drastic drop in revenues, and ubiquitous draft dodging. In a July 2015 speech Assad acknowledged the setbacks:

It was necessary to specify critical areas for our armed forces to hang on to. Concern for our soldiers forces us to let go of some areas [...]. There is a lack of human resources [...]. Everything is available [for the army], but there is a shortfall in human capacity.[5]

For the first time since the early days of the uprising, it seemed that the regime's days might be numbered.

But in September 2015 Russia intervened directly to support the Damascus authorities. The Russian air force turned the tide and bucked up their Syrian allies. The regime's manpower shortages were addressed by bringing in Shiite paramilitaries from elsewhere. Lebanese Hezbollah already had been active in military operations in Syria beginning in 2012. Subsequently, Iraqi Shiite militiamen and Iranian-commanded Afghan Shiites bolstered the Damascus government's forces and helped it to recapture and to hold territory.

By 2017 the combined arms of the government, its allied local paramilitaries, and foreign Shiite militias had opened up a tenuous land route linking government-controlled Syria, government-controlled Iraq, and Iran. This created a broad swath of territory that potentially could allow Iran to ferry arms and support overland to regime-controlled areas of Syria and into Hezbollah's Lebanon bases as well. As a sign of the government's growing confidence, in late 2016 government and allied militia forces besieged and retook eastern Aleppo after rebels had held these parts of the city since 2012.

Developments between 2015 and 2017 made it all but certain that the Assad regime would survive. The various opposition militias would at best hold discrete and scattered rural areas. Moreover, in some of these areas (Idlib/Zawiya, for instance) al Qaeda's affiliate (Nusra/Syrian Conquest Front) had established itself as the most significant military power on the ground, reducing the opposition's ability to mobilize Western support. The US feared that arms and supplies it provided would simply fall into the hands of al Qaeda. In July 2017 American President Donald Trump confirmed that the US would cease funding Syria's militant opposition, and would focus instead on fighting ISIS.

In 2017 the anti-Assad international coalition was coming apart. Turkey was at odds with the US over Washington's support for Kurdish Rojava, and Saudi Arabia imposed a blockade on Qatar accusing the small but rich emirate of supporting Muslim Brotherhood-linked forces. Saudi Arabia feared the Muslim Brotherhood because of the movement's historic organizational strength, and its ideological challenge to the Saudis' bid for Arab Muslim leadership. The Assad regime controlled all of Syria's major cities, including 80 percent of the country's remaining population, and the government (unlike the opposition as a whole) benefited from effective international and regional alliances.

10

SYRIA DIVIDED

The original Syrian uprising of 2011, with its national and popular democratic aspirations, became subsumed in a regional proxy war. By spring 2018, Syria as a unitary state no longer existed. The country was divided into a number of zones. The most populous and urbanized zone belonged to the Assad government. Another was the US-supported, predominantly Kurdish PYD which dominated a large swathe of northern and eastern Syrian territory, including the Tabqa Dam and major oil and gas fields. The Turkish-supported opposition, including significant al Qaeda elements, controlled rural areas around Idlib and in the Zawiya mountains. In the early months of 2018 Turkey also seized the western-most Kurdish enclave of Afrin, using both Turkish army units and Syrian proxy militias. In addition to these areas, other opposition zones included isolated and doomed pockets near Damascus, and areas in the south near Deraa and the Golan Heights, relying mostly on US support funneled through Jordan. Likewise, Israel offered assistance (supplies and medical aid) to 'friendly' rebels in the vicinity of the Golan Heights extending into Houran, to keep Iranian-supported or Syrian government forces away. Finally, ISIS still controlled some land in Syria's east, but 'the caliphate's' control of territory was rapidly eroding, squeezed as it was by the PYD in the north, the Syrian government in the west and the Iraqi government in the east.

The material and human costs, not yet fully tallied or ended, have set Syria back for decades. It will take years to return production, GDP and per capita incomes even to the modest levels of 2010. Nearly half of the country's population are displaced, and many of these are outside of Syria altogether, especially in the neighboring countries of Turkey, Lebanon and Jordan. In all likelihood the bulk of them will never return home, comparable to the experience of displaced and uprooted Palestinians from 1948 to 1949.

This condition of multiple Syrias (government, US-backed Kurdish, and Turkish-backed opposition and Islamist) will likely result in a long-term consolidation of

Iranian and Russian political influence in government-controlled areas. The Assad regime has survived and appears set to carry on, but will be more dependent than ever on its Russian and Iranian patrons. The Syrian government's connection to Iran may also bring China into the picture. Beijing sees Iran as an important part of its 'belt and road' initiative of solidifying trade and resource links along the old Silk Road, and the Syrian government will try to present its territory as a western extension of this project. China already has discovered a strategic interest in Syria, in light of Beijing's concern about Chinese Muslim fighters from Xinjiang trained by and embedded with ISIS. Good relations among Damascus, Baghdad and Tehran offer a tantalizing strategic possibility of Syria some day being a Mediterranean coastal terminus for the 'belt and road' plan – an ambition that the Syrian government, looking for reconstruction funds, will wish to encourage.

The Syrian government's vaunted 'freedom of action' in the Hafez al-Assad years, that is, its prickly independence, is likely ended. The core elements of the regime – the Alawite-dominated security services and praetorian military units – have survived, but resource shortages have compelled the government to delegate authority to local pro-government militias whose leaders have adopted the swagger and modus operandi of warlords. Likewise, Syria's Druzes formed militias of their own in order to defend their home territories and to avoid being used as cannon fodder in the government's conscript forces. So the tight centralization of the prewar regime may be difficult to restore. Local 'government' authority may be wielded in different regions by warlords who ultimately are answerable to Damascus, but who in the meantime will run their turfs like miniature fiefdoms. (In this sense the near future may almost be like a reprise of the pre-reform Ottoman system in Syria, at least for an interim period.) In the longer term an inflow of resources (but from where?) and shifting political winds may allow Damascus to assert firmer control over local strongmen. As a step toward addressing the resources issue and consolidating political control, the government introduced a law in April 2018 that paves the way for it to seize and sell off the properties of internal refugees, exiles, and those who are wanted by the security services. Since nearly half of the population has been displaced and will not be able to meet the criteria for proving their ownership, implementation of this law will allow the government to engineer an immense transfer of resources to friendly or dependent populations, disinheriting Syrians who live in opposition areas or in exile.

Kurdish controlled regions of Syria ('Rojava') are a sensitive flashpoint vis-à-vis Turkey. The PYD leadership in Rojava is organically and historically linked to the Turkish PKK, thus ensuring official Turkish hostility. In early 2018 the Trump Administration in Washington publicly declared that the US would maintain an open-ended military presence in northern Syria to strengthen the PYD administration, in the name of preventing a return of ISIS and of combating Iranian influence in Syria. PYD or Kurdish rule in northern Syria had unabashedly become a US bargaining chip. Rojava adjoins both Iraqi Kurdistan and Kurdish-populated districts of Turkey. The existence of an autonomous authority in Rojava ensures that the Kurdish question will remain alive as a regional issue, not restricted to just one or two countries. The Turkish government moved with alacrity in the wake of Washington's announcement, and began to attack and bomb the PYD-held Afrin enclave located to the west of the main PYD territory in the Jazira. The Turks' stated objective was to push toward the edge of the main PYD-held region at Manbij, north of the PYD-held Syrian provincial capital of Raqqa. Afrin fell to Turkish forces and their client militias in March 2018.

The PYD benefits, at the moment, from Washington's largesse, but at the same time the Kurdish leadership are wary of being set up and later abandoned. Washington's passivity during Turkey's seizure of Afrin reinforced Kurds' doubts about the reliability of American patronage. The PYD and Damascus have a common adversary in Turkey, and they may yet build on their wartime tacit alliance to arrive at a *de facto* arrangement for Kurdish self-rule within Syria's internationally recognized frontiers. Such a hypothetical understanding would have to overcome many hurdles, not only because of Turkish and US opposition to a PYD-Damascus entente, but also because Assad and the Baath are unlikely to make constitutional, institutional concessions to Kurdish autonomy in Syria.

Islamist controlled regions of Syria (primarily Idlib/Zawiya, and southern regions near the Jordanian border) allow continued influence for political movements inspired by the Muslim Brotherhood. However, the presence of al Qaeda, especially in Idlib/Zawiya, complicates internecine turf wars fueled by the Islamist opposition's various backers (Turkey, Qatar and Saudi Arabia). How this will all play out is difficult to say. Perhaps at one point the Islamic opposition's backers will throw in the towel and allow Damascus to retake these areas, subject to guarantees that Damascus may or may not be willing to give or be interested in respecting. Much will depend on how the Islamist opposition's regional backers assess their interests. At one point, if Kurdish matters can be settled to Ankara's satisfaction (but certainly not the satisfaction of the Kurds!), Ankara and Damascus might reconcile and this would likely bring an end to a substantial opposition presence in Idlib/Zawiya.

All told, this is a sad end to a popular movement that began with so much hope and enthusiasm in the spring of 2011. Syria as an entity on the map will likely survive, but precariously.

FRAGILE NATION, SHATTERED LAND

Taking a historical long view, Syria has been from the beginning a tenuous political construct, rooted mainly in the principal cities of the center and west. Even so, Aleppo was never fully a part of the project and its political leaders resented their city's subjection to Damascus after the demise of the Ottoman Empire. Created by the French, the modern Syrian state was practically designed to fail. France purposefully used tools of modern state building to perpetuate if not deepen pre-national and regional divisions and segmentation. Independent Syria was internally divided, a plaything for regional and international powers. The country's leadership solicited external intervention in Syrian affairs to fuel their factional battles, and at one point the leadership rushed to dissolve the country into a larger political entity, the Egypt-dominated United Arab Republic.

The semblance of a coherent and unitary Syrian state under Hafez al-Assad depended on the manipulation of existing identities (clan, tribe and sect) and regional loyalties, bolstered by fear-inducing authoritarianism. Encouraging Syrians to fear one another was a deft way of staying on top of the heap. As an accountant from Aleppo, now a refugee, said while reminiscing about the Hafez al-Assad years:

> We weren't educated about the different people in the country, so there wasn't real integration. Arabs didn't know about Kurdish culture. Arabs and Kurds knew nothing about Turkmens. We'd hear that there were people called Syriacs and Assyrians, but who are they and how do they live? We didn't know. The Druze? You know that they live in Syria, but what is their culture and what do they want? We were all just groups of strangers. A country of closed communities, held together by force.[1]

Many enduring or successful modern states had bloody, unsavory and arbitrary origins. But Syria had neither the resources nor the buy-in from regional elites and powerbrokers to build a hegemonic national identity within the boundaries bequeathed to it by France. This made it fragile. Syria as a discrete, stand-alone state lacked the anchors to withstand the disintegrative effects of regional wars and political-sectarian rivalries, especially after the ill-conceived US invasion of Iraq in 2003. The careless and arrogant behavior of the US government and its British ally shattered the Fertile Crescent's brittle political arrangements and unleashed the furies of sectarian discourse and rivalries. Political forces inside and outside of Iraq post-2003, including Saudi–Iranian rivalry, nurtured rival region-wide alliances built around sectarian distinctions.

Syria is a microcosm of the modern Arab national project, which sought to turn a venerable and transnational high-cultural tradition into a thriving cultural and political presence, able fully to claim a place in the international state system (cf. China). Syria was in many ways at the heart of the Arab project. It was a fulcrum of the Nahda, the center of Faisal's post-World War I administration, and it was the coveted 'prize' in rivalries between Egypt and Iraq in the 1950s. The cultural achievements of the Arab project are beyond dispute, and Syria (with its artists, writers, musicians, filmmakers and playwrights) is emblematic of the Arab movement's cultural achievements.

But the Arab *political* project was stillborn. Whether conceived as a union of Arab states, or as a coherent bloc of Arab states whose combined weight would count for something internationally, the Arab political dream never recovered from the Arabs' loss of the 1948–9 Palestine war (the 'first Arab–Israeli war') and the forced dispersion of the Palestinian Arab population. The successful mobilization of Jewish religious identity as a marker for political exclusion (of the Muslim and Christian Palestinians) set a powerful precedent for further fragmentation. The trauma of defeat triggered military coups, militarization, arms races and bitter internecine recriminations in newly independent and shallowly rooted Arab states.

For a while the Arab national dream appeared to receive a new lease on life with the rise of the Bandung non-aligned movement that advocated Global South solidarity and national liberation. But the Arab version of this aspiration fell afoul of quarrels between Nasser and his rivals, and shattered for good on the battlefields of the June 1967 war with Israel. Since then, in the place of modern Arabism and dreams of Arab solidarity, the field has been left to local identities and to states that are singly and collectively weak, along with an overarching religious (Islamic) nationalism that refutes much of the earlier effort to create and nurture a modern Arab cultural identity distinct from religion.

The record shows that Syrians as people(s) have many achievements to their name. Theirs is a land rich in historical associations, in cultural achievements, and in natural beauty. But often as not Syria the country has been a contested borderland possessed, dominated or divided by more powerful states.

Must it always be thus? Nothing is written or fated – 'men make their own history, but not exactly as they please,'[2] – but history is not so easily escaped.

CHRONOLOGY

1516	Battle of Marj Dabiq; Ottomans conquer Syria from Mamluks
1520	Janbirdi al-Ghazali's revolt in Damascus
1605	Rebellion of Janbulad Ali Pasha in the Aleppo region
1695	Introduction of *malikane* lifetime tax farms (good for provincial notables)
1699	Treaty of Karlowitz marks definitive end of Ottoman expansion
1725	Ismail Pasha becomes the first Azm governor of Damascus
1768–74	Ottoman–Russian war
1774–1804	Ascendancy of Ahmad Pasha al-Jazzar, based at Acre
1799	Napoleon Bonaparte unsuccessfully besieges Acre
1805	Muhammad Ali Pasha becomes governor of Egypt
1821	Greek Revolt shakes Ottoman Empire's foundations
1822	Devastating earthquake in Aleppo
1826	Sultan Mahmud II crushes Janissary revolt and disbands Janissary corps
1831–40	Syria is under Egyptian rule
1839	First Tanzimat decree marks beginning of reform era in Ottoman Empire
1848	Ottoman government officially recognizes Greek Catholic religious community
1850	Anti-Christian violence in Aleppo
1853–6	Crimean War pits Ottomans, French and British against Russians
1856	Second Tanzimat reform decree
1860	Anti-Christian violence in Damascus
1863	Telegraph line links Damascus and Istanbul
1865	Province of Damascus is reorganized as Province of Syria
1870	Alawite chieftains defeated by centralizing Ottoman government forces
1876–8	First Ottoman constitutional era
1876–1909	Reign of Sultan Abdulhamid II, who promoted Syrian notables
1878	Ottoman defeat in war with Russia raises Syrians' concerns
1877–9	First privately owned newspapers in Damascus and Aleppo
1889–90	Ottomans extend authority into Jabal Druze following peasant uprising
1908–14	Young Turk rebellion inaugurates Second Ottoman constitutional era
1914–18	World War I devastates Syria

1918–20	Sharif Hussein's son Faisal governs the Syrian interior from Damascus
1920	French victory over the Arab army at Maysaloun
1920–43	French Mandate in Syria
1925–7	Great Syrian Revolt challenges French rule
1928	Formation of the National Bloc
1930	Colonial constitution comes into force
1936	Franco–Syrian Treaty (never ratified) promises end of French Mandate
1939	Turkey annexes Iskanderun district (Hatay)
1939–45	World War II
1939	French suspend Syrian constitution and impose martial law
1941	British-supported Free French replace Vichy French in Syria
1943	Syria declares independence, with British support and against Free French wishes
1945	French forces bombard Damascus one last time
1945	Syria joins Arab League and the United Nations as charter member
1946	Final French withdrawal from Syria
1947	UN General Assembly votes to partition Palestine
1948–9	Syrian army seizes scattered pieces of northern Palestine in first Arab–Israeli War
1949	Three successive military coups bring the Syrian army into politics
1949–54	Col. Adib Shishakli dominates Syria's political life
1952	Merger of Akram al-Hourani's Arab Socialist Party with the Baath
1954–8	Renewal of party parliamentary life, emergence of politicized factions in the army officer corps
1958–61	Union with Egypt to form the United Arab Republic
1959	Syrian Baathist officers in Egypt form the clandestine Military Committee
1961–3	Secessionist regime in Damascus marks last gasp of political old guard
1963	Military coup brings the Baath to power
1964	Violent protests in Hama against Baathist nationalizations
1966	Internal party coup consolidates role of the 'Neo-Baath', a mostly Alawite military clique
1967	Israel defeats Syria in June and occupies the Golan Heights
1970	Defense Minister Hafez al-Assad seizes power in November
1973	October War pits Syria and Egypt against Israel
1976	Syrian army intervenes in Lebanon, then remains for 29 years
1982	Muslim Brotherhood uprising in Hama
1982	Israeli invasion of Lebanon
1983–4	Tense standoff in Damascus during President Assad's illness
1989	Taif Agreement ends Lebanon's civil war, leaves Syria predominant in the country
1990–1	Syria joins US-led alliance against Iraq's invasion of Kuwait

1991	Syrian–Israeli negotiations begin, and continue off and on until 2000 without a resolution
1991	New laws encourage private investment in industrial enterprises
2000	Hafez al-Assad dies and his son Bashar succeeds him as president
2000–1	'Damascus Spring,' a brief period of liberalization
2001	Al Qaeda attacks in New York and Washington cause US government to launch a global war on terror
2003	US invasion and occupation of Iraq puts US troops at Syria's border
2004	Clashes and protests in Qamishli over Kurdish rights
2005	Assassination of former Lebanese Prime Minister Rafiq Hariri; backlash forces Syrian army's withdrawal from Lebanon
2005	Baath party congress endorses economic liberalization: 'the social market economy'
2005	Iraqi refugees eventually totaling one million take shelter in Syria
2006	Syrian-backed Hezbollah in Lebanon withstands sustained Israeli offensive
2006–10	Devastating drought and crop failures drive thousands of rural people to cities
2011	Anti-government uprising begins in Syria, eventually leading to half a million deaths and displacement of half the country's population
2013	The US signals it will not intervene with its own armed forces in the Syrian conflict
2015	Russia intervenes in Syria to bolster Assad's government forces
2017	Assad government retakes Aleppo as divided opposition groups falter
2017	US-supported Kurds and Assad government reduce ISIS to a small pockets
2018	Clashes break out in Syria between Turkey and US-backed Syrian Kurds
2018	Assad government retakes Deraa town, cradle of the 2011 anti-government uprising

WHO'S WHO
(definite article *al-* ignored for alphabetizing surnames)

Abdulhamid II (r. 1876–1909), Ottoman sultan who revived the office of caliphate

Abdullah of Transjordan (d. 1951), son of Sharif Hussein and British-installed ruler of Transjordan, later Jordan

Abdulmejid I (r. 1839–61), Ottoman sultan who initiated the Tanzimat reforms

al-Abid, Ahmad Izzat (d. 1924), Abdulhamid loyalist who became one of the wealthiest and most powerful men in Ottoman Damascus

al-Abid, Nazik (d. 1959), pioneer of Syria's twentieth-century women's movement

Abu Bakr b. Abi al-Wafa (d. 1583), a celebrated Sufi of Aleppo

Abu Risha, Omar (d. 1990), Syrian poet of the mid-twentieth century

Adwan, Mamdouh (d. 2004), playwright who explored sociopolitical issues

Aflaq, Michel (d. 1989), a Damascene and co-founder of the Baath party

al-Ajluni, Ismail (d. 1749), a conservative jurist of Damascus

al-Ali, Saleh (d. 1950), Alawite sheikh who led resistance campaign against French in 1920

Ali Bey al-Kabir (d. 1773), independence-minded Mamluk ruler of Egypt, 1760–72

Alloush, Zahran (d. 2015), opposition militia leader in the post-2011 civil war

Amer, Abdel Hakim (d. 1967), Egyptian military associate of Nasser's who wielded authority in Syria during the last months of the union with Egypt

Amiralay, Omar (d. 2011), Syria's preeminent documentary filmmaker

al-Antaki, Abd al-Masih (d. 1923), Aleppo intellectual and journalist of the 1890s who saw modern Europe and France as social models for Syria

Arar, Maher (b. 1970), Canadian–Syrian engineer arrested in the US and sent to Syria for interrogation under torture

al-Arsuzi, Zaki (d. 1968), prominent Arab activist in Iskanderun during the 1930s

al-Assad, Anisa (née Makhlouf) (d. 2016), wife of Hafez al-Assad

al-Assad, Asma (née Akhras) (b. 1975), wife of Bashar and Syria's First Lady (2001–)

al-Assad, Bashar (b. 1965), president of Syria from 2000 onward

al-Assad, Basil (d. 1994), oldest son and heir-apparent of Hafez al-Assad

al-Assad, Hafez (d. 2000), Alawite air force general who ruled Syria from 1970 until his death al-Assad, Rifaat (b. 1937), Hafez's younger brother who commanded praetorian guard units until stripped of his military power in 1984

al-Atassi, Hashim (d. 1960), senior nationalist from Homs, and Syria's president during intervals from 1936 to 1955

al-Atassi, Nureddin (d. 1992), Sunni ally of Salah Jadid who was figurehead president of Syria, 1966–70

al-Atrash, Sultan (d. 1982), Druze leader of the Syrian revolt against France, 1925–7

al-Azm, Abdallah Pasha (d. 1809), last Azm governor of Damascus who held office in intervals, 1795–1807

al-Azm, Asaad Pasha (d. 1758), third and most illustrious Azm governor of Damascus, 1742–57

al-Azm, Ibrahim Bey, a local military commander active in the region between Hama and Aleppo in the seventeenth century, founder of the Azm family of Ottoman governors

al-Azm, Khalid (d. 1965), industrialist and independent politician who as premier was twice overthrown in military coups

al-Azmeh, Yusuf (d. 1920), commander of the Arab forces who fought the advancing French at Maysaloun in 1920

al-Bakri, Nasib (d. 1966), one of the few landowning notables of Damascus to participate in the anti-French revolt of 1925–7

Barakat, Halim (b. 1936), Syrian-born novelist from the coastal mountains

Barakat, Subhi (d. 1939), a pro-French politician from Antioch

al-Barazi, Muhammad Agha (d. 1891), a military figure who in 1880 became a major land-owner around Hama

al-Barazi, Najib (d. 1967), landowning notable of Hama who frustrated efforts to extend the anti-French revolt to the city in 1925

Barbar Agha (d. 1835), local Janissary and military strongman of Tripoli

Bashir II al-Shihab (d. 1850), emir of Mount Lebanon (1789–1840) who allied with the Egyptians in the 1830s and became identified with local Christian rule

Ben Ali, Zine El Abidine (b. 1936), president of Tunisia, 1987–2011

Beyhum, Muhammad Jamil (d. 1978), Beirut feminist, husband of Nazik al-Abid

al-Bouti, Mohamed Said Ramadan (d. 2013), prominent Sunni religious scholar and ally of Hafez al-Assad

al-Bukhari, Muhammad Murad (d. ca. 1720), a Central Asian scholar who established the Muradi family of *ulama* in Damascus

Burayk, Mikhail (fl. 1782), Christian chronicler of Damascus

Bush, George H. W. (b. 1924), US president, 1989–93

Bush, George W. (b. 1946), US president, 2001–9

al-Bustani, Salim (d. 1884), Beirut pioneer of the Arabic novel whose *Zenobia* (1871) lionized the Roman-era queen of Palmyra

Carbillet, Gabriel (d. 1940), a French officer whose ham-handed administration helped to spark the anti-French revolt in the Jabal Druze in 1925

Clinton, Bill (b. 1946), US president, 1993–2001

Darwish Pasha, governor of Damascus in 1574

de Gaulle, Charles (d. 1970), during World War II, leader of the Free French who ceded Syrian independence; later became president of France

al-Dimashqi, Zayn al-Din Muflih, one of the Damascus *ulama* in the sixteenth century

Erdoğan, Recep Tayyip (b. 1954), Turkish prime minister (2003–14) and president (2014–)

Faisal, son of Sharif Hussein (d. 1933), who established an Arab administration in Damascus from 1918 to 1920, then was made king of Iraq, 1921–33

Fakhr al-Din Ibn Maan (d. 1635), a Druze strongman of Mount Lebanon

Farhi, Haim (d. 1820), Jewish banker and administrator for Ahmad Pasha al-Jazzar and Suleiman Pasha

Farzat, Ali (b. 1951), the preeminent cartoonist in the Assads' Syria

Gaddafi, Muammar (d. 2011), leader of Libya, 1969–2011

Ghalioun, Burhan (b. 1945), exiled Syrian academic and early head (2011–12) of the opposition Syrian National Council

al-Ghawri, Qansuh (d. 1516), last Mamluk sultan of Syria (r. 1501–16)

al-Ghazali, Janbardi (d. 1521), former Mamluk official who rebelled against Sultan Suleiman

Ghul Aghasi, Mahmud 'Abu Qa'qa' (d. 2007), populist preacher in Aleppo

al-Hafez, Amin (d. 2009), Sunni Baathist president of Syria from 1963 to 1966, aligned with the Baath's civilian leadership in the National Command

Hamadas, a Shiite military clan who administered parts of the Lebanon region as Ottoman tax farmers in the seventeenth and eighteenth centuries

Hananu, Ibrahim (d. 1935), leading nationalist from Aleppo in the early years of French rule

al-Hariri, Rafiq (d. 2005), Sunni Lebanese politician and former prime minister, killed by a car bomb

Harfushes, a Shiite military clan who administered parts of rural Syria under Ottoman auspices from the sixteenth to eighteenth centuries

al-Hasani, Taj al-Din (d. 1943), a pro-French Damascene politician during the Mandate

al-Hasibi, Abu'l-Su'ud, Muslim notable of Damascus who witnessed the 1860 massacres

Hinnawi, Sami (d. 1950), colonel who led the second of three military coups in 1949

al-Hourani, Akram (d. 1996), socialist organizer from Hama whose agrarian party merged with the Baath in 1952

Hussein, King of Jordan (d. 1999), reigned from 1952 until his death

Hussein, Saddam (d. 2006), Baath dictator and president of Iraq, 1979–2003

Ibn Arabi (d. 1240), theosophist and saint who emphasized search for inner truths

Ibn Budayr (fl. 1762), a barber-chronicler of Damascus

Ibn Kannan, Muhammad (d. 1740–1), prolific writer and member of Damascene *ulama*

Ibn Khaldun (d. 1406), celebrated late medieval Arab Muslim thinker

Ibn Taymiyya (d. 1328), medieval thinker who emphasized literal and outward forms of scriptural understanding (contra Ibn Arabi)

Ibn Tulun, Muhammad (d. 1546), eyewitness to Ottoman conquest of Damascus

Ibrahim Pasha (d. 1848), Muhammad Ali Pasha's son and heir-apparent who governed Syria for his father in the 1830s

Ipshir Pasha (d. 1655), a governor of Aleppo between 1652–4

Ismail Pasha al-Azm, first Azm governor of Damascus from 1725 to 1730

al-Jaba'i, Ghassan (b. 1956), author of 1994 prison novel *Banana Fingers*

Jabiri, Saadallah (d. 1947), the leading nationalist in Aleppo after Hananu's death

al-Jabiri, Shakib (d. 1996), author of the first Syrian novel published in Syria (1937)

Jadid, Salah (d. 1993), Alawite military officer and principal figure in the Baath regime from 1963 to 1970, when Hafez al-Assad ousted him in an internal coup

Janbulad Ali Pasha (d. 1610), Kurdish strongman near Aleppo who rebelled in 1605

al-Jazairi, Abd al-Qadir (d. 1883), Algerian leader of anti-French resistance exiled to Damascus

al-Jazairi, Adila Beyhum (d. 1975), leader of the Syrian women's movement who advocated for 'patriotic motherhood' in lieu of political rights

al-Jazzar, Ahmad (d. 1804), Ottoman strongman of the Syrian coast, usually based at Acre

Jemal Pasha (d. 1922), Ottoman military commander in Syria during World War I

John Paul II (d. 2005), pontiff from 1978 to 2005, visited Syria 2001

al-Kawakibi, Abd al-Rahman (d. 1902), Aleppo legal scholar, journalist and dissident

Khaddam, Abdul Halim (b. 1932), civilian Baathist ally of Hafez al-Assad who held senior government posts including vice president until 2005

al-Khatib, Moaz (b. 1960), well-known Damascus cleric and later an opposition figure

Khoury, Colette (b. 1931), pioneering feminist novelist from Damascus

al-Khoury, Faris (d. 1962), principal Christian politician in the National Bloc

Khusrow Pasha (d. 1544), high-ranking Ottoman official who built Aleppo's first Ottoman landmark, completed in 1546

Kuftaro, Sheikh Ahmed (d. 2004), long-serving Mufti of the Republic and ally of the Assad regime

Kurd Ali, Muhammad (d. 1953), journalist, intellectual, and founding head of the Arab Academy in Damascus

La La Mustafa Pasha (d. 1580), governor of Aleppo and Damascus from 1563 to 1568

Lahham, Duraid (b. 1934), Damascus-born comedian famous for his satirical movies

Lahoud, Emile (b. 1936), pro-Syrian president of Lebanon, 1998–2007

Maans, a Druze military clan who administered parts of the Lebanon region as Ottoman tax farmers, sixteenth–seventeenth centuries

Mahmud II (d. 1839) Ottoman sultan (1808–39) who abolished the Janissaries in 1826

Makhlouf, Rami (b. 1969), Bashar al-Assad's cousin and prominent crony capitalist

al-Makki, Muhammad (fl. 1688–1722), court scribe in Homs

Malas, Mohammad (b. 1945), prominent film director

al-Maliki, Nouri (b. 1950), Iraqi prime minister, 2006–14

al-Malki, Adnan (d. 1955), a pro-Baath, pro-Nasser military officer assassinated at a sensitive moment in Syria's Cold War political life

Mardam Bey, Jamil (d. 1960), principal figure in the National Bloc in the 1930s

Masharqa, Zuhair (d. 2007), Baath functionary who served as a vice president of Syria from 1984 to 2006

Mina, Hanna (b. 1924), pioneer of socialist-realist novels in Syria, born in Latakia

Mishaqa, Mikhail (d. 1889), Christian chronicler and American consular agent in Syria

Mohammed, Ossama (b. 1954), prominent film director

Mubarak, Hosni (b. 1928), president of Egypt, 1981–2011

Muhammad Ali Pasha (d. 1848), autonomous governor of Egypt, 1805–48

Murad Pasha, governor of Damascus, 1568–9.

Mussolini, Benito (d. 1945), Fascist dictator of Italy, 1922–43

Mustafa Kemal (d. 1938), Ottoman general who led the Turkish resistance movement after World War I and became Kemal Ataturk, Turkey's first president

al-Nabulusi, Abd al-Ghani (d. 1731), the towering Damascene polymath of his day

al-Nahrawali, Qutb al-Din (d. 1582), chronicler and envoy who traveled in Syria

Nasrallah, Sayyid Hasan (b. 1960), leader of Lebanon's Hezbollah 1992–

Nasser, Gamal Abdul (d. 1970), president of Egypt from 1954 to 1970 and of Syria when it was part of the UAR, 1958–61

Obama, Barack (b. 1961), US president, 2009–17

al-Qabbani, Abu Khalil (d. 1902), the first modern Damascene playwright

Qabbani, Nizar (d. 1998), prominent literary figure from Damascus, popularly identified as Syria's national poet

Qastun, Fathallah (d. ca. 1920s?), Catholic newspaper editor of Aleppo during the later Ottoman and early French eras

al-Qawuqji, Fawzi (d. 1977), anti-colonial military officer who fought in Syria and in Palestine

al-Qudsi, Nazim (d. 1998), Aleppo politician who served as Syria's president during the post-UAR 'secessionist regime', 1961–3

al-Quwatli, Shukri (d. 1967), National Bloc leader who became independent Syria's first president

Rabbath, Edmond (d. 1991), prominent Catholic nationalist, from Aleppo

al-Rukayni, Haydar Rida (d. 1783), a Shiite chronicler from Jabal Amil

al-Rumi, Jalal al-Din (d. 1273), Konya (Turkey) mystic who inspired the Mawlawiyya Sufis

Saadeh, Antoun (d. 1949), political theoretician and founder of the Syrian Social National Party (SSNP)

Sabbagh, Ibrahim (d. 1775), treasurer and administrator for Zahir al-Umar

Sadat, Anwar (d. 1981), president of Egypt, 1970–81

Safavi, Ismail (d. 1524), founder of Iranian Safavid dynasty (1501–1722)

Safi al-Din (d. 1334), Kurdish sheikh and ancestor to Ismail Safavi

Said, Ali Ahmad 'Adonis' (b. 1930), widely recognized modernist poet from Latakia

Saladin (d. 1193), medieval Muslim warrior and founder of the Ayyubid dynasty

Saleh, Ali Abdullah (d. 2017), president of North Yemen, 1978–90, of Yemen, 1990–2012

al-Sarraj, Abdel-Hamid (d. 2013), Syrian intelligence officer who exercised authority in the country during the years of union with Egypt

Sayfas, a Turcoman military family who administered the Tripoli region for the Ottomans from 1579 to 1625

al-Sayyadi, Abu al-Huda (d. 1909), Sufi sheikh from Aleppo and Sultan Abdulhamid loyalist

Seif, Riyad (b. 1946), independent parliamentarian, businessman and dissident

Selim I, Ottoman sultan who conquered Syria (r. 1512–20)

Shahbandar, Abd al-Rahman (d. 1940), Damascene founder of the first nationalist party in French-ruled Syria, the People's Party

Shallah, Badr al-Din (d. 1996), longtime head of the Damascus Chamber of Commerce and ally of Hafez al-Assad

Shallah, Rateb (b. 1932), son of Badr al-Din, head of the Federation of Syrian Chambers of Commerce and ally of Bashar al-Assad

Sharif Hussein (d. 1931) of Mecca launched the Arab Revolt in league with Britain during World War I

Shihabs, the dominant political family in Mount Lebanon from 1697 to 1842, initially Sunni Muslims but later convert to Maronite Christianity

Shishakli, Adib (d. 1964), colonel who led the third of three military coups in 1949 and ruled as a military strongman until 1954

al-Shufi, Hammud (b. 1927), Baathist diplomat who resigned as Syria's ambassador to the UN in 1979

al-Sibai, Mustafa (d. 1965), legal scholar and founder of the Syrian Muslim Brotherhood

Sinan Pasha (d. 1596), governor of Damascus in 1586–7 and in 1588

Suleiman 'the Magnificent', (d. 1566), Ottoman sultan, 1520–66

Suleiman al-Murshid (d. 1946), charismatic advocate of self-rule for the Alawite coastal region

Suleiman Pasha al-Azm (d. 1743), second Azm governor of Damascus (1734–8, 1741–3)

Suleiman Pasha (d. 1819), a Mamluk of al-Jazzar's who succeeded him at Acre, 1804–19

Suwaydan, Ibrahim Agha (d. 1709), a local military figure in Homs

Taja, Khalid (d. 2012), veteran actor

Tamerlane (d. 1405), Central Asian conqueror who waged war in Syria

Tlas, Mustafa (d. 2017), officer colleague of Hafez al-Assad and long-serving Defense Minister, 1972–2004

Trump, Donald (b. 1946), US president, 2017–

Wannous, Saadallah (d. 1997), prominent playwright, born in the coastal mountains

Weizmann, Chaim (d. 1952), Zionist leader who secured British support for a Jewish national home in Palestine

Yusuf, Ibrahim (d. 1980), captain in the Syrian Army who set up a massacre of Alawite military cadets in Aleppo in 1979

Zahir al-Umar (d. 1775), warlord and tax farmer of the Galilee

Zahlawi, Elias (b. 1932), Catholic priest and founder of a prominent choir

Zaim, Husni (d. 1949), Syrian officer who led the first of three military coups in 1949

Zain al-Din, Nazira (d. 1976), campaigned for modern Islam and against the veil during the French Mandate years

Zeidan, Jurji (d. 1914), Syrian émigré in Egypt who popularized the genre of the historical novel in Arabic

GLOSSARY

A'yan: provincial notables and powerbrokers who become important in the eighteenth century

Agha: military title, often associated with the Janissary corps

Amal: 'hope'; Lebanese Shiite political party and militia, founded in the 1970s

Anaza: Bedouin tribes who displaced older pastoralist communities in the eighteenth century

Assyrians: Syriac-rite Christians affiliated with the Church of the East and its offshoots, formerly called 'Nestorians'

Baath: 'resurrection'; Arab nationalist party est. 1947, has ruled Syria since 1963

Bashibazouks: Ottoman paramilitaries who complemented regular forces in the nineteenth century, often rough and ill disciplined

Bey: high military rank or title, below that of pasha

Bilad al-Sham: 'Lands of Damascus', Arabic equivalent to geographic Syria

Capitulation Agreements: treaties that defined foreigners' privileges in Ottoman lands

Dabka: a popular style of Syrian folk dance

al-Dawla: 'the state' (also a reference to the Ottoman sultanate)

Dhimmi: a Christian or Jew offered protection in return for his/her recognition of Muslim rule

Druze(s): a monotheistic faith community in geographic Syria with distant roots in Islam

Effendi: title denoting an 'urban gentleman': learned, literate, and non-military

Emir: prince or commander

Grand Vizier: the highest-ranking political–military administrator in the Ottoman Empire

Hadith: canonical accounts of Prophet Muhammad's life and words

Hanafi: favored by the Ottomans, one of four schools of law (or 'rites') in Sunni Islam

Hashemites: dynasty founded by Sharif Hussein of Mecca

Hezbollah: 'party of God'; Lebanese Shiite political party and guerrilla movement, founded in the early 1980s

Irhal: 'go away'; slogan directed at Bashar al-Assad in demonstrations

Ismailis: followers of a branch of Shiite Islam headed by the Aga Khan

Janissary/-ies: Ottoman infantry

Jizya: poll tax paid by non-Muslim subjects (*dhimmis*) of a Muslim ruler

Kadi: judicial officer, and judge in the Ottomans' sharia law courts

Khan: caravanserai or merchants' emporium

Khanqah: a Sufi meeting-place ('lodge')

Khedive: ruler of Egypt after Muhammad Ali Pasha establishes hereditary Ottoman governorship

Madrasa: 'school'; in Ottoman times refers to schools that taught Islamic knowledge

Majalla: reform-era Ottoman civil law code, based on the sharia

Majdhub: a living saint, whose unusual behavior shows s/he is 'seized' by the Divine

Majous: 'magi'; Sunni militants' derogatory word for Shiites lampooned as anti-Arab 'Persians'

Malikane: lifetime tax farm, introduced in 1695

Mamluk: a 'slave soldier'; manumitted Mamluks formed powerful military retinues

Maronites: Arabic–Syriac rite Christians in communion with Rome, concentrated in Lebanon

Mawlawis: a Sufi order traced to the medieval mystic Jalal al-Din al-Rumi, also called the 'Whirling Dervishes'

Melkites: also called Greek Catholics, Orthodox-rite Christians in communion with Rome

Millet: Ottoman-recognized religious community

Mizrahis: Ottoman and Middle Eastern Jews of Arab ancestry

Mufti: Muslim jurisconsult; 'Mufti of the Republic' = Syria's highest-ranking Muslim cleric

Mutasarrifiyya: autonomous district of Mount Lebanon created in 1861

Mutawila: an old name for Shiites of the Lebanon region, today considered pejorative

Nahda: 'renaissance'; name given to the Arabic literary movement of the nineteenth and early twentieth centuries

Nakba: 'catastrophe'; Israel's dispossession of 700,000 Palestinian Arabs during the 1948–9 war that accompanied the creation of Israel

Naqib al-Ashraf: head of the Ashraf (Prophet's descendants) in a particular city

Naqshbandi: a Sufi order significant in Syria since the seventeenth century

Nasserist: Arab nationalist supporting the leadership of Egypt's President Nasser

Nawruz: Kurdish and Persian new year, corresponding to the spring equinox

Nusaryis: an old name for Alawites, today considered pejorative

Nusra: the Syrian al Qaeda franchise, est. 2012 and later renamed Syrian Conquest Front

Pasha: military rank or title held by senior officials including provincial governors

Phanariots: aristocratic Greek families of Istanbul who played important roles in Ottoman administration (administrators, diplomats, tax farmers)

Qadiriyya: a Sufi order originating in medieval Iraq, associated with leadership of the Kaylani family

Al Qaeda: 'the base'; international Muslim militant group founded in 1988 during the war against the USSR in Afghanistan

Rafidis, Rafida: 'rejectors'; pejorative Sunni term for Shiites

Rojava: 'western Kurdistan'; Kurdish nationalists' name for northern Syria

Rumi: a Turk from Anatolia, derived from *Rum* (= Rome = Byzantium)

Safarbarlik: Syrians' experiences of conscription, flight and famine during World War I

Salafiyya: movement of Islamic intellectual revival and reform beginning in the late nineteenth century, advocates called Salafis

Sephardis: Ottoman and Middle Eastern Jews of Spanish (Andalusian) ancestry

Shabiha: paramilitary enforcers, derived from criminal gangs, working for the Bashar al-Assad government

Sharia: Islamic law

Sharif (pl. Ashraf): recognized descendant(s) of the Prophet Muhammad

Sheikh al-Islam: the highest-ranking religious-legal authority in the Ottoman Empire

Sipahi: a soldier-administrator granted revenues of land in return for military service to the Ottoman sultan

Sufi/-ism: Islamic mystic/mysticism

Suq: market or bazaar

Suryani: a reference to the Syriac-rite Syrian Orthodox Church (formerly called 'Jacobites')

Tahqiq: study ('verification') of earlier writers and their treatises

Takiyya: a Sufi meeting-place ('lodge')

Tanzimat: 'renovations'; Ottoman reform program beginning in 1839

Tariqa: a Sufi order

al-Tariq al-Sultani: Ottoman royal road extending from north to south in Syria

Ulama: Muslim scholars and men of religion, comparable to clergy

Umayyads: first dynasty of Arab caliphs (661–750 CE), based at Damascus

Vilayet: Ottoman province

Wahhabis: Muslim revivalists in Arabia who challenged Ottoman legitimacy

Waqf: an endowment dedicated to charitable purposes, or to keep intact a family's property

Watan: 'homeland'; in modern times became Arabic equivalent to French *patrie*

Yazidis: a distinct religious community, predominantly Kurdish and Iraqi, rooted in Mesopotamian religious traditions

Zawiya: a Sufi meeting-place ('lodge'); also the name of a rugged region in north-central Syria

Ziamet: revenue-yielding lands, controlled and administered by a Zaim in return for military services to the Ottoman sultan

Zionism: Jewish national movement that aimed to build a Jewish homeland in Palestine

NOTES

1. SYRIA BECOMES OTTOMAN, SIXTEENTH–SEVENTEENTH CENTURIES

1 The origins of the difference lay in the fact that Shiites believed leadership of the Muslim community was rightly vested in direct descendants of the Prophet Muhammad, called Imams, who were gifted with esoteric religious knowledge. The first such Imam was Ali, Muhammad's son-in-law. In contrast Sunnis believed that community leadership was open to any pious man, known as a caliph, selected by learned men of the community conversant with the practices and traditions (Sunna) of Muhammad.

2 Pronounced 'room' where the word *Rum* (Rome) referred to the former realm of the Byzantines. People from Anatolia (today usually called 'Turks') were for the Syrians *Rumis* – Romans.

3 Qutb al-Din al-Nahrawali, in Richard Blackburn, *Journey to the Sublime Porte: The Arabic Memoir of a Sharifian Agent's Diplomatic Mission to the Ottoman Imperial Court in the Era of Suleyman the Magnificent* (Beirut: Orient-Institut, and Würzburg: Ergon Verlag, 2005), 35.

4 Ibid., 39.

5 Religious pluralism was deeply entrenched in the cities of Ottoman Syria. Protected non-Muslim religious communities (principally Christians and Jews) were permitted to retain their distinct communal identities in return for political loyalty and the payment of special taxes. These protected non-Muslim communities were called *dhimmis* – non-Muslims who accepted Muslim rule. Because the Ottomans had assumed the mantle of Byzantium (both lands and peoples), Orthodox Christians were an especially important part of the Ottomans' consolidated imperial structure.

6 Quoted in James Grehan, *Everyday Life and Consumer Culture in 18th-Century Damascus* (Seattle: University of Washington Press, 2007), 148–9.

7 Quoted in Steve Tamari, 'The 'alim as public intellectual: 'Abd al-Ghani al-Nabulusi (d. 1731 CE) as a scholar-activist,' in Mohammed A. Bamyeh (ed.), *Intellectuals and Civil Society in the Middle East: Liberalism, Modernity and Political Discourse* (London: I.B.Tauris, 2012), 99–100.

8 Ibid., 104.

9 Quoted in Toru Miura, *Dynamism in the Urban Society of Damascus: The Salihiyya Quarter from the Twelfth to the Twentieth Centuries* (Leiden: Brill, 2016), 202.

2. SYRIA'S 'LONG' EIGHTEENTH CENTURY: POLITICAL CRISES AND LOCAL RULERS

1 Quoted in James A. Reilly, 'The universal and the particular: a view from Ottoman Homs ca. 1700', *The Journal of Ottoman Studies* 44 (2014), 348.
2 Quoted in ibid., 347.
3 Quoted in Steve Tamari, 'Between the "golden age" and the Renaissance: Islamic higher education in eighteenth-century Damascus', in Osama Abi-Mershed (ed.), *Trajectories of Education in the Arab World: Legacies and Challenges* (New York: Routledge, 2010), 46.
4 Quoted in Steve Tamari, 'Biography, autobiography, and identity in early modern Damascus', in Mary Ann Fay (ed.), *Auto/Biography and the Construction of Identity and Community in the Middle East* (New York: Palgrave, 2001), 45.
5 Quoted in ibid., 46.
6 Quoted in Dana Sajdi, *The Barber of Damascus: Nouveau Literacy in the Eighteenth-Century Ottoman Levant* (Stanford: Stanford University Press, 2013), 183.
7 Quoted in ibid., 152.
8 Quoted in ibid., 79.
9 Quoted in Tamari, 'Biography, autobiography', 45.
10 Quoted in Sajdi, *Barber of Damascus*, 23.
11 Quoted in James Grehan, *Everyday Life and Consumer Culture in 18th-Century Damascus* (Seattle: University of Washington Press, 2007), 141.
12 Quoted in ibid., 149–50.
13 Quoted in ibid., 150.
14 Ismailis are followers of a branch of Shiite Islam headed by the Aga Khan.
15 Translated by and quoted in Sajdi, *Barber of Damascus*, 83–4. The words in quotation marks are phrases from the Qur'an.
16 Ibid., 85.
17 Quoted in Thomas Philipp, *Acre: The Rise and Fall of a Palestinian City, 1730–1831* (New York: Columbia University Press, 2002), 109.
18 Quoted in ibid., 126.
19 Quoted in ibid., 148.

3. SYRIA BETWEEN EUROPE AND THE OTTOMANS, 1820s–1900s

1 Mount Lebanon refers to the high coastal mountains that are within today's Lebanon, but Mount Lebanon covers less territory than does the modern Lebanese state. Formerly the Ottomans had called these coastal mountains the 'Druze mountain', because of the preeminence of Druze feudal intermediaries and tax farmers there.

2 Mikhayil Mishaqa, *Murder, Mayhem, Pillage, and Plunder: The History of the Lebanon in the 18th and 19th Centuries*, translated by Wheeler M. Thackston, Jr (Albany: State University of New York Press, 1988), 255.

3 Ibid., 257–8.

4 Estimates and statistics are discussed in Leila Tarazi Fawaz, *An Occasion for War: Civil Conflict in Lebanon and Damascus in 1860* (Berkeley: University of California Press, 1994), 132–3.

5 Theodoros Kolokotronis, quoted in David Brewer, *The Flame of Freedom: The Greek War of Independence 1821–1833* (London: John Murray, 2001), 71.

6 Quoted in Khaled Fahmy, *All the Pasha's Men: Mehmed Ali, His Army and the Making of Modern Egypt* (Cairo: American University in Cairo Press, 2002), 115.

7 Neophytes of Cyprus, quoted in Norman N. Lewis, *Nomads and Settlers in Syria and Jordan, 1800–1980* (Cambridge: Cambridge University Press, 1987), 38.

8 Quoted in Bruce Masters, *Christians and Jews in the Ottoman Arab World: The Roots of Sectarianism* (Cambridge: Cambridge University Press, 2004), 162.

9 Quoted in Fawaz, *An Occasion for War*, 90.

10 Quoted in Kamal S. Salibi, 'The 1860 upheaval in Damascus as seen by al-Sayyid Muhammad Abu'l-Su'ud al-Hasibi, notable and later *Naqib al-Ashraf* of the city', in William Polk and Richard Chambers (eds), *Beginnings of Modernization in the Middle East: The Nineteenth Century* (Chicago: University of Chicago Press, 1968), 190.

11 Quoted in Salibi, 'The 1860 upheaval in Damascus', 188–9.

12 Quoted in Eugene L. Rogan, 'Sectarianism and social conflict in Damascus: the 1860 events reconsidered', *Arabica* 51 (2004), 505.

13 Quoted in Rogan, 'Sectarianism and social conflict', 496.

14 Quoted in Lewis, *Nomads and Settlers*, 72.

15 The Barazis' fiefdom in Hama would be targeted by populist radicals beginning in the 1950s. The subsequent (1960s) dispossession and marginalization of old landed elites including the Barazis turned the traditional market and residential quarters of their urban bastions into hotbeds of anti-government opposition, culminating in Hama's bloodily suppressed anti-government uprising in 1982.

4. THE IDEA OF SYRIA AND WORLD WAR I

1 Quoted in Nadia Bou Ali, 'Butrus al-Bustani and the Shipwreck of the Nation', *Middle Eastern Literatures* 16, 3 (2013), 275.

2 Quoted in Keith David Watenpaugh, *Being Modern in the Middle East: Revolution, Nationalism, Colonialism, and the Arab Middle Class* (Princeton, NJ: Princeton University Press, 2012), 42–3.

3 The figure 300,000 is cited in Najwa al-Qattan, 'Fragments of wartime memories from Syria and Lebanon', in M. Talha Çiçek (ed.), *Syria in World War I: Politics, Economy,*

and Society (London: Routledge, 2016), 131. The figure of half a million, which 'might be conservative,' is cited in Leila Tarazi Fawaz, *A Land of Aching Hearts: The Middle East in the Great War* (Cambridge: Harvard University Press, 2014), 277.

4 Quoted in Fawaz, *A Land of Aching Hearts*, 105.

5 Quoted in Salim Tamari, 'Muhammad Kurd Ali and the Syrian–Palestinian intelligentsia in the Ottoman campaign against Arab separatism', in Çiçek, *Syria in World War I*, 47.

5. FRANCE AND THE CREATION OF THE SYRIAN TERRITORIAL STATE

1 Quoted in Michael Provence, *The Great Syrian Revolt and the Rise of Arab Nationalism* (Austin: University of Texas Press, 2005), 82.

2 Quoted in Watenpaugh, *Being Modern in the Middle East: Revolution, Nationalism, Colonialism, and the Arab Middle Class* (Princeton: Princeton University Press, 2006), 141.

3 Quoted in Philip S. Khoury, *Urban Notables and Arab Nationalism: The Politics of Damascus, 1860–1920*, 147–8, re-quoted in Watenpaugh, *Being Modern*, 141.

4 Rushdi Duhna quoted in Watenpaugh, *Being Modern*, 147–8.

5 Nearly a century later, in the 2010s, the Zawiya region and its district center of Idlib would once again be a stronghold of rebellion, this time against the Damascus government of Bashar al-Assad.

6 Years later, in the Syrian civil war of the 2010s, the Jazira would mostly be lost to Damascus, becoming terrain fought over between the jihadist Islamic State movement and the Kurdish-dominated Syrian Democratic Forces militia.

7 Philip S. Khoury, *Syria and the French Mandate: The Politics of Syrian Nationalism* (Princeton: Princeton University Press, 1987), 237.

8 One of his partners was Khalid al-Azm (d. 1965), scion of the famous Ottoman-era political family and a leading proponent of industrialization in mid-twentieth-century Syria.

9 Quoted in Watenpaugh, *Being Modern*, 5.

10 Quoted in ibid., 215.

11 Quoted in Elizabeth Thompson, *Colonial Citizens: Republican Rights, Paternal Privilege, and Gender in French Syria and Lebanon* (New York: Columbia University Press, 2000), 121.

12 Quoted in Thompson, *Colonial Citizens*, 144. The editorial interjection is mine. The phrase 'patriotic motherhood' is Thompson's.

13 Quoted in ibid., 132.

14 For a video of the older Abu Risha reciting a poem of heartbreak, with English translation superimposed, see 'Omar Abu Risha – Go Back! Arabic poetry translated', https://www.youtube.com/watch?v=_M0r_wH9Lgc.

15 Quoted in Khoury, *Syria and the French Mandate*, 602.

6. CRISES OF INDEPENDENT STATEHOOD

1 Its name evoked Shahbandar's original People's Party, which dissolved after his unsolved assassination in 1940. Shahbandar's supporters, and French intelligence, accused his National Bloc rivals of responsibility for the death.

2 Quoted in Hanna Batatu, *Syria's Peasantry, the Descendants of its Lesser Rural Notables, and their Politics* (Princeton: Princeton University Press, 1999), 24.

3 The League, established in 1945, was an instrument for Egyptian leadership of independent Arab states.

4 Quoted in Patrick Seale, *The Struggle for Syria: A Study of Post-War Arab Politics, 1945–1958* (London: I.B.Tauris, 1965, 1986), 125.

5 Quoted in Seale, *Struggle for Syria*, 87.

6 Quoted in Joshua Landis, 'Shishakli and the Druzes: integration and intransigence', in Thomas Philipp and Birgit Schaebler (eds), *The Syrian Land: Processes of Integration and Fragmentation: Bilad al-Sham from the 18th to the 20th Century* (Stuttgart: Franz Steiner Verlag, 1998), 390.

7 Quoted in Tabitha Petran, *Syria* (London: Ernest Benn, 1972), 175.

8 Quoted in Batatu, *Syria's Peasantry*, 173.

9 Quoted in Petran, *Syria*, 248.

10 Paul Starkey, *Modern Arabic Literature* (Edinburgh: Edinburgh University Press, 2006), 76.

11 Qabbani's status as a national icon is represented, for instance, by his image on the wall of a Syrian café that opened in a vibrant neighborhood of Toronto in 2017.

12 Roger Allen, *The Arabic Novel*, quoted in Starkey, *Modern Arabic Literature*, 129.

7. THIRTY YEARS OF HAFEZ AL-ASSAD

1 Quoted in Nikolaos van Dam, *The Struggle for Power in Syria: Politics and Society under Asad and the Ba'th Party,* 4th edn (London: I.B.Tauris, 2011), 90.

2 Ibid., 93.

3 Ibid., 106.

4 Acting 'as if' – a concept applied to Syria and the Assad cult by Lisa Wedeen, 'Acting "as if": symbolic politics and social control in Syria', *Comparative Studies in Society and History* 40 (1998), 503–23.

5 miriam cooke, *Dissident Syria: Making Oppositional Arts Official* (Durham, NC: Duke University Press, 2007), 16.

6 Quoted in Volker Perthes, *The Political Economy of Syria under Asad* (London, I.B.Tauris, 1995), 262.

7 Quoted in Hanna Batatu, *Syria's Peasantry, the Descendants of its Lesser Rural Notables, and their Politics* (Princeton: Princeton University Press 1999), 329.

8 Quoted in cooke, *Dissident Syria*, 58–60.

9 Ibid., 131.

10 Ibid., 72–7.

11 Rasha Salti, 'Critical nationals: the paradoxes of Syrian cinema', in Rasha Salti (ed.), *Insights into Syrian Cinema: Essays and Conversations with Contemporary Filmmakers* (New York: Rattapallax Press, 2006), 21–44.

12 Quoted in cooke, *Dissident Syria*, 4.

13 Ibid., 92–9.

14 Ibid., 87–92.

8. A FALSE 'SPRING' AND GATHERING STORMS

1 Quoted in Eyal Zisser, *Commanding Syria: Bashar al-Asad and the First Years in Power* (London: I.B.Tauris, 2007), ix.

2 Quoted in David W. Lesch, *Syria: The Fall of the House of Assad* (New Haven, CT: Yale University Press, 2012), 4.

3 Quoted in Zisser, *Commanding* Syria, 82.

4 Quoted in ibid., 84.

5 Quoted in Volker Perthes, *Syria under Bashar al-Asad: Modernisation and the Limits of Change* (New York: Oxford University Press, 2004), 17.

6 Quoted in ibid., 17.

7 Quoted in Christa Salamandra, *A New Old Damascus: Authenticity and Distinction in Urban Syria* (Bloomington: Indiana University Press, 2004), 159, cited in Miriam Cooke, *Dissident Syria: Making Oppositional Art Official* (Durham: Duke University Press, 2007), 162.

8 Statistic cited in Perthes, *Syria under Bashar al-Asad*, 29.

9 Statistic cited in Zisser, *Commanding Syria*, 115.

10 Statistic cited in ibid., 116.

11 Phil Sands, 'Syrian actor champions slum dwellers' plight', 12 November 2009, https://www.thenational.ae/world/mena/syrian-actor-champions-slum-dwellers-plight-1.538318.

12 Quoted in Thomas Pierret, 'Merchant background, bourgeois ethics: The Syrian *ulama* and economic liberalization', in Christa Salamandra and Leif Stenberg (eds), *Syria from Reform to Revolt*, vol. 2, *Culture, Society and Religion* (Syracuse, NY: Syracuse University Press, 2015), 144.

9. UPRISING, CIVIL WAR AND FRAGMENTATION

1 Assad must go, Obama says *Washington Post* 18 August 2011, https://www.washingtonpost.com/politics/assad-must-go-obama-says/2011/08/18/gIQAelheOJ_story.html?utm_term=.8e9dc4f122c0.

2 Quoted in David W. Lesch, *Syria: The Fall of the House of Assad* (New Haven, CT: Yale University Press, 2012), 237.

3 Quoted in Joshua Landis, 'Zahran Alloush: His Ideology and Beliefs', *Syria Comment* 15 December 2013, http://www.joshualandis.com/blog/zahran-alloush/.

4 Quoted in Harriet Allsopp, *The Kurds of Syria: Political Parties and Identity in the Middle East* (London: I.B.Tauris, 2014), 200.

5 'Assad admits army struggling for manpower', *al-Jazeera* 26 July 2015, http://www.aljazeera.com/news/2015/07/syria-assad-speech-150726091936884.html.

10. SYRIA DIVIDED

1 Quoted in Wendy Pearlman, *We Crossed a Bridge and it Trembled: Voices from Syria* (New York, 2017), 7.

2 Karl Marx, *The Eighteenth Brumaire of Louis Napoleon*, quoted in Wikipedia, 'The Eighteenth Brumaire of Louis Napoleon', https://en.wikipedia.org/wiki/The_Eighteenth_Brumaire_of_Louis_Napoleon.

SELECTED BIBLIOGRAPHY

WEBSITES

'Assad must go, Obama says', *Washington Post* 18 August 2011, https://www.washington post.com/politics/assad-must-go-obama-says/2011/08/18/gIQAelheOJ_story.html? utm_term=.8e9dc4f122c0.

Haddad, Bassam, 'The Syrian regime's business backbone', *Middle East Report* 262 http:// www.merip.org/mer/mer262/syrian-regimes-business-backbone.

Landis, Joshua, 'Zahran Alloush: His Ideology and Beliefs', *Syria Comment* 15 December 2013, http://www.joshualandis.com/blog/zahran-alloush/.

Marx, Karl, *The Eighteenth Brumaire of Louis Napoleon*, quoted in Wikipedia, 'The Eighteenth Brumaire of Louis Napoleon', https://en.wikipedia.org/wiki/The_ Eighteenth_Brumaire_of_Louis_Napoleon.

'Omar Abu Risha – Go Back! Arabic poetry translated', https://www.youtube.com/ watch?v=_M0r_wH9Lgc.

Provence, Michael, 'French Mandate counterinsurgency and the repression of the Great Syrian Revolt', *The Routledge Handbook of the History of the Middle East Mandates*, https://www.routledgehandbooks.com/doi/10.4324/9781315713120.ch8.

Sands, Phil, 'Syrian actor champions slum dwellers' plight', 12 November 2009, https://www. thenational.ae/world/mena/syrian-actor-champions-slum-dwellers-plight-1.538318.

'Syria's Assad admits army struggling for manpower', *al-Jazeera* 26 July 2015, http://www. aljazeera.com/news/2015/07/syria-assad-speech-150726091936884.html.

ARTICLES AND CHAPTERS

Bandak, Andreas, 'Performing the nation: Syrian Christians on the national stage', in Christa Salamandra and Leif Stenberg (eds), *Syria from Reform to Revolt*, vol. 2, *Culture, Society and Religion* (Syracuse, NY: Syracuse University Press, 2015), 110–29.

Bou Ali, Nadia, 'Butrus al-Bustani and the shipwreck of a nation', *Middle Eastern Literatures* 16, 3 (2013), 266–81.

Chagas, Gisele Fonseca, 'Muslim women and the work of *da'wa*: the female branch of the tariqa Naqshbandiyya-Kuftariyya in Damascus, Syria', *Middle East Critique* 20, no. 2 (Summer 2011), 207–18.

de Elvira, Laura Ruiz, 'Christian charities and the Ba'thist regime in Bashar al-Asad's Syria', in Christa Salamandra and Leif Stenberg (eds), *Syria from Reform to Revolt*, vol. 2, *Culture, Society and Religion* (Syracuse, NY: Syracuse University Press, 2015), 92–109.

Della Ratta, Donatella, 'The "whisper strategy": how Syrian drama makers shape television fiction in the context of authoritarianism and commodification', in Christa Salamandra and Leif Stenberg (eds), *Syria from Reform to Revolt*, vol. 2, *Culture, Society and Religion* (Syracuse, NY: Syracuse University Press, 2015), 53–76.

El-Rouayheb, Khaled, 'Opening the gate of verification: the forgotten Arab–Islamic florescence of the 17th century', *International Journal of Middle East Studies* 38 (2006), 263–81.

Haddad, Bassam, 'Syria's state bourgeoisie: an organic backbone for the regime', *Middle East Critique* 21, no. 3 (Fall 2012), 231–57.

Hinnebusch, Raymond, 'Modern Syrian politics', *History Compass* 6/1 (2008), 263–85.

Hourani, Albert, 'Ottoman reform and the politics of notables', in William R. Polk and Richard L. Chambers (eds), *Beginnings of Modernization in the Middle East: The Nineteenth Century* (Chicago: University of Chicago Press, 1968), 41–68.

Kafescioğlu, Çiğdem, '"In the image of Rum": Ottoman architectural patronage in sixteenth-century Aleppo and Damascus', *Muqarnas* 16 (1999), 70–96.

Khoury, Philip S., 'Continuity and change in Syrian political life: the nineteenth and twentieth centuries', *American Historical Review* 96, no. 5 (1991), 1374–95.

Landis, Joshua, 'Shishakli and the Druzes: integration and intransigence', in Thomas Philipp and Birgit Schaebler (eds), *The Syrian Land: Processes of Integration and Fragmentation: Bilad al-Sham from the 18th to the 20th Century* (Stuttgart: Franz Steiner Verlag, 1998), 369–96.

Lesch, David W., 'Anatomy of an uprising: Bashar al-Assad's fateful choices that launched a civil war', in Mark L. Haas and David W. Lesch (eds.), *The Arab Spring: The Hope and Reality of the Uprisings* (Boulder, CO: Westview, 2017), 91–112.

Masters, Bruce, 'The political economy of Aleppo in an age of Ottoman reform', *Journal of the Economic and Social History of the Orient* 53 (2010): 290–316.

Meier, Astrid, 'Perceptions of a new era? Historical writing in early Ottoman Damascus', *Arabica* 51, no. 4 (2004), 419–34.

Pfeifer, Helen, 'Encounter after the conquest: scholarly gatherings in 16th-century Ottoman Damascus', *International Journal of Middle East Studies* 47 (2105), 219–39.

Pierret, Thomas, 'Merchant background, bourgeois ethics: the Syrian ulama and economic liberalization', in Christa Salamandra and Leif Stenberg (eds), *Syria from Reform to Revolt*, vol. 2, *Culture, Society and Religion* (Syracuse, NY: Syracuse University Press, 2015), 130–46.

Al-Qattan, Najwa, 'Fragments of wartime memories from Syria and Lebanon', in M. Talha Çiçek (ed.), *Syria in World War I: Politics, Economy and Society* (London: Routledge, 2016), 130–49.

Rafeq, Abdul-Karim, 'Craft organization, work ethics, and the strains of change in Ottoman Syria', *Journal of the American Oriental Society* 111, no. 3 (1991), 495–511.

——, 'Relations between the Syrian ulama and the Ottoman state in the eighteenth century', *Oriento Moderno* 18, no. 1 (1999), 67–95.

Reilly, James A., 'The universal and the particular: a view from Ottoman Homs ca. 1700', *The Journal of Ottoman Studies* 44 (2014), 341–56.

Rogan, Eugene L., 'Sectarianism and social conflict in Damascus: the 1860 events reconsidered', *Arabica* 51 (2004), 493–511.

Sajdi, Dana, 'In other worlds? Mapping out the spatial imaginaries of 18th-century chroniclers from the Ottoman Levant (Bilad al-Sham)', *The Journal of Ottoman Studies* 44 (2014), 357–92.

Salamandra, Christa, 'Syria's drama outpouring: between complicity and critique', in Christa Salamandra and Leif Stenberg (eds), *Syria from Reform to Revolt*, vol. 2, *Culture, Society and Religion* (Syracuse, NY: Syracuse University Press, 2015), 36–52.

Salibi, Kamal S., 'The 1860 upheaval in Damascus as seen by al-Sayyid Muhammad Abu'l-Su'ud al-Hasibi, notable and later *naqib al-ashraf* in the city', in William R. Polk and Richard L. Chambers (eds), *Beginnings of Modernization in the Middle East: The Nineteenth Century* (Chicago: University of Chicago Press, 1968), 185–202.

Salti, Rasha, 'Critical nationals: the paradoxes of Syrian cinema', in Rasha Salti (ed.), *Insights into Syrian Cinema: Essays and Conversations with Contemporary Filmmakers* (New York: Rattapallax Press, 2006), 21–44.

Schilcher, Linda Schatkowski, 'The Hauran conflicts of the 1860s: a chapter in the rural history of modern Syria', *International Journal of Middle East Studies* 13 (1981), 159–79.

Stenberg, Leif, 'Muslim organizations in Bashar's Syria: The transformation of the Shaykh Ahmad Kuftaro Foundation', in Christa Salamandra and Leif Stenberg (eds), *Syria from Reform to Revolt*, vol. 2, *Culture, Society and Religion* (Syracuse, NY: Syracuse University Press, 2015), 147–68.

Tamari, Salim, 'Muhammad Kurd Ali and the Syrian–Palestinian intelligentsia in the Ottoman campaign against Arab separatism', in M. Talha Ciçek (ed.), *Syria in World War I: Politics, Economy and Society* (London: Routledge, 2016), 37–60.

Tamari, Steve, 'Between the "golden age" and the Renaissance: Islamic higher education in eighteenth-century Damascus', in Osama Abi-Mershed (ed.), *Trajectories of Education in the Arab World: Legacies and Challenges* (New York: Routledge, 2010), 36–58.

——, 'Biography, autobiography, and identity in early modern Damascus', in Mary Ann Fay (ed.), *Auto/Biography and the Construction of Identity and Community in the Middle East* (New York: Palgrave, 2001), 37–49.

———, 'The 'alim as public intellectual: 'Abd al-Ghani al-Nabulusi (d. 1731 CE) as a scholar-activist', in Mohammed A. Bamyeh (ed.), *Intellectuals and Civil Society in the Middle East: Liberalism, Modernity and Political Discourse* (London: I.B.Tauris, 2012), 93–109.

Totah, Faedah M., 'The memory keeper: gender nation, and remembering in Syria', *Journal of Middle East Women's Studies* 9, 1 (Winter 2013), 1–29.

Wedeen, Lisa, 'Acting "as if": symbolic politics and social control in Syria', *Comparative Studies in Society and History* 40 (1998), 503–23.

BOOKS

Abu-Husayn, Abdul-Rahim, *Provincial Leaderships in Syria 1575–1650* (Beirut: American University of Beirut Press, 1985).

Allsopp, Harriet, *The Kurds of Syria: Political Parties and Identity in the Middle East* (London: I.B.Tauris, 2014).

Batatu, Hanna, *Syria's Peasantry, the Descendants of its Lesser Rural Notables, and their Politics* (Princeton: Princeton University Press, 1999).

Blackburn, Richard, *Journey to the Sublime Porte: The Arabic Memoir of a Sharifian Agent's Diplomatic Mission to the Ottoman Imperial Court in the Era of Suleyman the Magnificent* (Beirut: Orient-Institut and Würzburg: Ergon Verlag, 2005).

Brewer, David, *The Flame of Freedom: The Greek War of Independence 1821–1833* (London: John Murray, 2001).

Commins, David, *Islamic Reform: Politics and Social Change in Late Ottoman Syria* (New York: Oxford University Press, 1990).

cooke, miriam, *Dancing in Damascus: Creativity, Resilience, and the Syrian Revolution* (New York: Routledge, 2017).

———, *Dissident Syria: Making Oppositional Arts Official* (Durham, NC: Duke University Press, 2007).

Fahmy, Khaled, *All the Pasha's Men: Mehmed Ali, His Army and the Making of Modern Egypt* (Cairo: American University in Cairo Press, 2002).

Fawaz, Leila Tarazi, *A Land of Aching Hearts: The Middle East in the Great War* (Cambridge, MA: Harvard University Press, 2014).

———, *An Occasion for War: Civil Conflict in Lebanon and Damascus in 1860* (Berkeley: University of California Press, 1994).

Gelvin, James L., *Divided Loyalties: Nationalism and Mass Politics in Syria at the Close of Empire* (Berkeley: University of California Press, 1998).

Grehan, James, *Everyday Life and Consumer Culture in 18th-Century Damascus* (Seattle, WA: University of Washington Press, 2007).

Harris, William, *Lebanon: A History, 600–2011* (New York: Oxford University Press, 2012).

Heydemann, Steven, *Authoritarianism in Syria: Institutions and Social Conflict, 1946–1970* (Ithaca, NY: Cornell University Press, 1999).

Holt, P. M. *Egypt and the Fertile Crescent 1516–1922: A Political History* (Ithaca, NY: Cornell University Press, 1966).

Khatib, Line, *Islamic Revivalism in Syria: The rise and Fall of Ba'thist Secularism* (New York: Routledge, 2011).

Khoury, Philip S., *Syria and the French Mandate: The Politics of Syrian Nationalism* (Princeton: Princeton University Press, 1987).

———, *Urban Notables and Arab Nationalism: The Politics of Damascus, 1860–1920* (New York: Cambridge University Press, 1983).

Lesch, David W., *Syria: The Fall of the House of Assad* (New Haven, CT: Yale University Press, 2012).

Lewis, Norman N. *Nomads and Settlers in Syria and Jordan, 1800–1980* (Cambridge: Cambridge University Press, 1987).

Malek, Alia, *The Home that Was Our Country: A Memoir of Syria* (New York: Nation Books, 2017).

Marcus, Abraham, *The Middle East on the Eve of Modernity: Aleppo in the Eighteenth Century* (New York: Columbia University Press, 1989).

Masters, Bruce, *Christians and Jews in the Ottoman Arab World: The Roots of Sectarianism* (Cambridge: Cambridge University Press, 2004).

———, *The Arabs of the Ottoman Empire, 1516–1918* (Cambridge: Cambridge University Press, 2013).

———, *The Origins of Western Economic Dominance in the Middle East: Mercantilism and the Islamic Economy in Aleppo, 1600–1750* (New York: New York University Press, 1988).

Meriwether, Margaret L., *The Kin Who Count: Family and Society in Ottoman Aleppo, 1770–1840* (Austin, TX: University of Texas Press, 1999).

Mishaqa, Mikhayil, *Murder, Mayhem, Pillage, and Plunder: The History of the Lebanon in the 18th and 19th Centuries*, trans. Wheeler M. Thackston, Jr (Albany, NY: State University of New York Press, 1988).

Miura, Toru, *Dynamism in the Urban Society of Damascus: The Salihiyya Quarter from the Twelfth to the Twentieth Centuries* (Leiden: Brill, 2016).

Parsons, Laila, *The Commander: Fawzi al-Qawuqji and the Fight for Arab Independence 1914–1948* (New York: Hill and Wang, 2016).

Pearlman, Wendy, *We Crossed a Bridge and it Trembled: Voices from Syria* (New York: HarperCollins, 2017).

Perthes, Volker, *Syria under Bashar al-Asad: Modernisation and the Limits of Change* (New York: Oxford University Press, 2004).

———, *The Political Economy of Syria under Asad* (London: I.B.Tauris, 1995).

Petran, Tabitha, *Syria* (London: Ernest Benn, 1972).

Philipp, Thomas, *Acre: The Rise and Fall of a Palestinian City, 1730–1831* (New York: Columbia University Press, 2002).

Provence, Michael, *The Great Syrian Revolt and the Rise of Arab Nationalism* (Austin, TX: University of Texas Press, 2005).

Rabo, Annika, *A Shop of One's Own: Independence and Reputation among Traders in Aleppo* (London: I.B.Tauris, 2005).

Raymond, André, *The Great Arab Cities in the 16th–18th Centuries: An Introduction* (New York: New York University Press, 1984).

Reilly, James A., *A Small Town in Syria: Ottoman Hama in the Eighteenth and Nineteenth Centuries* (Oxford: Peter Lang, 2002).

Rogan, Eugene, *Frontiers of the State in the Late Ottoman Empire* (Cambridge: Cambridge University Press, 1999).

Sajdi, Dana, *The Barber of Damascus: Nouveau Literacy in the Eighteenth-Century Ottoman Levant* (Stanford, CA: Stanford University Press, 2013).

Salamandra, Christa, *A New Old Damascus: Authenticity and Distinction in Urban Syria* (Bloomington, IN: Indiana University Press, 2004).

Schilcher, Linda Schatkowski, *Families in Politics: Damascene Factions and Estates of the 18th and 19th Centuries* (Wiesbaden: F. Steiner, 1985).

Seale, Patrick, *Asad: The Struggle for the Middle East* (Berkeley: University of California Press, 1988).

———. *The Struggle for Syria: A Study of Post-War Arab Politics, 1945–1958* (London: I.B.Tauris, 1965, 1986).

Semerdjian, Elyse, *'Off the Straight Path': Illicit Sex, Law, and Community in Ottoman Aleppo* (Syracuse, NY: Syracuse University Press, 2008).

Shannon, Jonathan Holt, *Among the Jasmine Trees: Music and Modernity in Contemporary Syria* (Middletown, CT: Wesleyan University Press, 2006).

Sorensen, David S., *Syria in Ruins: The Dynamics of the Syrian Civil War* (Santa Barbara, CA: Praeger, 2016).

Starkey, Paul, *Modern Arabic Literature* (Edinburgh: Edinburgh University Press, 2006).

Tejel, Jordi, *Syria's Kurds: History, Politics and Society* (London: Routledge, 2009).

Thompson, Elizabeth, *Colonial Citizens: Republican Rights, Paternal Privilege, and Gender in French Syria and Lebanon* (New York: Columbia University Press, 2000).

Totah, Faedah M., *Preserving the Old City of Damascus* (Syracuse, NY: Syracuse University Press, 2014).

Van Dam, Nikolaos, *The Struggle for Power in Syria: Politics and Society under Asad and the Ba'th Party*, 4th edn (London: I.B.Tauris, 2011).

Watenaugh, Heghnar Zeitlian, *The Image of an Ottoman City: Imperial Architecture and Urban Experience in Aleppo in the 16th and 17th Centuries* (Leiden: Brill, 2004).

Watenpaugh, Keith David, *Being Modern in the Middle East: Revolution, Nationalism, Colonialism, and the Arab Middle Class* (Princeton: Princeton University Press, 2012).

White, Benjamin Thomas, *The Emergence of Minorities in the Middle East: The Politics of Community in French Mandate Syria* (Edinburgh: Edinburgh University Press, 2011).

Wilkins, Charles L. *Forging Urban Solidarities: Ottoman Aleppo 1640–1700* (Leiden: Brill, 2010).

Winter, Stefan, *A History of the 'Alawis from Medieval Aleppo to the Turkish Republic* (Princeton: Princeton University Press, 2016).

Zachs, Fruma and Sharon Halevy, *Gendering Culture in Greater Syria: Intellectuals and Ideology in the Late Ottoman Period* (London: I.B.Tauris, 2015).

Zisser, Eyal, *Asad's Legacy: Syria in Transition* (London: Hurst & Co., 2001).

———, *Commanding Syria: Bashar al-Asad and the First Years in Power* (London: I.B.Tauris, 2007).

INDEX